THE CAMBRIDGE COMPANION TO
KEYNES

John Maynard Keynes (1883–1946) was the most important
economist of the twentieth century. He was also a philosopher who wrote on ethics and the theory of probability and
was a central figure in the Bloomsbury Group of writers and
artists. In this volume, contributors from a wide range of
disciplines offer new interpretations of Keynes's thought,
explain the links between Keynes's philosophy and his
economics, and place his work and Keynesianism – the economic theory, the principles of economic policy and the
political philosophy – in their historical context. Chapter
topics include Keynes's philosophical engagement with
G. E. Moore and Franz Brentano, his correspondence,
the role of his *General Theory* in the creation of modern
macroeconomics and the many meanings of Keynesianism.

New readers will find this the most convenient, accessible
guide to Keynes currently available. Advanced students and
specialists will find a conspectus of recent developments in
the interpretation of Keynes.

ROGER E. BACKHOUSE is Professor of the History and Philosophy of Economics at the University of Birmingham.

BRADLEY W. BATEMAN is Gertrude B. Austin Professor of
Economics at Grinnell College, Iowa.

THE STOICS *Edited by* BRAD INWOOD
WITTGENSTEIN *Edited by* HANS SLUGA *and*
DAVID STERN

The Cambridge Companion to

KEYNES

Edited by

Roger E. Backhouse
University of Birmingham

and

Bradley W. Bateman
Grinnell College

CAMBRIDGE UNIVERSITY PRESS
Cambridge, New York, Melbourne, Madrid, Cape Town, Singapore,
São Paulo

CAMBRIDGE UNIVERSITY PRESS
The Edinburgh Building, Cambridge CB2 2RU, UK
Published in the United States of America by Cambridge University Press,
New York

www.cambridge.org
Information on this title: www.cambridge.org/9780521600606

First published 2006

Printed in the United Kingdom at the University Press, Cambridge

A catalogue record for this book is available from the British Library

ISBN-13 978-0-521-84090-3 hardback
ISBN-10 0-521-84090-2 hardback
ISBN-13 978-0-521-60060-6 paperback
ISBN-10 0-521-60060-X paperback

For Ann, Robert, and Alison, R. E. B.
For Sheryl, Thomas, Henry, and Lydia, B. W. B.

CONTENTS

CONTRIBUTORS

ROGER E. BACKHOUSE is Professor of the History and Philosophy of Economics at the University of Birmingham. He is the author of *The Penguin History of Economics* and *The Ordinary Business of Life*.

THOMAS BALDWIN is Professor of Philosophy at the University of York. He is editor of *The Cambridge History of Philosophy 1870–1945*.

BRADLEY W. BATEMAN is the Gertrude B. Austin Professor of Economics at Grinnell College, Iowa. He is the author of *Keynes's Uncertain Revolution*.

SAMUEL BRITTAN has been one of the *Financial Times'* leading columnists for nearly thirty years. He is the author of *Against the Flow*.

DONALD GILLIES is Professor of the Philosophy of Science and Mathematics at University College London. He is the author of *Philosophical Theories of Probability*.

CRAUFURD D. GOODWIN is James B. Duke Professor of Economics at Duke University. He is the author of *Art and the Market: Roger Fry on the Commerce in Art*.

KEVIN D. HOOVER is Professor of Economics at the University of California, Davis. He is the author of *Causality in Macroeconomics*.

MATTHIAS KLAES is Professor of Commerce at the University of Keele. He is the author of *Transactions Costs: A Conceptual History.*

DAVID LAIDLER is Professor Emeritus at the University of Western Ontario. He is the author of *The Golden Age of the Quantity Theory* and *Fabricating the Keynesian Revolution.*

AXEL LEIJONHUFVUD is Professor of Monetary Theory and Policy at the University of Trento. He is the author of *On Keynesian Economics and the Economics of Keynes* and *Macroeconomic Instability and Coordination: Selected Essays.*

MARIA CRISTINA MARCUZZO is Professor of Economics at the University of Rome, La Sapienza. She is co-editor of *Economists in Cambridge: A Study through their Correspondence, 1907–1946.*

D. E. MOGGRIDGE is Professor of Economics at the University of Toronto. He is co-editor *The Collected Writings of John Maynard Keynes* and the author of *Maynard Keynes: An Economist's Biography.*

GEORGE C. PEDEN is Professor of History at the University of Stirling. He is the author of *Keynes, the Treasury and British Economic Policy* and *The Treasury and British Public Policy, 1906–1959.*

TIZIANO RAFFAELLI is Professor of the History of Economic Thought at the University of Pisa. He is the author of *Marshall's Evolutionary Economics.*

LIST OF ABBREVIATIONS

1   A cunning purchase: the life and work of Maynard Keynes

Yet I glory
More in the cunning purchase of my wealth
Than in the glad possession

Ben Jonson, Volpone

PORTRAIT OF THE ECONOMIST AS A YOUNG MAN

On 21 June 1921, Maynard Keynes delivered the presidential address
to the annual reunion of the Apostles – a secret society of the
Cambridge University students and alumni which included such
luminaries as Alfred North Whitehead, Bertrand Russell, G. E.
Moore and Henry Sidgwick.[1] What had united the Apostles of
Keynes's own generation were their commitments, learned from
G. E. Moore, to absolute truth and to the search for friendship and
beauty. The ideal career for Keynes's cohort of Apostles would
have been to become an artist, creating beauty and living in a
community of other artists with whom one had close bonds of
friendship. But what should one do if one simply did not have the
talent to become an artist? In his address, Keynes seems to suggest that the best option for those who lack artistic talent may be
to use their talents to pursue a career in finance or business.
Quoting Ben Jonson, Keynes argued that the true reward of such
activity lay not in wealth itself so much as in the 'the cunning
purchase of . . . wealth'.

It is hard to know why he picked out finance and business rather
than, say, engineering. However, in citing Jonson's *Volpone* to make
his argument, Keynes demonstrates that he has not completely
severed his Moorean roots. For the *state of mind* that one achieves

in the pursuit of money is all important. Keynes spurns the money-making motive as it is commonly understood (the desire for money for its own sake) and embraces something more subtle and complex: the enjoyment obtained in using one's talents to pursue an end.

By 1921, when he delivered his address, Keynes had come through Eton (where he had won numerous prizes) and King's College Cambridge, graduating with first-class honours in mathematics (twelfth wrangler, the twelfth person on the first-class honours list, a place he had forecast precisely). He had then learned economics studying for the Civil Service examinations, in which he came in second place overall. Second place meant that he had missed out on the one position open that year at the Treasury and that he had to be content, instead, with a position in the India Office. There, he had written his first book on economics, *Indian Currency and Finance*, while continuing to work on his study of the philosophical foundations of the theory of probability, work which gained him a Fellowship at King's in 1909 (and was later published in an expanded form as the *Treatise on Probability*). Eventually he had been able to move to the Treasury (1915), which had sent him with the British negotiating team to the Versailles Peace Conference. His resignation in protest, the reasons for which had been written up in *The Economic Consequences of the Peace* (1919), turned him into an instant celebrity, and the book's royalties (it was a bestseller on both sides of the Atlantic) had given him financial security. However, despite having experienced what many would have considered a meteoric rise to prominence as an economist, he was still experiencing doubts about his vocation.

His outlook in 1921 can profitably be juxtaposed alongside the retrospective view expressed in the much better-known 'My early beliefs' (1938). By the time he wrote this essay, he had established his reputation as an economist with his great trilogy: *A Tract on Monetary Reform* (1923), *A Treatise on Money* (1930) and *The General Theory of Employment, Interest and Money* (1936). The first of these, originally published as articles in the *Manchester Guardian Commercial*, used the monetary theory of his teacher, Alfred Marshall, to launch a sharp attack on government policy of returning to the Gold Standard at the pre-war exchange rate. It marked a further stage in the marriage of economics with a polemical critique of economic policy that had started with *The Economic*

Consequences of the Peace and that continued, in *The Economic Consequences of Mr. Churchill* (1925), his support for the Liberal Party's public works policies in such pamphlets as 'Can Lloyd George do it?' (1929), 'Proposals for a revenue tariff' (1931) and 'The means to prosperity' (1933). By 1938, he had also been heavily involved in advising government, as a member of the Macmillan Committee and the newly formed Economic Advisory Council.[2] His *Treatise on Money* marked a change in audience: it was a two-volume work aimed at academic economists, and it involved theoretical innovations in the field of monetary economics that went beyond anything found in his earlier work. Though analyzing policy under the restored Gold Standard, he was turning his attention to the theoretical foundations in a way he had not done before. However, though this was to have been his *magnum opus*, he soon became disillusioned with it and embarked on the change of direction that led to the *General Theory*. In the present volume, Maria Cristina Marcuzzo's essay on Keynes's correspondence with other Cambridge economists shows how he used the intricate web of economists at Cambridge as a sounding-board for developing his last great work in economics.

By the time Keynes had finished the *General Theory* and turned his attention, in 'My early beliefs', back to his earlier work in philosophy, he no longer felt the need to apologize for his pursuit of money-making and a career in finance, as he had when he had given his address to the Apostles sixteen years earlier. He did, however, want to reflect upon how far he and the others had come from their earlier foundation in the work of G. E. Moore. He had by this time served for many years as the bursar of King's, he was the portfolio manager for two large insurance companies and he had served as the personal financial adviser to a number of people. He had given generously to the arts, including his work on establishing the Arts Council and the Cambridge Arts Theatre. As Donald Moggridge's essay here shows, his academic work and his business life came together in the way he managed his intellectual property, negotiating contracts with his publishers that gave him a degree of involvement (and consequent financial rewards) that were entirely atypical of most author–publisher relationships. Money-making might, indeed, involve a degree of cunning and brilliance that was worthy of an Apostle, but by now it was *also* clear that it was a necessary activity for supporting the good things in life, including the arts.

In his theoretical work and his policy-making experience, he had learned to make the lives of working people more stable and so to create a better material life for them. The long genesis of his trilogy, culminating in the *General Theory*, no longer required an apologia.

Keynes's role as an economic problem-solver and a patron of the arts would continue through his last decade, despite his poor health. Tragically, he never reached old age, dying at the age of 63 in 1946. However, by then he could already look back on a career that included more than most economists manage, quite apart from his other roles. By 1946, he could see Keynesianism emerging and his disciples using his theories to argue for policies that went beyond anything he had envisaged. By the time of his death, his *General Theory* had already achieved its dominant place in economics, and the process of constructing the new Keynesian orthodoxy that dominated economic thinking for the next thirty years was well under way. His ideas had successfully been used to solve the problem of finding non-inflationary ways to finance the Second World War. The construction of national income statistics (along lines inspired by his theory) had become firmly established as a responsibility of government and was about to be taken up by the newly formed United Nations. And he had served as diplomat, economist and negotiator as head of the British teams that had negotiated with the United States over wartime finance and the postwar economic order.

KEYNES THE PHILOSOPHER

In the last two decades, a rich literature has developed in the study of Keynes's philosophical work.[3] The primary focus of this material has been on explicating his theory of probability. But not surprisingly, given the weight of Keynes's name, there has been controversy over the nature of his early work in philosophy. The official biography by Roy Harrod (1951), although an indispensable account of Keynes's life, minimized the connection between Keynes's philosophy and his economics. Discussion of Keynes's early beliefs might have led to open discussions of his homosexuality and so, for Harrod's iconographic purposes, the early interest in philosophy had to be dismissed as a youthful enthusiasm that the mature Keynes, the economist, had left behind. Much of the 'Keynes and philosophy' literature starts with the early life. It explores the beliefs of Keynes and his friends as they were formed under Moore's tutelage; it explores his relationships with Bertrand Russell, Ludwig Wittgenstein and Frank Ramsey.[4] This is a literature in which ethics is central, though tied up with epistemology and induction. A major strand in it is Keynes's work on uncertainty which came out of the same context, his ideas on uncertainty arising as part of his critique of Moore's ethics. This is potentially of great importance because of his claims about the role played by uncertainty in his mature economics; when defending his *General Theory* in 1937, he brushed aside the technical points made by his critics to argue that his main point was that we know very little about the future, in a way that appears to connect very easily with his *Treatise on Probability*.

One way into these controversies is to consider Ramsey's devastating critique of Keynes's *Probability*, which levelled Keynes's attempt to build a theory of probability on Platonic foundations. Until the past twenty years, philosophers always took at face value Keynes's capitulation to Ramsey in his review of Ramsey's critique (1931), published after Ramsey's death. However, during the 1980s, two Cambridge doctoral dissertations argued that Keynes had not, in fact, capitulated to Ramsey. One of these, by Anna Carabelli, argued that Keynes had always held the subjectivist position traditionally attributed to him *after* his capitulation. The other, by Roderick O'Donnell, argued that Keynes continued to hold what has traditionally been taken to be his *earlier* objectivist position and so that he never capitulated. In the present volume, Tiziano Raffaelli and Donald Gillies take the more traditional position, carefully explaining how Keynes formed his early objectivist position and how Ramsey's critique changed this in fundamental ways.[5] Raffaelli also shows how Keynes's argument for a new understanding of probability drew on several strands of Cambridge philosophy. In trying to act well, just as much as in trying to make money, one is always forced to make decisions that will play out in a world that one cannot foresee perfectly. Gillies shows convincingly that while this concern with an uncertain future never disappeared, Keynes's understanding of probability itself changed considerably over time. Whereas he had started in his early work with a Platonic idea of probability in which one can act on the basis of the future through knowledge of these objectively defined probabilities, his thinking evolved, in response to Ramsey's criticism, to encompass an idea of probability based on the idea that people tend to follow the herd and to make their estimates of the future in the hope that what the crowd is thinking can protect them.

Another way to frame Keynes's interest in philosophy is to look at his interest in ethical theory and the influences on this concern of his. Thomas Baldwin's essay takes a dispassionate look at one of the ideas in G. E. Moore that most fascinated Keynes and his contemporaries in the Apostles, the concept of the naturalistic fallacy. Moore argues in *Principia Ethica* (1903) that virtually all previous ethical theories have been erroneously based upon the fallacy that there is some thing in the world (e.g. utility) that always entails the good. In place of this view, Moore argues that good is an indefinable entity that cannot always be attached to some thing in the world. Utility may be good, or it may be bad. Only good is always good. This reductionism had the perverse effect of both freeing the Apostles to examine everything in the world afresh, to determine if it was, indeed, good, and also of releasing them from the traditional demands of ethical inquiry. 'By contrast if one adopts the traditional view that ethical values connect with possibilities for human fulfillment, the question of the value of love and beauty should be, in principle, susceptible of explication and sensible discussion' (see p. 239).

But there is much more to Keynes's early work in philosophy and the influences that shaped him during his undergraduate years. Keynes also wrote on Edmund Burke during his philosophical apprenticeship, and this influence shaped his later work in economics. Thomas Baldwin writes in his essay on Keynes's ethical concerns of how they were also shaped by Franz Brentano, while Tiziano Raffaelli in his essay discusses Burke's conservative influence.

Craufurd Goodwin's essay breaks new ground in showing how Keynes's economic thinking was influenced by the ideas of his fellow Bloomsburys, especially Roger Fry and Leonard Woolf. Goodwin shows that after leaving Cambridge, Keynes continued to develop his ethical thinking and arrived at a position that posits levels of ethical concern. First, one must meet the material concerns that sustain life (the actual life); but then, once these concerns are met, one is obliged to consider a larger set of human needs and activities (the imaginative life). These richer schemata must certainly have influenced Keynes's evolution from seeing money-making and financial knowledge as a good exercise of the mind to his more mature position in which he could appreciate it as a means to help workers achieve more stable lives and to support the arts. It also echoes the observation made in Baldwin's essay that Keynes was influenced by Moore to look beyond the simple calculus of utilitarianism.

THE PHILOSOPHER AS ECONOMIST

The question of how Keynes's work in philosophy influenced his work in economics has been complicated in recent years by the discovery that during the central years of his career as an economist, he explicitly eschewed the kind of rhetoric about uncertainty and expectations that so clearly influenced his *General Theory*. Early in his career, Keynes was a close adherent of the Cambridge theory of the trade cycle, which depended crucially on the roles of uncertainty and expectations. But as he progressed through the *Tract* and the *Treatise*, he turned against this earlier inheritance and became a sharp critic of the argument that either uncertainty or expectations have any important role in macroeconomic phenomena. By the time that he became a member of the Macmillan Committee in 1930, his commitment to a mechanistic model of the business cycle (driven by changes in the interest rate) was so strong that he engaged his fellow Cambridge economist A. C. Pigou in an acerbic exchange before the Committee, and tried to force him to admit that uncertainty and expectations were no part of a proper understanding of the current environment.[6] Pigou, however, refused to give up on the older Cambridge arguments that expectations were a central cause of the business cycle. Keynes was running an argument that the level of interest rates was the only factor necessary to understanding the business cycle, but Pigou would have none of it, believing that profit expectations of entrepreneurs were as important as interest rates.

Keynes held on to his mechanistic explanations of the business cycle until late 1933, a year into the composition of the *General Theory*. During this time, they led him into another disagreement, this time with Hubert Henderson. In 1929, the two had collaborated on 'Can Lloyd George do it?', but by 1932 they were diametrically opposed about the efficacy of loan-financed public works projects. Henderson had come round to the position that running large budget deficits would frighten investors, dampening their expectations of future profits and causing investment to fall off. This was anathema to Keynes, who stated in his letters to Henderson that arguments about the importance of expectations to the business cycle were ridiculous. Perhaps in response to his exchanges with Henderson, however, Keynes suddenly started to reclaim his youthful heritage in Cambridge business cycle theory, introducing expectations into several of his functions in the lectures he gave at Cambridge in the autumn of 1933. He had not then accepted Henderson's point about frightening investors with his policy initiatives, but he did come round to acknowledging the possibility in his final arguments in 1936, and he reiterated them in the year immediately following the publication of the *General Theory*.[7]

THE POLITICAL PHILOSOPHY OF KEYNESIANISM

Keynes wrote at a time when the British political system was undergoing profound changes. In Keynes's childhood, government alternated between the Liberal and Conservative Parties, this period culminating in the great Liberal administration of 1906. This administration marked a significant change, with the Liberal Party adopting more radical stances towards social reform, breaking away from Gladstonian Liberalism to introduce progressive income taxation, old age pensions, unemployment insurance and a raft of other measures. The intellectual counterpart to this was the so-called New Liberalism, represented by such thinkers as L. T. Hobhouse and J. A. Hobson, offering an alternative to the socialism of the emerging Labour Party. The interwar period was one of Conservative dominance, the left being divided between the Liberals, who were fatally split between Old and New Liberals, and the rising Labour Party.

Keynes was a Liberal, siding with the radical ex-Prime Minister David Lloyd George when the Asquith and Lloyd George wings of the party split. He is famous for saying that 'when the revolution comes, you will find me on the side of the educated bourgeoisie'. He described his own politics as firmly to the left: 'I fancy that I have played in my mind with the possibility of greater social changes than come within the present philosophies of, let us say, Mr Sidney Webb, Mr Thomas, or Mr Wheatley.[8] The republic of my imagination lies on the extreme left of celestial space' (JMK IX: 309). However, his home lay in Liberalism. Referring to Socialists ('who believe the economic foundations of modern society are evil, yet might be good', *ibid.*),[9] he contended that 'their historic creed of State Socialism, and its newer gloss of Guild Socialism' no longer interested them any more than it interested Liberals. Both parties of the left should continue, and should work together. His philosophical defence of this conclusion is worth quoting in full.

The political problem of mankind is to combine three things: economic efficiency, social justice, and individual liberty. The first needs criticism, precaution, and technical knowledge; the second, an unselfish and enthusiastic spirit, which loves the ordinary man; the third, tolerance, breadth, appreciation of the excellencies of variety and independence, which prefers, above everything, to give unhindered opportunity to the exceptional and the aspiring. The second ingredient is the best possession of the great party of the proletariat. But the first and third require the qualities of a party which, by its traditions and ancient sympathies, has been the home of economic individualism and social liberty.

(JMK IX: 311)

But if we can trace Keynes's concerns with socialism, the exact nature of his commitment to capitalism has never been well understood. Craufurd Goodwin's essay, however, would seem to suggest a broad Bloomsbury framework for understanding his commitment to capitalism that would also connect his commitment with his earliest concerns in G. E. Moore's work. Eventually, Keynes seemed to have come to a mature understanding of capitalism that saw it as the system most likely to sustain the 'actual life' of basic economic existence as well as the one most apt to create an adequate surplus for sustaining the 'imaginative life'. As Goodwin shows, these schemata reflect the art critic Roger Fry's vision of modern life, and also allowed Keynes to argue for capitalism as the best means to Moore's ends of art and friendship.

Likewise, the problems of capitalism that became leitmotifs in Keynes's writings drew, at least in part, from his experience as a main figure in Bloomsbury. As the chapters on both his aesthetics (Goodwin) and his economics (Leijonhufvud and Hoover) show, one of his central concerns regarding capitalism was that information was not well co-ordinated, and that this led to inevitable disruptions in output and employment. As his outlook matured during the creation of the *General Theory*, Keynes came to see the behaviours fostered by this lack of co-ordination as the source of additional economic problems. Faced with the uncertain future caused by repeated co-ordination failures, investors and financiers were reduced to behaving in ways that seemed to resemble those of gamblers at a casino. Keynes came to believe that the outcomes of investments rested largely on luck: on whether other investors making the same gamble stuck with it. If one's fellow investors lost confidence, this could easily cause a collapse in the value of one's own investments.

Keynes did not believe that this potential for the system to collapse necessarily meant that the system was liable to continual, unpredictable swings. While swings in behaviour *could* lead to swings in output and employment in his basic model, the problem on which he focused most intensely was the possibility that the whole system might swing into a state of low output and low employment from which it would become difficult to lift people's expectations. Should this happen, the whole system could get stuck near this low point and stay there indefinitely. Keynes saw this as the best explanation of the back-breaking stagnation that characterized the late 1920s and the 1930s in Britain. The biggest problem was not swinging up and down but becoming stuck at a low point.

Keynes's concern with the possibility of being stuck for long periods in a low-employment equilibrium position led to one of his best-known depictions of capitalists, as being driven by 'animal spirits'. He saw the collapsed expectations and the consequent economic depression as unnecessary aspects of modern capitalism, an unreasonable response to the abundance and possibilities available to entrepreneurs. He likewise saw the optimism and sanguine expectations necessary to an upswing as essentially a matter of outlook and 'animal spirits': what was really necessary for prosperity was not public works projects and government budget deficits, but hope and optimism on the part of capitalists. Thus, in a news broadcast on the occasion of Britain's departure from the Gold Standard in 1931, he focused on the psychological importance of the change:

'It is a wonderful thing for our business men and our manufacturers and our unemployed to taste hope again. But they must not allow anyone to put them back in the gold cage, where they have been pining their hearts out all these years.'[10] In the end, public works and deficits were merely short-term palliatives that might be successful in helping to bolster 'animal spirits'. Bradley Bateman argues in his essay that much of the focus on demand management in the Keynesian literature produced after Keynes's death distorts this focus in Keynes's own writings.

Perhaps because Keynes saw that improved 'animal spirits' could solve the problem of economic depression and unemployment, he argued, later in his life, that it would be possible to eliminate scarcity within the foreseeable future. Today, when we are conscious of the dreams and aspirations of an entire global community to ever higher levels of material wealth, such aspirations seem quixotic; however, Keynes lived in an age when it was possible for him to believe that it would take no more than a century to eliminate the worst poverty in the industrial world. This position was almost certainly influenced by the schemata he had drawn from Roger Fry. Since he believed that there was already some surplus beyond the most basic needs of the British population – the actual life – and that this surplus supported the important experiences in the imaginative life, it cannot have been too hard to believe that all the needs within the actual sphere might be met when the regular downturns of the business cycle had been ameliorated and 'animal spirits' had been held at a high level for several generations. His love for art and literature must have made him hope fervently for such a world, despite the difficulty that others had with envisaging it.

One might think that this would have placed him within the orbit of the New Liberals, but he remained outside that group. Socially, culturally and intellectually, there was a marked gap between them and the Bloomsbury set to which Keynes belonged. Though Keynes attached great importance to remedying the defects of capitalism, he did not share the New Liberals' keen concern for social justice and regarded the so-called New Liberalism as 'a typical example of Oxford Idealist muddle' (Skidelsky 1992: 134). He became briefly involved in the Summer Schools, which were established by the New Liberals to formulate a set of policies for the 1920s, but this served only to make clear his differences from them.

In 1922 he became involved in the takeover of the journal *Nation and Athenaeum*, ruthlessly pushing out the representatives of the Summer School movement and installing his Cambridge colleague Hubert Henderson as editor and Leonard Woolf as literary editor. In place of the Oxford and Manchester New Liberalism, Keynes made it an organ of Cambridge economics (including many of his pieces on policy) and Bloomsbury.[11]

Though elements of Keynes's vision were shared by many of the 'Keynesians' who took up his ideas in the 1940s and after, they were taken up selectively. Samuel Brittan's essay questions the degree to which Keynes had a vision that is compatible with the subsequent social democratic bent of much of Keynesian economics. But clearly, Keynes's vision of capitalism influenced his economic theory. However, it is necessary to be careful here, for his vision was largely reflected in the *interpretation* he placed on the mathematical apparatus he helped to create, *not* in the mathematical apparatus itself. His 'model' *could* be interpreted in terms of his vision, but there was no necessity to do so. Moreover, certain parts of his vision could be represented in the model better than others. His ideas about the way spending generated further demand were fairly faithfully represented by the mathematical device of the multiplier, but his ideas about 'animal spirits' and investment were all 'off stage', for uncertainty did not appear anywhere in his mathematics.

KEYNES'S SCIENTIFIC METHODOLOGY

Kevin Hoover's essay draws on a distinction between aiming for a comprehensive theory and working with theories that are purpose-built to solve particular problems, seeing the latter as the hallmark of a diagnostic science. This was Keynes's method, his theories being made out of building-blocks (the consumption function, liquidity preference) that had been created for the purpose. This was the method of his teacher Alfred Marshall. Axel Leijonhufvud's essay makes the point that one reason for such a methodology was that both Keynes and Marshall were analyzing systems in motion: equilibrium was but a point attractor in such a process. When systems are in motion in this way, providing a comprehensive model of their dynamics is almost impossible, something of which Marshall had been well aware; systems have to be cut into pieces, using simplifications. Thus the capital stock may be taken as constant, on the grounds that it changes too slowly for such changes to be a significant factor in variations in employment. Similarly, other variables may be taken to adjust sufficiently fast that their adjustment can be taken to be instantaneous.

However, when economists came to make sense of the *General Theory*, they interpreted it in a different way – in terms of theories that aimed at comprehensiveness, as is explained in Roger Backhouse's essay. General equilibrium theory, interest in which was revived by John Hicks, Paul Samuelson and others in the 1940s, was such a theory and, from the 1940s, was increasingly the framework within which Keynesian ideas were developed. This was known as the project of providing microeconomic foundations for Keynesian economics, and it involved many of the most prominent postwar macroeconomic theorists. David Laidler's essay explains the connections between Keynes's own work, that of his predecessors in macroeconomic theorizing and his many successors'. Though his successors were concerned with policy, they sought to find policy prescriptions within a type of theory that was very different from that used by Keynes. As this theory became the generally accepted way to do economics, Keynes came to be seen, not as having had a different type of theory, but as not having had a theory at all. Frank Hahn has gone so far as to say that Keynes did not know how to theorize rigorously (Blaug 1990: 74). This is the change that has been called 'the formalist revolution', and some economists have been very critical of it (Blaug 1999). It is no doubt the case that the demand for general theories, and a reluctance to engage in what Hoover calls diagnostic science, has been an important factor behind certain Keynesian themes ('animal spirits' and co-ordination failures) being pushed out of macroeconomics.

Another dimension to this is Keynes's treatment of individual behaviour. In modern economics it has become standard practice to model agents as utility maximizers. Consumption is modelled by assuming that agents maximize utility over their lifetimes, or even over an infinite horizon that includes the lifetimes of their descendants. Demand for money is the result of selecting an optimal portfolio of assets given the need to finance transactions and expectations of the future. Keynes, however, did not view things this way; but contemporary economists are wrong to claim that he

had no microfoundations for his macroeconomics. He rejected utilitarianism, and with it the notion of rational behaviour that in
modern economics is considered virtually synonymous with microfoundations, but that was because he had his own microfoundations, that were built on a very different foundation, perhaps closer
to that of modern behavioural economics. His theories of consumer behaviour and of behaviour in securities markets were both
based on a mixture of intuitions about how sensible people would
behave when faced with the situations he believed them to face (no
doubt informed by his own involvement in such activities), and
what he had learned through observing behaviour close at hand. It
was an almost casual use of evidence, reminiscent of his teacher,
Marshall. Though he paid great attention to the collection and
compilation of statistics, he did not believe that there was much
scope for formal statistical methods, such as were beginning to be
used in economics in the 1930s and which dominated the subject in
the postwar period.

In 1939, the Dutch physicist-turned-economist Jan Tinbergen
published, for the League of Nations, an econometric model. This
turned out to be the forerunner of many such models, built using
more sophisticated techniques and becoming larger and larger from
the late 1940s to the early 1970s. During this period, such models
were almost always structured along Keynesian lines, to such an
extent that large-scale macroeconometric modelling seemed the
natural empirical extension of Keynesian economics. Keynes's response to Tinbergen's early work is of great interest because it is the
only published example of his reaction to the type of empirical work
that later came to be linked to his name.[12]

At one level this was a dispute between Keynes and Tinbergen
over the specific techniques used by Tinbergen. Keynes offered what
could be seen as technical criticisms of certain statistical techniques, whether data admitted the interpretations Tinbergen placed
on them, and so on. However, beneath this lay philosophical differences. Though Keynes believed statistical data were important (he
had been responsible for encouraging wartime work on the construction of the national accounts), he was wary of placing too much
weight on them and at times would choose to rely, instead, on his
own intuition. There is room for debate over what epistemology

underlay Keynes's thinking: whatever it was, it was certainly neither the empiricism associated with the Cowles Commision in the 1940s nor the positivism propagated by Milton Friedman during the 1950s. Keynes was a Marshallian in his use of formal techniques as a means for handling ideas that were too complex to be captured completely within the mathematics. He used formal theory, but the need to keep the complications continually in the back of one's mind severely constrained how such theory could be used.

There are clear parallels here between what was happening in economic theory and in applied economics. During the 1930s and 1940s, there were moves towards more formal methods in both fields. At the risk of oversimplification, they could be summed up as the movement away from Marshall. Marshall used formal theory, but because his ideas were rooted in an evolutionary understanding of human nature and of social organization, he remained sceptical about it, holding that the world was too complex for mathematical models, which were necessarily simple, to encompass its ramifications. His knowledge of this complexity derived not from statistical evidence so much as from careful observation; it was what might nowadays be considered, at best, historical methods or, at worst, casual empiricism. Keynes occupies a paradoxical position here: his ideas fuelled the formalization of both macroeconomic theory and econometrics, but at the same time he remained profoundly sceptical of both developments. Methodologically he remained closer to Marshall (as both Hoover and Leijonhufvud argue) than to those contemporaries whose work he was inspiring.

WHO WAS KEYNES?

Only when we see Keynes in this light, as someone whose ethical, philosophical and economic thinking was shaped fully by his encounters with life, can we understand what he wrote and theorized. It is a brittle victory to explicate his scholarly work in isolation from his engagement with the world. As a young man, Keynes had tried to live on the theoretical level and describes some of these early efforts in a humorous light in 'My early beliefs'; but with experience and maturity he was able to build a set of moral commitments out of those early experiments that he believed held the potential to improve the world.

Keynes is one of a handful of economists whose life was rich enough to warrant the extensive biographical treatment he has received. The official biography, by Roy Harrod (1951), has already been mentioned. Harrod was a friend and colleague of Keynes, and had been prominent in the propagation of Keynesian economics. His biography, as mentioned earlier, conformed to the Victorian ideas about biography, perhaps ironically given Bloomsbury's attack on such values. The Keynes who emerged from Harrod's biography was a brilliant figure who rose above his Victorian origins to save Britain from the dark forces of economic ignorance, but who retained a measure of Victorian dedication to duty in his work to fashion the postwar financial world – a task in which, given the weakness of his bargaining position *vis à vis* the Americans, he was remarkably successful. Robert Skidelsky's three-volume biography (1983, 1992, 2000)[13] attempted to offer a 'Bloomsbury Keynes' who had completely escaped Harrod's Victorian 'taint'. Skidelsky's Keynes is both brilliant and civilized, humane and complex. In revealing Keynes's homosexuality and taking seriously his commitments to art, Skidelsky offered a fuller and richer vision than Harrod's. But Skidelsky also sought to 'save Keynes from the economists', believing that such a brilliant and complex man was above the mundaneness of contemporary economics. This left space for Donald Moggridge's (1992) insightful exploration, with the benefit of forty more years of hindsight than were available to Harrod, of Keynes as fully a part of the world of mid-century economics, shaping it theoretically and morally. Each picture contains a piece of Keynes, and each reminds us of how much he did to temper and shape his understanding of ethics, economics and finance, and of how hard he worked to bring them into the service of what is really important in life.[14] Keynes's involvement in Bloomsbury goes further than being influenced by Bloomsbury: he was himself a major part of the group. As such it is reasonable to imagine that Keynes was a modernist. And yet his writing on uncertainty has often been used to describe him as a post-modernist. Matthias Klaes explores the implication that Keynes must be seen as lying somewhere between modernism and post-modernism.

The present volume does not claim to offer either a comprehensive survey of these studies of Keynes's intellectual development or an alternative to them. Rather it takes up a number of themes from this literature, taking stock in certain areas, and it introduces some new ones. It spans Keynes's intellectual development and the context (economic and social as well as philosophical) in which that development took place, and it explores the way people responded to Keynes's ideas.

CONCLUSIONS

Keynes is one of the few people of the twentieth century who had influence across many spheres. He made important contributions to the theoretical understanding of how to lift an economy out of mass unemployment. Even more importantly, he helped shape a commitment within the British government to acknowledging the terrible dislocations and wastefulness of mass unemployment. And he helped to shape a nascent public commitment to the support of the 'imaginative life'. He did not simply exercise his talents – he saw and understood the potential for building a better world. Keynes always saw this potential humbly and with detachment – 'Economists are not the makers of civilization, but the custodians of the possibilities of civilization' – but he was fervently committed to the principle of making civilization possible. Without pretending to offer a definitive biographical treatment, even to have the last word on which Keynes was the real Keynes, our point is that it is possible to see, in the complexity of his life, the forces that shaped a man and his moral commitments, which in turn motivated his economics.

NOTES

1   This occasion is discussed in more detail in the Prologue to Skidelsky (1992), entitled 'What is one to do with one's brains?'
2   The most complete account of Keynes's work on the Economic Advisory Council is Howson and Winch (1977). Clarke (1988) provides the best account of the cut and thrust of his work in advising government.
3   Gillies and Ietto-Gillies (1991), Davis (1994b), O'Donnell (1989), Carabelli (1988), Bateman (1988), Andrews (2000), Runde and Mizuhara (2003), Bateman (1996), Bateman and Davis (1991), Coates (1996).

4   This literature is discussed below.

5   Bateman (1987) is the first defence in the literature of the traditional position that Keynes had, in fact, capitulated to Ramsey.

6   See Bateman (1996) for a full explanation of Keynes's changing attitudes to uncertainty and the business cycle.

7   JMK VII: 162.

8   James Henry Thomas (1874–1949) and John Wheatley (1869–1930) were both Labour MPs. Sidney Webb (1859–1947) was also a Labour MP and is perhaps best known for founding the Fabian Society with his wife, Beatrice.

9   Communists, so called, went further, believing that evil had to be created so that good might come out of it.

10 British Movietone News; extract included in video, John Maynard Keynes, edited by Mark Blaug.

11 Skidelsky (1992: 134ff).

12 JMK XIV: 306–20; Tinbergen (1940). See Patinkin (1982), Lawson and Pesaran (1989) and Bateman (1990).

13 Abridged as Skidelsky (2003).

14 It is also worth drawing attention to several studies of the development of Keynes's economic ideas that, though they are not biographies, explore an important part of his intellectual development in detail. Three of the best are Patinkin (1976) and Clarke (1988, 1998). Dostaler (2005) is a very recent study that provides much background information and an introduction to French-language literature on Keynes.

2 The Keynesian revolution

I believe myself to be writing a book on economic theory, which will largely revolutionise – not, I suppose, at once, but in the course of the next ten years – the way the world thinks about economic problems.

Keynes to George Bernard Shaw
(quoted in Skidelsky 1992: 520)

[A]n element of myth-making is involved whenever the phrase 'Keynesian revolution' is deployed . . . the re-arrangement of ideas to which it refers was neither revolutionary in the usual sense of the word nor by any means uniquely Keynesian in origin.

(Laidler 1999: 3)

INTRODUCTION

The Keynesian revolution is the central feature of twentieth-century macroeconomics. It has been praised, condemned and subjected to extensive historical analysis, sometimes being used as a case study in the philosophy of science. The aim of this essay is not to ask what the Keynesian revolution 'really' was, for that would be to add but one more turn to a debate that has continued for seven decades, but to explore how and why economists' understanding of the Keynesian revolution has changed in the seventy years since the publication of the *General Theory*. This is important for at least three reasons. It demonstrates some of the many ways in which Keynesian economics has been understood, for though there may be near universal agreement that there was, for good or ill, a Keynesian

19

revolution, there has been little agreement over precisely what it comprised. It helps distinguish Keynes's economics from the 'Keynesian economics' of his successors; and it helps explain why it is superficially easy to use Keynes to illustrate propositions about the philosophy of science but very difficult to make such applications convincing.

Before moving on to discuss the Keynesian revolution, it is important to clarify what is being discussed in this chapter. The term Keynesian economics (and by implication the Keynesian revolution) has been used to refer to three very different things. The first is an approach to government policy – the use of monetary and fiscal policy to control the level of aggregate demand and hence the level of unemployment. The second is a political philosophy to which both Marxists and devotees of free markets objected equally strongly. The third is a type of economic theory. Keynes, in his *General Theory*, was concerned with changing economic theory. This chapter is concerned with the last of these. Of course, Keynesian economic theory had implications for policy and, arguably, for political philosophy, but it is helpful to consider these three revolutions separately, for understanding them requires different types of analysis.

FROM 'NEW ECONOMICS' TO A KEYNESIAN ORTHODOXY

Keynes made a point of emphasizing the revolutionary nature of his own theory and his battle with orthodox economics, describing his book as the result of a long struggle to escape from such beliefs (JMK VII: xxiii). In adopting this strategy, Keynes was taking up a theme that had become established during the early 1930s (the years of the Great Depression). By 1936, the phrase the 'New Economics' had come to mean theories based on the idea that monetary expansion could cure depression. Kitson, Soddy and Major Douglas were referred to as 'the new economics school' (Bradford 1935). This was not the first time there had been a search for a 'New Economics'. Referring to the 1880s, Ely (1936: 144–5) had written:

The most fundamental things in our understanding were the ideas of evolution and of relativism . . . A new world was coming into existence and if this world was to be a better world, we believed we must have a new economics to go along with it. The old economists, however, held the idea of a body of established truths arrived at chiefly by deduction, based upon certain traits of human nature and familiar observations.

Though Keynes and his contemporaries may not have shared either Ely's relativism or his belief in evolution, they shared his beliefs that the world required a fresh economics; that orthodoxy was abstract and based on premises that were irrelevant to the modern world; and that the new theory would make the world a better place. However, though the idea of a 'New Economics' was established before 1936, Keynes rapidly came to be seen as its leader – as having provided its theoretical foundations. Within a decade, the 'New Economics' had come to be synonymous with Keynesian economics (Haberler 1946: 187; Dillard 1948: viii).

At the same time as talking of the 'New Economics', economists also began to talk of a Keynesian revolution. The book that popularized this term was Lawrence Klein's *The Keynesian Revolution* (1944), originally a PhD thesis submitted to MIT, where he had been influenced by Paul Samuelson. In this book, Klein laid out much of what was to become the standard interpretation of the Keynesian revolution. Starting his career as a classical economist, Keynes developed practical policies to cure unemployment, even though he did not have a satisfactory theoretical account of why these policies would work. The resulting inconsistency between his theory and his policy recommendations was resolved when, some time in 1933, he developed a new theoretical framework that broke with the classical tradition. Klein dated the transition by comparing two articles that Joan Robinson (a close colleague of Keynes) published in 1933: the first was in the classical framework of Keynes's *Treatise on Money* (1930), but the second contained a clear statement of how saving and investment determined the level of output, as in the *General Theory*.

Klein then justified describing this change as a revolution: he reviewed the pre-Keynesian literature looking for evidence of the classical view that there could not be a prolonged period of deficient aggregate demand and that fiscal policy would not raise the level of employment; he reviewed the controversies over the *General Theory* to show that there was a fundamental difference between the Keynesian outlook and that of classical economics; he reviewed the extent to which various 'heretics' identified by Keynes had anticipated the *General Theory*; he rebutted the charge that the *General Theory* was relevant only to times of depression; and he discussed the implications of the book for social reform. Klein offered a view of the Keynesian revolution that was very close to Keynes's own, and in which Keynes himself played the leading role.

In the *General Theory*, Keynes offered two accounts of the relationship between his economics and that of the classics, both of which had a profound effect on the subsequent literature. He identified what he claimed were the key classical postulates, the denial of which led to his own, more general theory; and he argued that, if government policy could achieve full employment, the classical theory would come into its own. There were three classical postulates, any one of which implied the other two: (1) the wage rate equals the value of the output produced by a day's extra labour; (2) there is no such thing as involuntary unemployment (everyone who wants work at the going wage can get it); (3) when the economy is taken as a whole, there is no shortage of demand for goods and services. He then constructed a theory, based on certain assumptions about consumers' expenditure, investment and the demand for money in which there might be an equilibrium where people were involuntarily unemployed.

This way of formulating the difference between his work and previous theories led economists to ask what were the key assumptions that caused Keynes to reach different conclusions. To identify these would be to identify the revolutionary element in Keynes's theory. Almost immediately the *General Theory* had been published, economists started formulating mathematical models of the relationship between saving, investment, the rate of interest, wages and the level of employment, working out when they yielded classical results and when they yielded Keynesian ones. The most successful of these models was produced by John Hicks (1937), who reduced it to a pair of curves; these were later developed by Alvin Hansen (1953), who labelled them the IS and LM curves, giving the model a name that stuck (this story is told in Young 1987. In this context, the Keynesian revolution involved making different (and arguably more realistic) assumptions about the slopes of these curves, and hence about the underlying relationships. Of these, the main ones were the responsiveness of investment (in physical capital goods) and of the demand for money to the rate of interest.

During the 1940s, there was a revival of interest in general equilibrium theory. This was a theory of how prices would adjust to bring about equilibrium (where demand and supply were equal) in a large number of markets simultaneously. Essentially the mechanism was that if demand for one good were greater than the quantity firms wished to supply, its price would rise; this would affect demands for and supplies of other goods, affecting their prices; this process of adjustment would continue until, assuming all went well, all markets were in equilibrium. This was becoming the standard way to think about economic problems, so it was natural to ask how Keynesian economics could be fitted into this framework. The most direct way was to see the IS-LM model as a miniature general equilibrium model, in which there were four markets (goods, labour, money and bonds) and three prices (the wage, the price of goods and the rate of interest) (see Modigliani 1944). The problem for Keynesian economics was that in equilibrium there was full employment, so in order to explain Keynesian phenomena it was necessary to explain why markets did not achieve equilibrium. Economists had always accepted that if the wage rate was inflexible, the result might be unemployment, so economists sought other explanations. Possibilities considered by Hicks, Hansen, Modigliani and others included a floor to the rate of interest (the liquidity trap) and a limit to the amount of investment that firms were willing to undertake, however low the rate of interest.

An important step in the interpretation of Keynes came in Patinkin (1948) with the introduction of the so-called real balance effect. This was a highly technical point, but with important implications for the way Keynesian economics was conceived. The 'classical' mechanism (quotation marks are needed, because it was a mechanism postulated by Keynes, following Hawtrey, and was not to be found in Marshall or Pigou) for eliminating unemployment was that the existence of unemployment would cause wages (and hence prices) to fall, raising the real value of the money supply and pushing down the rate of interest. This fall in the rate of interest would stimulate spending, especially investment, thereby raising demand and hence employment. If there were a liquidity trap, or if firms were simply unwilling to invest, this mechanism would not work. Patinkin's observation was that as deflation raised the real value of money balances, it would make people wealthier; even if the rate of interest did not fall, this would cause them to spend more. This led to the conclusion that, provided wages could fall, unemployment would not occur in equilibrium. Unemployment must be a disequilibrium phenomenon. This contrasted with Keynes's claim, thought by many to be central to the Keynesian revolution, that there could be an equilibrium in which there was unemployment. These ideas were most fully developed in Patinkin's *Money, Interest and Prices* (1956, 1965) which became the leading graduate textbook on macroeconomics in the 1960s and early 1970s. Patinkin did not minimize the importance of unemployment: far from it. Though there might exist forces that would bring the economy back to full-employment equilibrium, these might be very weak or operate very slowly. As a result, unemployment might persist for socially unacceptable periods of time and it might be necessary to take corrective action. Keynesian policies might be justifiable to eliminate unemployment that persisted for too long. This led to the consensus view that though Keynes may have been wrong to argue that his theory represented the general case, it was the one that was relevant for policy.

This interpretation of Keynesian economics, though it may seem a long way from Keynes (it certainly conflicts with much that he said about unemployment equilibrium) fits in well with the second of Keynes's statements about the relationship between his theory and the classical. At the end of the *General Theory* (JMK VII: 377–81), Keynes speculated that if government policy could ensure that resources were fully employed, the classical theory would come into its own. The mechanism of supply and demand was an efficient way of allocating resources between different activities (it could ensure that the right mix of goods was produced): its defect was simply that it could not ensure full employment. This distinction formed the basis of what Samuelson, who had done as much as anyone to propagate Keynesian economics, termed 'the neoclassical synthesis' in the third (1955) edition of the textbook *Economics*, the book that had done more than any other to popularize Keynesian economics. By the 1960s, though economists might disagree over such points as the importance of the real balance effect or the liquidity trap, and hence whether it was right to talk about 'equilibrium' unemployment, this was the standard way to think about Keynesian economics and hence the Keynesian revolution. Keynesian economics had become assimilated into the new orthodoxy.

DISSENTING INTERPRETATIONS OF THE KEYNESIAN REVOLUTION

Shortly after the *General Theory* was published, the *Quarterly Journal of Economics* published a symposium on the book, containing critiques by several distinguished economists. These offered long and detailed criticisms, but rather than get embroiled in details, Keynes chose to respond by saying what he considered the most important point about his theory. He wrote:

> I am more attached to the comparatively simple fundamental ideas which underlie my theory than to the particular forms in which I have embodied them. . . [For the classical economists] facts and expectations were assumed to be given in a definite and calculable form. . . The calculus of probability . . . was supposed to be capable of reducing uncertainty to the same calculable status as that of certainty itself. . . Actually, however, we have, as a rule, only the vaguest idea of any but the most direct consequences of our acts. . . I accuse the classical theory of being itself one of those pretty, polite techniques which tries to deal with the present by abstracting from the fact that we know very little about the future.
>
> (JMK XIV: 112–13, 115)

In these passages he was taking up the ideas on investment he had proposed in chapter 12 of the *General Theory*. There he had argued that investment depended on what he called the state of long-term expectations – expectations about what the world would be like in twenty or thirty years' time. This depended on things such as whether there was a European war, to which it was impossible to attach probabilities. People simply did not know.

Keynes's claim that the existence of uncertainty, in the sense of uncertainty that cannot be reduced to probability, has provided the justification for a more radical interpretation of the Keynesian revolution, which has been described in such terms as 'fundamentalist' or 'chapter 12' Keynesianism (cf. Coddington 1983: ch. 6). Where Hicks, Samuelson, Modigliani, Patinkin and the other architects of the neo-classical synthesis interpreted the

Keynesian economics using standard price theory, in which supply and demand depend on the actions of rational, maximizing agents, fundamentalist Keynesianism claimed that Keynes was challenging the foundations of the orthodox price theory; orthodox Keynesians were therefore missing the point of Keynes's revolution. Fully specified, determinate models such as the IS-LM model or Patinkin's model miss the point of the *General Theory*, for Keynes's argument is that no model can be specified (Loasby 1976: 167).

The first fundamentalist interpretation of the Keynesian revolution came from Hugh Townshend (1937). He started from Keynes's theory of liquidity preference, making the case that it applied to all goods. All valuations depended on expectations and were therefore conventional. The most elegant, and perhaps furthest-reaching, exponent of this view, however, was George Shackle. In a series of books (e.g. 1967, 1973) Shackle argued that the Keynesian revolution concerned time. The essence of time is that it is irreversible and that we can know nothing about the future. Furthermore, human creativity and free will imply that indeterminacy is inherent in human behaviour, providing a theoretical explanation of why the future cannot be known. However, the most widely cited exponent of this view was probably Joan Robinson (1974), who drew a distinction between history and equilibrium, or historical and logical time. The Keynesian revolution was about breaking with equilibrium, which can occur only in logical time, and creating a theory about how economic activity took place in historical time that was relevant to the real world. This view has since then been developed by Paul Davidson (1972) and some other post-Keynesian economists (cf. King 2002). The common feature of all such interpretations is that they see the Keynesian revolution as overthrowing precisely the type of rational-choice theory on which the neoclassical synthesis was based. This explains why Robinson coined the phrase 'bastard Keynesianism' to describe the postwar Keynesian orthodoxy.

There are certainly passages written by Keynes that point towards a fundamentalist interpretation of the Keynesian revolution. On top of those mentioned already, the *General Theory* contains a chapter, puzzling to most economists, on 'The essential properties of interest and money', which can easily be read as providing support for this view. It fits well with much of Keynes's earlier work, such as his *Treatise on Probability* (1921) and *The End of Laissez-Faire* (1926). The *General Theory* could be construed as providing a theoretical justification for his earlier claim that 'many of the greatest evils of our time [including unemployment of labour] are the fruits of risk, uncertainty and ignorance', and that it was necessary for the state to control money and credit, and to decide on the appropriate scale of saving and where those savings should be directed (JMK IX: 291–2).

On the other hand, the textual evidence against this interpretation is also very strong. The IS-LM model is built from elements that are all found in the *General Theory*: evidence for this is found in the number of economists who, when faced with the *General Theory*, independently came up with essentially the same set of equations. When Hicks showed Keynes his article on IS-LM, Keynes responded that he had next to nothing to say by way of criticism. Keynes's clear statement that the classical theory comes into its own once full employment is achieved is clearly incompatible with a fundamentalist interpretation.

A completely different critique of what by then had become the Keynesian orthodoxy was opened up by Robert Clower (1965). He shared the fundamentalist Keynesian conviction that the Keynesian revolution was about a monetary economy, and that conventional models did not deal adequately with this, but he developed the idea in a different way. The essence of a monetary economy is that goods are exchanged for money, not directly for other goods. This meant, amongst other things, that goods cannot be bought with labour: labour has first to be sold for money, and that money used to buy the goods. The implication of that is that if workers cannot sell their labour, they will be unable to buy goods. Clower then added the observation that if there is unemployment, workers cannot (by definition) be able to sell the quantity of labour they want to sell, which means that they cannot buy the quantity of goods they would ideally like to buy. He called this the 'dual decision hypothesis' – the notion that consumption is constrained first by households' resources (the hours available in the day and their wealth) and second by the labour they manage to sell. Without the dual-decision hypothesis, Clower argued, Keynesian theory simply did not make sense.

The reason why this was such a radical idea was that it challenged the standard conceptions of what lay behind supply and demand. If markets were all in equilibrium, everyone would be able to buy and sell as much as they wished at the going prices, and orthodox theory was fine. However, out of equilibrium (when there was unemployment), additional constraints came into operation that meant that effective demands would be different from the 'notional' demands of orthodox theory. The Keynesian revolution, therefore, involved a new view of how markets operated. It turned out that Clower's dual-decision hypothesis was similar to an idea that Patinkin had proposed when dealing with disequilibrium in *Money, Interest and Prices*; he had proposed that if firms cannot sell all the goods they wish to sell at the prevailing prices, they will cut back on their hiring of labour. Put together, these led to a view of how economies might get stuck with high levels of unemployment: employment was low because firms could not sell enough goods; and sales of goods were low because workers could not sell their labour. It was a vicious circle.

The book that addressed the revolutionary implications of these ideas was Axel Leijonhufvud's *On Keynesian Economics and the Economics of Keynes* (1968). As the title stated, he argued that Keynesian economics, as it had come to be understood, bore no relation to the economics of Keynes. The conventional view attributed unemployment to wages being inflexible; as Leijonhufvud pointed out, the idea that wage rigidity might cause unemployment was hardly revolutionary. What was revolutionary about the *General Theory*, and which justified the word 'general' in Keynes's title, was that it was about economics 'without the auctioneer'. His reasoning was that in classical theory it is assumed that markets are in equilibrium – as in markets where an auctioneer calls out prices, allowing trade to take place only when supply and demand balance. In markets without an auctioneer, trade will take place at prices that are not equilibrium prices; as a result, agents will find that they cannot buy or sell all that they wish to sell at the going prices; and the constraints analyzed by Clower and Patinkin will come into operation. Disequilibrium, far from being a special case caused by failure of the wage rate to adjust, was in fact the general case. Keynes was justified in the revolutionary claims he made for his theory.

Leijonhufvud also reassessed the arguments over expectations and the rate of interest that are central to the *General Theory*. In the same way that he placed arguments about quantity constraints in the broader context of economics when markets are not co-ordinated, he placed Keynes's arguments about interest rates into a broader context by arguing that Keynes was talking about an 'inter-temporal disequilibrium'. Because of the way expectations were formed, the rate of interest could not co-ordinate decisions to save and to invest, with the result that there could emerge a deficiency of aggregate demand. This took up themes that Swedish economists such as Erik Lindahl and Gunnar Myrdal, following Wicksell, had pursued in the 1930s. The significance of Leijonhufvud's argument about interest rates was that he was providing reasons why it might be reasonable to consider the failure of markets to equilibrate the system to be the normal, more general case. Keynesian economics was not simply about what happened when, because of some institutional constraint, either the wage rate or the interest rate could not adjust to bring about equilibrium.

For a brief period, Leijonhufvud's book was widely read and discussed. However, in the longer term, its influence was much less. In the mid-1970s, his work, along with that of Clower and Patinkin, was seen as providing the justification for what came to be called 'disequilibrium macroeconomics', or 'fix-price' macroeconomics. Following an earlier paper by Solow and Stiglitz (1968), Robert Barro and Herschel Grossman (1971) constructed a model where consumers were constrained by actual sales of labour and firms employed no more labour than needed to produce the goods they actually sold. It was therefore possible for an economy to get stuck in a low-level equilibrium where there was unemployment and, at the same time, firms could not sell all the goods they wanted to sell. This was labelled Keynesian unemployment. Though this type of model could be interpreted as a way of analyzing the implications of markets where trading took place in real time, and in which there were many imperfections, it came to be interpreted as exploring the implications of rigid prices in a Walrasian general equilibrium model. This confirmed what by then had become the standard 'textbook' interpretation of the Keynesian revolution that Leijonhufvud had sought to disprove.

THE KEYNESIAN REVOLUTION AFTER LUCAS

The economic crisis that followed OPEC's decision to raise crude oil prices in 1973-4 marked the end of what has been called 'the age of Keynes'. Not only was Keynesian policy called into question – it could not provide guidance when unemployment and inflation were both rising sharply – but the theoretical framework that underlay Keynesian economics was challenged. The main architect of this challenge was Robert Lucas, whose work laid the foundations for what came to be called the New Classical Macroeconomics. Where previous challengers (such as Milton Friedman) had worked within a theoretical framework that had much in common with the Keynesian, and was arguably strongly influenced by it, the foundations of the New Classical Macroeconomics were radically different. Where Keynesian economics was based on the existence of empirical regularities such as the marginal propensity to consume, the New Classical Macroeconomics argued that the one thing that could be relied upon was that individuals were rational and took up all profitable opportunities open to them. This meant that markets had to be modelled as being in equilibrium, because if supply and demand were not equal, anyone who could not buy (or sell) all that they wanted had merely to raise the price they offered (or lower the price they were asking).

Perhaps more important, where Keynesian economists had viewed government policy as something that could be manipulated to ensure that desired outcomes were reached (raise spending to stimulate spending and employment; cut interest rates to get the optimal level of investment; and so on), the New Classicals argued that private agents would see any patterns in government policy and take account of them. Unless the government took private agents by surprise, the private sector would neutralize the effects of policy changes. Policy would be ineffective. From this perspective, which spread through economics in the late 1970s and 1980s, Keynesian economics was completely misconceived. It was based on premises both about the economy and about how to do economics that were fatally flawed. Keynesian economics seemed to be dying, if not dead, and the Keynesian revolution to have been a harmful detour.

However, Keynesian economics did not die. The problem of persistent unemployment did not disappear, but re-emerged, especially in Europe, in the 1980s. There was also dissatisfaction with the new theories at a theoretical level. Economists could not believe that markets worked like perfectly competitive auction markets where a single price was determined by supply and demand. They began to find reasons why markets might work differently: workers might have more information about their own abilities than the firms with whom they were trying to find a job; firms and workers might have an element of monopoly power; firms might not be able to observe how hard workers were working. When these effects were taken into account, economists began to build models that, though based on completely rational agents, exhibited Keynesian features. This led to the New Keynesian Macroeconomics. Problems also arose within the New Classical research programme: the timing of changes in output and price changes did not fit what the New Classical models predicted would happen if changes were driven by money-supply shocks. This was the rationale for the move towards so-called real business-cycle models. These were methodologically very similar to New Classical models but were driven by supply-side shocks. This helped resolve the lack of fit between theory and data, but there were still problems. As a result, over the years, even those economists who started building pure real business-cycle models began to introduce more and more 'Keynesian' features, such as wage stickiness; this helped explain why unemployment persisted for longer than pure real business-cycle models suggested it should.

From the perspective of the New Keynesian Macroeconomics, the Keynesian revolution looked different yet again. The Keynesian revolution may not have yielded theoretically rigorous models, but the intuitions on which it was based were essentially correct. Economies could fail to generate high levels of employment. The New Keynesian economics provided detailed microeconomic explanations of why this might be so, most of which related to the labour market, but the results were substantially the same as those reached by the early Keynesians, with important differences. There was much greater awareness that Keynesian results (such as that expanding the money supply might raise employment) applied only in the short run, and that the long-run effects (inflation) might arise much sooner than early Keynesians thought. There was also a belief that the public would try to anticipate government policy, which might therefore have less effect than if it did not.

THE KEYNESIAN REVOLUTION AS AN EPISODE IN THE HISTORY OF SCIENCE

Thomas Kuhn's *The Structure of Scientific Revolutions* was published in 1962, with a revised edition in 1970, with profound effects on the philosophy of science (see Suppe 1977). Early on, attempts were made to apply Kuhn's ideas to economics, trying to identify periods of normal science and scientific revolutions (Coats 1965). The Keynesian revolution was, along with the so-called 'marginal revolution' of the 1870s, one of the prime candidates for a Kuhnian scientific revolution in economics. In the 1970s, concern with Kuhn's philosophy of science was supplemented and partly displaced by interest in Imre Lakatos's (1970) methodology of scientific research programmes (aided perhaps by Lakatos's position at the LSE, and Spiro Latsis's (1976) success in drawing together a very distinguished group of economists to explore the relevance of the methodology of scientific research programmes to economics). The Keynesian revolution became one of the main candidates for analysis in terms of the transition from one research programme to another. This had great advantages over Kuhn's paradigms as a framework, for it was consistent with the fact that 'classical' economics did not die after the Keynesian revolution, but continued, in competition with it.

If the Keynesian revolution was a switch from one scientific research programme in the sense described by Lakatos, it must be possible to identify the hard cores of the classical and Keynesian programmes, and the transition must have taken place because Keynesian economics predicted important novel facts that classical economics could not. Hands (1985) claimed that mass unemployment, the phenomenon explained by the *General Theory*, was not a novel fact. Blaug, who had previously (1975) cited the Keynesian revolution as illustrating Lakatos's claim that scientists change allegiance from degenerating to progressive research programmes, responded (1990b) that the main novel fact predicted by the *General Theory* was that the expenditure multiplier was greater than one: that a rise in investment or government spending would produce a rise in income that was larger than the initial increase in spending. On top of this, the model could be used to predict a host of other novel facts, and was so used during the 1940s.

These debates were largely taken up by a newly emerging group of scholars who, though largely based in economics departments (and many of whom were trained in economics), were approaching economics from the perspective of philosophy. Their main commitment was to provide a rigorous philosophical account of what had happened in economics. They were not trying to argue that a particular approach to economics was correct; this was not their task. There were, however, other economists who used arguments about the Keynesian revolution being a paradigm shift in the sense of Kuhn to argue for a new way of doing economics. One of the earliest was Jan Kregel, whose *Reconstruction of Political Economy* (1973) argued that implicit in the *General Theory* was a critique of the theory of supply and demand itself: the dependence of economic behaviour on expectations of the future meant that changes in relative prices would not have the effects postulated by traditional theory. However, rather than aim at this fundamental target, Keynes adopted the pragmatic strategy of conceding everything he could to the tradtional view, in order to persuade economists that something could be done about mass unemployment. The result of this was that Keynes opened the way for traditional theory to be restored, and a revolution in economic theory was avoided. The way to a revolution was to embrace Keynes's critique of the price theory (the traditional theory of supply and demand). Following Joan Robinson, Kregel called this new economics 'post-Keynesian' economics, claiming that it amounted to a Gestalt shift, such as characterized a Kuhnian paradigm shift.

Looking at an abstract figure I may be able to see the outlines of a rabbit. Someone else . . . may believe it to be an elephant. But for me to see the elephant implies losing the image of the rabbit; both cannot be seen at once. So it seems also with economic theory. . . So I ask you to do your best to try and see my rabbit.

(Kregel 1973: 4)

Post-Keynesian economists are not the only ones to have argued that Keynes's introduction of radical uncertainty implies a profound rupture in economic theory. Verdon (1996) has drawn parallels with the revolution wrought by Einstein in physics. (It is perhaps worth comparing this with Pigou's (1936: 115) claim that 'Einstein actually did for Physics what Mr. Keynes believes himself to have done for Economics'.) Keynes's discussions of uncertainty have prompted others to talk of 'postmodern moments' in Keynes's theory (Ruccio and Amariglio 2003: ch. 2).This emphasizes the variety of ways in which the *General Theory* can be read, for although there are passages that can be read this way, there are others where Keynes appears to be arguing in just the way claimed by more mainstream Keynesians, such as the architects of the neo-classical synthesis.

THE KEYNESIAN REVOLUTION: RHETORIC AND REALITY

The task of disentangling what the Keynesian revolution was is beset by pitfalls. One of the main barriers to understanding it has been the large number of economists for whom Keynes has iconic status, representative of an age and a political philosophy as much as of a technical change in the way economics has been done. Keynes rapidly became regarded as the leading representative of a particular political philosophy, criticized by the left for being too supportive of capitalism, and by the right for being tantamount to socialism. Keynes himself encouraged this with his provocatively entitled 'The end of laissez-faire' and with a chapter in the *General Theory* in which he speculated on the implications of his theory for the long-run organization of society. His only rivals in this respect are Adam Smith, David Ricardo and Karl Marx (and nowadays perhaps Friedrich Hayek). It was this canonization of Keynes to which Paul Samuelson (Blang 1990a: 58) referred when he wrote:

> I actually did not like a certain note that I thought I detected at the hundredth anniversary of Keynes's birth, celebrated at the holy of holies, King's College, Cambridge. Person after person got up, walked the sawdust trail and said: 'I am just as firm a Keynesian as I ever was. I am an unreconstructed Keynesian.' And I finally exploded and said: 'We don't want unreconstructed Keynesians. We want people who will carry the scientific analysis further.'

However, this is not the only reason why the task is difficult. Three statements about the Keynesian revolution are undoubtedly correct: (1) Keynes claimed to be making a revolutionary break with the economics of the past. (2) Keynesian economics was welcomed enthusiastically by a large part of the economics profession, with the result that his *General Theory* had an effect on the subject that was unprecedented in both its speed and its depth. Within a decade, it was clear that Keynes had been the leading economist of his generation, eclipsing his rivals Schumpeter and Hayek, and that he was probably one of the most influential economists of all time. (3) Economics was done very differently indeed from the way it had been done before the *General Theory* was published. The problem is in knowing how to relate the third of these to the first two. It can be posed in two ways, starting either from Keynes or from economics after Keynes.

Keynes emphasized the revolutionary nature of his theory, and when pushed to sum up what was revolutionary about it, he talked about his theory being relevant for a world in which there is true uncertainty. However, it is arguable that these aspects of his theory were taken up by only a few economists. Many economists ignored these aspects of the book, focusing on the mathematical relationships (the consumption, investment and demand-for-money functions) that could be used to construct formal models. Those mathematical relationships, though they could be interpreted using the verbal reasoning that Keynes offered, did not have to be interpreted that way. They could be justified using more conventional arguments, as happened during the 1940s and 1950s. Post-Keynesians were, therefore, able to claim that the Keynesian revolution had been aborted, or that there had been a counter-revolution, arguing that his verbal arguments about the implications of uncertainty had been pushed aside. Against this, it was possible to argue that the new theories were genuinely Keynesian because they built directly on the mathematical framework around which Keynes constructed his *General Theory*. As Laidler (1999) summed it up, with the Keynesian revolution came a new model: a set of equations (drawn out of the *General Theory*) that could be used to analyze macroeconomic phenomena.

One reason why the *General Theory* could be interpreted in so many ways was that it contained many different lines of reasoning. Joan Robinson (1974: 261), hardly a defender of orthodox economics, argued that, amongst the many lines of argument in the book, there was one that provided a logically firm connection between Keynes's assumptions and his conclusions, but that the book also contained many separate lines of argument that Keynes should have removed, but did not. This may be one reason why, following

Ricoeur, Gerrard (1991) could argue that the *General Theory* was a rich text, capable of many interpretations.

If, instead, the problem of the Keynesian revolution is approached from the starting-point of modern economics, further problems arise. Macroeconomics in the 1950s was dramatically different from what it was like in the early 1930s – so much so that economists believed it was reasonable to claim that the field had been newly created. Keynes was everywhere. However, these changes were caused by much more than Keynes's work. The main change was the use of formal mathematical models and the move to a style of reasoning where deriving the properties of such models was central to economic analysis. There were similar changes in other fields: economics generally became more technical, a process that has continued since then (cf. Solow 1997). This is a process that cannot be attributed entirely to Keynes. Indeed, Keynes was very ambiguous in his attitude towards mathematical economics (cf. Patinkin 1976). On the one hand, he wrote about the importance of intuitive arguments that cannot be completely formalized (cf. Moggridge 1992: 551–71; Skidelsky 1992: 539–48; Backhouse 1997: 34–6), and his criticism of the use of techniques based on the assumption that we know more about the future than we do was implicitly a criticism of mathematical modelling. He was also very critical of the mathematical models constructed by his contemporaries. On the other hand, he placed functional relationships and their properties, very much a mathematical-style argument, at the heart of his book.

This change in the way economists used mathematics took place simultaneously with the Keynesian revolution, to such an extent that the two are difficult to separate. However, there are many reasons to argue that mathematics was coming into economics for reasons completely unconnected with Keynes. The Econometric Society, committed to applying to economics the formal methods that had proved successful in natural science, had been founded in 1930, and different traditions of mathematical economics arose in Europe and the United States. Yet, as regards certain types of mathematical economics (macroeconomics and econometrics), this mathematical revolution is almost inseparable from the Keynesian. What happened was that, though economists had already started to develop mathematical models, Keynes's *General Theory* provided concepts that proved so suitable for these models that within a short period it became hard to see that the move towards using such methods had started before 1936.

Similar remarks can be made about the revolution in national income accounting that took place between the 1930s and 1950s. The first official measures of US national income were not produced till 1933, and these, when they appeared, were for four years only and were not very detailed. By the 1950s, national income was being collected systematically in many countries, and the United Nations was involved in establishing international standards that would ensure different countries' accounts were comparable. These accounts were compiled on Keynesian lines, hiding their pre-Keynesian origins. The availability of detailed, regular statistics transformed the context in which macroeconomics was done. Beneath all these developments lay important political developments: during the Second World War, governments became far more involved in the economy than ever before, and the war, combined with memories of the Great Depression, had a dramatic effect on society in many countries. The political environment was thus completely different from that of the 1930s.

The problem, therefore, with the Keynesian revolution is that there are many explanations and interpretations that, at one level, seem to fit what happened. The Keynesian revolution is the name given to one aspect of a much larger intellectual change with many dimensions. However, because of the immense interest in Keynes, as much for ideological as for any other reasons, there has been a search for simple summaries of the phenomenon that supporters and critics have been happy to label the Keynesian revolution. The Keynesian revolution has become so stuck in economists' collective consciousness that it has proved difficult to question, even though questioning it might help to remove some of the confusion that surrounds it.

CONCLUSIONS

There are several reasons why arguments about the Keynesian revolution have failed to converge on an agreed consensus. The first reason is the complexity of the set of changes that the term has been used to describe. The Keynesian revolutions in economic theory, in macroeconomic policy and in political philosophy are intimately connected with each other. Furthermore, they rest on much broader changes, both within economics and within society more generally: the role of the state was transformed by the Second World War; the political landscape in many countries was changed, as was the international environment; within economics there were important changes involving both the collection and use of statistics and in the extent to which economists used mathematical methods. Keynesian economics did not cause the ideological shift that came about after the Depression and during the Second World War, but it was such an integral part of that shift that the two became hard to disentangle. Right from the start, it was never possible for debates over the Keynesian revolution to be separated from ideology. The immodesty of Keynes's own claims for what his book was going to achieve may have been part of the problem.

3 Keynes and the birth of modern macroeconomics

KEYNES AND MACROECONOMICS

Keynes's *General Theory of Employment, Interest and Money* (1936) was about the role of the monetary system in general, and the rate of interest in particular, in causing the overall level of employment in a market economy to fall short of its full potential. A sub-set of its ideas were systematized by a younger generation of economists and introduced to the textbooks, just as the word *macroeconomics* began to be widely used to distinguish the analysis of the economy as a whole from *microeconomics*, which dealt with individual households, firms or even industries. Not without justification, macroeconomics soon became a synonym for *Keynesian economics*; and in the late 1970s, when the influence of Keynes's specific ideas on the sub-discipline had long since waned, he was still commonly credited with having founded it (Lucas and Sargent, 1978).

MYTHS ABOUT KEYNES AND THE CLASSICS

Myth-making about Keynes's role in the creation of modern macroeconomics began with his own 1936 account of the work of his predecessors and older contemporaries, to whom he affixed the blanket label the 'Classical economists'. He attributed a fundamental weakness to their economic theory: namely, that it encompassed the postulate – known as Say's Law – that an economy-wide excess supply of output, and therefore of labour, was a logical impossibility, and that it was incapable of explaining economy-wide unemployment.

Keynes's account of classical economics was a caricature, but most of his interpreters accepted it and supplemented it with distortions of his own work to produce a myth about the development of macroeconomics that still dominates many economists' beliefs. In this myth, classical economics argued that if more people sought work than there were jobs available, a fall in wages would not only suffice to restore full employment but would in fact occur. The relevant wage was the *real* wage, the *nominal* wage adjusted for variations in the purchasing power of the money in terms of which it was actually set, but, so the myth continued, the classical economists had failed to notice that, in the modern world, a wide variety of contractual rigidities prevented nominal wages from falling in the face of an excess supply of labour. Keynes, however, did notice this, and deduced that real wages could therefore not be relied on to adjust according to classical principles. He proposed that, in these circumstances, the government should fight unemployment by increasing its own spending on goods and services, and perhaps by cutting taxes to encourage households to increase their spending, and should be prepared to run budget deficits to finance such measures.

According to this myth, then, Keynes's originality in 1936 lay first in recognizing that the labour market was subject to wage rigidities that other economists had overlooked; and second in proposing that unemployment resulting from these rigidities be dealt with by an active programme of deficit spending by governments. This simple tale is implausible. It is unlikely that economists, whose discipline had existed since at least the second half of the eighteenth century, had failed to notice so salient a feature of labour markets as wage stickiness in the intervening years, and it is hard to see, for example, where the first Roosevelt administration's New Deal could have come from, if Keynes was not to invent expansionary fiscal policy until 1936. Finally, if this is nevertheless what Keynes's book was really about, why did he not give it some such title as *Employment, Wages and Fiscal Policy*? After all, the above account credits it with only superficial theoretical content and mentions neither interest nor money at all.

SAY'S LAW AND MONEY

Keynes's caricature of classical economics nevertheless captured certain salient features of its subject. For a century after the publication of the *Wealth of Nations* (Smith 1776), its centrepiece was a theory of economic growth that was indeed underpinned by a version of Say's Law. Smith had argued that income not spent by landowners and capitalists on consumption, and hence saved, would be channelled into supporting labour in the production of goods for future consumption, and that, therefore, there would be no chance of output going to waste. With certain qualifications having to do with the production of machinery, David Ricardo (1817, 1821) also subscribed to this view. More generally, he also argued that though goods were not bartered, but bought and sold in exchange for money, monetary exchange was purely an intermediate activity that did not alter the essential nature of market activity, namely that it was goods and services that ultimately bought goods and services, so that a general oversupply of them, and hence of labour, was impossible.

Ricardo, however, wrote in the second decade of the nineteenth century, a period marked by unemployment and social unrest, and some commentators, notably his friend Thomas Malthus (1820), attributed these problems to a flaw in the mechanisms of economic growth that somehow caused rapid capital accumulation and output growth to outrun the capacity of *effective demand* to absorb it, leading to a *general glut* of commodities on the market. Ricardo's counter-argument to this, namely that unemployment reflected a *mis-allocation* of labour among industries brought about by postwar changes in the *structure* of demand and would in due course be cured by an adjustment of *relative* prices, is generally judged to have carried this debate, but the dissenting position never quite died out, subsequently enabling Keynes to claim – whether accurately or not is another matter, though Steven Kates (1994) mounts a strong defence of Keynes's claim – that his *General Theory* was but the latest, but finally a logically coherent, manifestation of it.

Had there been no more to classical economics than the views expressed in Ricardo's *Principles*, there would be much to be said for Keynes's 1936 critique. However, it also encompassed a more pragmatic literature, dealing with cyclical economic instability, which has a strong claim to be treated as the true antecedent of modern macroeconomics, and to which, incidentally, Ricardo was also an early contributor. It was in this context that John Stuart Mill (1844, 1848) pointed to an essential role for money in qualifying Say's Law as it was generally understood, explicitly connecting his insights to the Malthus–Ricardo debate. Mill reaffirmed the impossibility of excessive capital accumulation creating a general glut of output but noted that the proposition that agents would always bring goods and services to market with a view to buying other goods and services was true of logical necessity only in an economy where trade was by barter. Under monetary exchange, agents might sometimes try to sell goods to acquire money for its own sake, and when they did, there would be a general oversupply of goods on the market relative to money.

Mill associated such behaviour with financial crises. He thought that a desire to accumulate cash at such times was a reaction to acute uncertainty about the near-term future, and would be short-lived; and he did not make any more of his insights than this. But those insights were nevertheless of profound theoretical importance: they suggested that markets where exchange was mediated by money could sometimes behave in ways that would be impossible under barter, and that such behaviour stemmed from the uncertainty to which economic activity co-ordinated by monetary exchange was subject. In short, they suggested that monetary exchange was anything but an inessential feature of the economy. Much generalized, and their potential implications worked out in great detail, these insights would ultimately inform the *General Theory*.

MONEY WAGE STICKINESS

Even so, when Mill's successors began to study unemployment, they did not directly associate it with the efforts of agents to build up their money-holdings but began to rely instead on nominal wage stickiness. Following Alfred Marshall and Mary Marshall (1879), it was often argued that, when, over the course of the cycle, the price level rose and fell, money wages would follow only sluggishly, so that real wages would fall and rise, inducing fluctuations in the demand for labour and therefore employment. Post-1936 myths were thus badly wrong to suggest that nominal wage stickiness as an explanation of unemployment was original to Keynes. On the contrary, in 1936 he pointed to a serious logical incompleteness in the above argument, which seemed to imply that the implementation of nominal wage cuts, a policy to which he had been strongly opposed from the mid-1920s onwards, was a sure cure for unemployment.

This incompleteness arose because the argument assumed that the demand for labour varied inversely with the real wage, a relationship that would hold for an individual firm, or even a single industry, but not necessarily for the economy as a whole. Here, a sequence of effects running from fluctuations in employment to incomes, from incomes to expenditure, and from expenditure to the demand for labour and hence back to employment, had to be taken into account. In fact, Keynes asserted, there might be no way to restoring full employment to an economy by money wage cuts. Their implementation might set in motion a downward spiral of wages and prices, with no well-determined effect on quantities. He treated this last conclusion as a logical possibility, however, not a necessity, because, as we shall now see, he did recognize the existence of a mechanism whereby money wage cuts, whether market- or policy-induced, might indeed cause employment to rise.

An essential component of Keynes's (1936) theory was that employment depended on the economy-wide demand for labour, which in turn depended on *effective demand*, the economy-wide volume of expenditure on goods and services. He claimed that this insight had informed Malthus's theory of the general glut, but that the concept of effective demand had been lost sight of in the wake of Ricardo's victory in their debate, only now to be rediscovered by himself. He argued that money wage cuts might cure unemployment, not because they would lead to lower real wages, but because they might increase effective demand.[1] Such cuts would reduce firms' costs, enabling them to reduce prices, hence causing the general price level to fall. If the stock of nominal money in circulation was held constant as this happened, then its real purchasing power would increase, agents would find their money-holdings excessive, their expenditure on goods and services would go up and employment would therefore increase; and this would happen even though downward pressure on prices would tend to mute any direct effects on real wages.

Where the Marshalls and their successors had explained unemployment as the consequence of money wage stickiness in the face of falling prices, then, Keynes stressed that a failure of prices to fall induced by money wage stickiness could force output and employment (rather than the price level) to bear the burden of adjustment to a discrepancy between the supply and demand for money. He noted that wage cuts might, therefore, help to reduce unemployment, but he presented this effect as an unreliable one on which any case for attempting to reduce unemployment by inducing money wage cuts would nevertheless have to rely. It might, for example, be overwhelmed by depressing expectational effects on effective demand, associated with a *falling* (as opposed to a *lower*) price level, and it might be short-circuited by a monetary policy regime that permitted the nominal money supply to contract as the price level fell. Furthermore, in Keynes's view, the experience of the United States in the early years of the Depression, when the price level fell dramatically, ruled out wage–price stickiness as a plausible explanation of the occurrence of large-scale unemployment, and wage cuts as a reliable cure for it.

Keynes concluded that increasing the supply of money was a better remedy for unemployment than money wage cuts, but he had little more enthusiasm for this alternative. Rather, he argued that the causes of unemployment lay deeper in the mechanisms of monetary exchange than the effects of wage and price frictions on the workings of markets for currently produced goods and services, and that neither wage flexibility nor simple monetary measures would reliably counter them.

SAVING AND INVESTMENT, UNCERTAINTY AND THE MONETARY SYSTEM

When Adam Smith (1776) argued that a decision to abstain from current consumption (to *save*) was simultaneously a decision to employ labour in the production of goods for future consumption (and hence to *invest*), he was thinking of a choice made by an individual capitalist about the allocation over time of his own income. By Keynes's time, however, it had been a commonplace for more than a century that saving and investment decisions were typically made by different agents, and that the co-ordination of their choices about the intertemporal allocation of resources was a task for the capital market, in which the relevant equilibrating price was the rate of interest. By then, too, it had long been agreed that the rate of interest that investors were willing to pay for borrowed funds derived from their expectations about the profitability of the investments that they intended to make, and that the rate that lenders demanded depended upon their assessment of the sacrifices involved in deferring current consumption into the future. Within this broad consensus, however, the classical literature accommodated many important variations in the treatment of the interactions of saving and investment. One of these – felicitously called 'The Wicksell Connection' by Axel Leijonhufvud (1981) – focused on the role of the monetary system in these matters, and it is worth particular attention at this point.

Gold coinage and notes convertible into gold played a subordinate role in the late nineteenth-century monetary system. It was dominated by commercial banks whose lending created, as a by-product, deposits that were then used as a means of exchange. Of course, the role of banks in the monetary system had been much discussed throughout the century, but Knut Wicksell's *Interest and Prices* (1898) brought a new element to its analysis. Instead of concentrating on banks' capacity to create means of exchange *per se*, he focused on the effects on prices of the rate of interest at which they made loans, the *market rate*, and its interaction with the *natural* rate, which he usually identified with the rate of interest that would equilibrate the savings and investment at a full-employment level of output, and sometimes with the marginal productivity of capital.[2]

The banking system, Wicksell saw, was capable of keeping the market rate of interest away from the natural rate because of its capacity to create and destroy credit, and hence induce variations in the rate of flow of lending in the capital market that were independent of the economy's underlying saving rate. For him, the main point was that any discrepancy between these rates would have inflationary or deflationary consequences for the price level. By the 1920s, however, Wicksell's successors were beginning to stress that if the actions of the banks in creating and destroying credit could prevent the rate of interest settling at its natural level, a monetary economy could offer no guarantee that decisions about saving would always and automatically be translated into matching decisions about investment, that Say's Law would thus be violated and that things could perhaps go badly wrong on the employment front.

In his (1930) *Treatise on Money*, Keynes tried to create a theory of the business cycle partly, but explicitly, grounded in Wicksell's analysis. His basic thesis was that cyclical fluctuations stemmed from swings in investment that were in turn driven by variations in investors' perceptions of the profitability of investment. In times of optimism, the natural rate of interest rose, and in times of pessimism it fell, and the market rate of interest failed to keep up with its fluctuations. Even in the *Treatise*, Keynes's discussions of investors' perceptions stressed that they were influenced as much by psychology as by rational calculation, but he pushed this theme further in the *General Theory*, where he argued explicitly that investment was dominated by what he called 'animal spirits'. Though investors might act with a view to maximizing the present value of an expected flow of profits, and to that extent act rationally, the expectations on which they had to base their decisions, each one of which was likely to have unique features, could rely only to a very limited extent on hard information about their likely outcomes. Hence the calculus of probabilities could not be applied to the analysis of investment decisions, and they were bound to be dominated by psychology.

Some commentators trace Keynes's views on investment to ideas about fundamental uncertainty that he developed in his (1921) *Treatise on Probability*. However, as Bradley Bateman (1996) has noted, Keynes downplayed the importance of uncertainty in economic life in many of his writings in the 1920s, so this link is at best indirect. It is just as likely that Keynes's 1936 view of investment derived from the earlier work of his Cambridge colleagues, notably Arthur Pigou and Frederick Lavington, for as both Bateman and Laidler (1999) have pointed out, they raised such issues in the explicit context of business cycle theory in 1912 and 1922 respectively. They had argued that the longer the horizon of any investment decision, the more prone to error it became, and that errors of optimism and pessimism alike would be correlated across agents, and have market consequences which caused them to feed on themselves over time. Thus, they had postulated that successive waves of optimism and pessimism underlay the business cycle, in a manner that to some extent anticipated Keynes's treatment in the *Treatise*, albeit without the latter's explicitly Wicksellian monetary apparatus.

The discussion of investment in the *General Theory* is supplemented by a lengthy and justly famous account of why the characteristics of modern financial markets make the problems to which the foregoing arguments point worse rather than better. According to this account, access to markets in which shares may be actively and easily traded, in which there exists considerable *liquidity*, enables agents to make their savings available for investment without simultaneously having to tie them up for long periods in specific projects. Though this might encourage saving, it also ensures that short-term prospects for gains and losses in financial markets will come to dominate decisions about how to hold existing wealth and how to allocate new saving, thus ensuring that these choices remain disconnected from any careful assessment of the long-term prospects for particular investment projects.

Keynes's theory of *liquidity preference* was also developed in the *Treatise* before being given a crucial role in the *General Theory*, and is closely related to his scepticism about the capacity of financial markets to co-ordinate saving and investment in a world characterized by uncertainty. Alfred Marshall (1871) had argued that agents desire to keep by them a certain stock of money, which represents readily available and general purchasing power, in order to facilitate their transactions in markets for goods and services, and so matters had stood in Cambridge monetary theory until Lavington (1921) suggested that they might also hold money as a protection against the uncertainties to which their participation in financial markets exposed them. Keynes developed this insight in the *Treatise*, when he dealt with what he called the *financial circulation*. Specifically, he related changes in the amount of money that agents would want to hold for *speculative* (here I use the vocabulary of the *General Theory*) purposes to their swings between moods of pessimism and optimism. In times of pessimism, investment would shrink, and savers would simultaneously build up money-holdings in the *financial circulation*. When optimism returned, investment would pick up, and some of the funds needed to finance it would simultaneously be released from the financial circulation into the *industrial circulation*, where they would circulate in exchange for currently produced output. Crucially, these monetary movements would dampen the very swings in the market rate of interest needed to match those in the natural rate induced by successive waves of optimism and pessimism, and hence interfere with the mechanisms whereby investment might be kept in harmony with the economy's underlying saving rate.

This analysis too was pushed further in the *General Theory*. There, Keynes argued that agents always have the option of holding money as a store of wealth, and that money, being the economy's means of exchange and hence the most *liquid* (easily marketed) of all assets, they would demand a premium in order to part with it. Hence, the very presence of money in the economic system put a positive floor under the rate of interest, so that when investors' 'animal spirits' were depressed, it could not fall low enough to generate the volume of investment needed to absorb the economy's full-employment level of savings.

THE MULTIPLIER

The *General Theory* was by no means the first work to argue that: (a) the co-ordination of saving and investment at full employment by the rate of interest might break down because of the working on the monetary system; and that (b) this breakdown would probably result in unemployment. Earlier work, however, had failed to explain just how (b) in fact followed from (a). For example, the *Treatise on Money* itself had presented many verbal arguments about why output and employment might fluctuate as waves of optimism and pessimism caused the natural rate of interest to move away from the market rate, but that book's underlying theoretical framework nevertheless yielded cycles only in prices. That was because, as Keynes's younger colleagues at Cambridge had been quick to point out, the framework had implicitly assumed output and employment to be constant. In the *General Theory*, Keynes filled this gaping hole in his previous analysis with the *multiplier*, a mechanism which he did not originate, but for which he found a new and profoundly important theoretical use.

The idea that cumulative spillovers among firms, industries and even sectors of the economy might be a feature of economy-wide variations in output and employment made sporadic appearances in classical economics from the late nineteenth century onwards and attracted increasing attention in the 1920s, when the likely effectiveness of using variations in government spending on public works as a counter-measure to unemployment was frequently debated. The analysis of spillover effects remained disturbingly vague, however, inviting ridicule even from staunch supporters of the policies themselves. Pigou, for example, was still suggesting as late as 1933 that some arguments seemed to imply that, were the government to spend but one extra pound on increasing employment, that sum would be spent and re-spent in a never-ending sequence until full employment had been achieved (Pigou 1933).

Richard Kahn, Keynes's younger colleague and sometime student, had already played a prominent role in criticizing the theoretical structure of the *Treatise*, and it was he who finally put the analysis of spillovers onto a firm foundation and simultaneously disposed of this *reductio ad absurdum*. In an article published in 1931 he suggested that there would be leakages at each step in the sequence of expenditures: only a fraction of any injection of funds aimed at putting the unemployed to work would be re-spent by its recipients in ways that would put others to work, only a fraction of this already reduced amount would be spent at the next round, and so on. The effects on employment of the initial expenditure would certainly be multiplied by spillovers, therefore, but the multiplying factor would be finite, its size varying inversely with the fraction of expenditure that leaked away at each stage of the process.

Kahn analyzed the creation of employment and emphasized leakages from the multiplier sequence that arose because the government would no longer be obliged to pay unemployment relief (the dole) to newly employed workers, and because some of the expenditures of the latter would be directed at imports rather than domestic production. It was left to the Danish economist Jens Warming (1932) to restate the basic argument in the form in which Keynes would then use it.[3] Warming suggested that the multiplier was better understood if formulated in terms of income rather than employment, because the critical leakages in the process were not those that Kahn had emphasized but rather arose from the tendency of households to save a fraction of any income they received, an issue that Kahn had only touched on. For example, said Warming, if households saved 25 per cent of any increment to their income, and if this was the only leakage from the system, then the multiplier process would result in any new injection of government expenditure creating an increase in the economy's output four times bigger than that injection.

The emphasis on saving in Warming's version of the multiplier process was crucial in enabling Keynes to bring together his ideas about the instability of investment behaviour and its dependence on 'animal spirits', and about the role of uncertainty in creating liquidity preference, the key ingredients of his case for the failure of Say's Law to apply in a monetary economy, into a coherent account of how, nevertheless, such an economy coped with the problem of co-ordinating savings and investment. If households saved a stable fraction of any increment to their income, then a fall in investment spending would set in motion a downward multiplier process that would continue until income had contracted sufficiently to ensure that savings once again just matched investment.

Thus, the central theoretical revelation of the *General Theory* was that, in a money economy, variations in income and employment, not in the rate of interest, are the primary factor co-ordinating saving and investment. At the same time, there seemed to be no reason why the level of investment would, except by chance, be sufficient to require the volume of savings that the economy would generate at full employment. Indeed, in mature economies such as Keynes took those of Europe and the United States to be in the 1930s, the availability of profitable investment projects was bound to be low and shrinking, 'animal spirits' were likely to be permanently depressed, effective demand would fall short of the economy's capacity to produce goods and services, unemployment would be chronic, and far from being a symptom of some kind of disequilibrium soon to be eliminated by market forces, it would also be an equilibrium phenomenon.

Keynes's policy recommendations, which he developed only briefly, followed immediately: it was the role of government to fill, with its own expenditure, the gap between the level of investment required to generate full employment and that which 'animal spirits' alone would induce. There was nothing new about recommending increased public expenditures in 1936, but the foundation that Keynes provided for this advice, embedded as it was in a new theory that challenged the relevance of Say's Law to the workings of a monetary economy, was of the highest originality.

THE SUCCESS AND SIMPLIFICATION OF KEYNESIAN MACROECONOMICS

The *General Theory*'s rapid success owed much to the intellectual support it provided for an already popular approach to policy. In the early 1930s, another explanation of the economic troubles of the times, also grounded in an analysis of the workings of the monetary system that derived from Wicksell, had begun to capture many imaginations. But *Austrian* theory, as it was known, yielded nihilistic policy conclusions.[4] It argued that credit creation by the banking system enabled firms to command the production of investment goods without any voluntary act of saving on the part of households, that this command could only be sustained at the cost of ever-rising inflation, and that when the process came to its inevitable end in economic crisis, the economy would be burdened with stocks of unfinished capital equipment and hence unable to satisfy the demand for consumption goods. This imbalance could only be righted over time by labour force growth and depreciation of the capital stock. Any attempts by activist governments to hurry matters along would be destructive. Expansionary monetary impulses had caused the problem in the first place, so more of the same was the last thing needed; the capital stock was already overexpanded, so government-sponsored investment would worsen the situation; and there was no point in taking measures to stimulate consumption expenditure when the economy was already unable to meet existing demands.

It is easy enough nowadays to find theoretical weaknesses in this Austrian story, most of which stem from its protagonists' tendency to treat logical possibilities as if they were logical necessities, but it was based on apparently rigorous economic theory (by the standards of its time), and it also provided intellectual respectability to arguments for a 'hands-off' policy towards the Depression that were extremely popular in the financial community, and conservative political circles more generally, on both sides of the Atlantic. For economists who also wished to be policy activists, therefore, the arrival of Keynes's alternative theoretical vision was an event of singular importance, and it quickly drove Austrian ideas into professional obscurity.

Another factor contributed to the success of Keynes's analysis, however: namely, that its essential properties seemed capable of formal expression in terms that were only a very little more difficult to grasp than supply and demand analysis. The simplifications that enabled its message to be so expressed, though they had Keynes's own sanction, nevertheless distracted attention from the key role that the *General Theory* attributed to the facts of monetary exchange and their consequences for the economic system's behaviour, and they helped to ensure that macroeconomics began to lose sight of this essential feature of his contribution, as we shall now see.

Underlying Keynes's analysis of the role of money in disrupting the co-ordination of saving and investment by the interest rate were informational problems associated with the simple fact that economic activity takes place over time and that actions have to be based on expectations. Before 1936, many, including Keynes himself in the *Treatise on Money*, had treated the evolution of expectations as integral to the processes generating cyclical swings in unemployment, and the passage of time was thus always a central feature of their discussions, but a formal treatment of these matters was prevented by the lack of a technical apparatus that was up to the task. In 1936, Keynes dealt with this problem by resorting to a ruthless simplification: he divided expectations into two categories: *short-term* and *long term*, and then proceeded 'as if' the former were always fulfilled and the latter exogenous. In so doing, he created a manageable framework for analyzing how an economy in which choices were co-ordinated by output changes, rather than price-level or interest rate movements, would respond to various shocks.

But, paradoxically, that analytic framework now abstracted from the passage of time, and hence from any *raison d'être* for the very phenomena that were in the first place responsible for output changes, rather than interest rate movements, being at the heart of a monetary economy's co-ordination mechanisms. It thus only partially encompassed the ideas of the *General Theory*, but because it proved amenable to algebraic and geometric expression in the form of the so-called IS-LM (investment = saving, liquidity preference = money stock) model, it in due course became the workhorse of the textbooks.[5] IS-LM could be used to demonstrate some of Keynes's key conclusions: depressed 'animal spirits' would lead to a low level of income and employment; monetary policy could offset this only to the extent that the interest rate could be driven down; a fiscal response would be more reliable; etc. But the reasons why the equations of the system took the forms needed to produce such results could not be developed within it, and other forms seemed just as admissible.

Some of these alternatives, moreover, yielded very 'classical' results, in the sense of showing that Say's Law might hold after all, even in the presence of money. The best-known of these alternatives, developed in various degrees of detail by Gottfried von Haberler (1937), Pigou (1943) and Don Patinkin (1948), among others, involves the system's properties when it is postulated that: (a) the price level will fall if the level of income is below full employment; (b) the nominal supply of money is given; and (c) expenditure increases with the real purchasing power of that given nominal money supply. On these assumptions, for a given level of 'animal spirits' and degree of liquidity preference, and with any possibility for expectations to respond to falling prices elimi-nated by assumption, the system's only equilibrium is at full employment. Hence it appears to show that there is no fundamental 'flaw' in the workings of the market economy. But what this result really demonstrates is that if a model abstracts from the fact that economic activity takes place in real time, and hence from all the forces that make monetary exchange essential in any actual economy, it will also abstract from the factors the can cause Say's Law to fail.

As a critique of Keynes's contribution to macroeconomic analy-sis, this is hardly an earth-shattering result, then, useful though it is in confirming his insights about just where the fundamental mone-tary problems he thought worthy of his attention reside; but it was precisely this result that yielded the myth – once termed a 'useful fiction' by Paul Samuelson – that Keynes's explanation of unem-ployment relied on the assumption of money wage stickiness; more important, it provided a basis for the belief, widely held even among those who have taken the trouble to read the *General Theory*, that even though Keynes had indeed claimed that wage stickiness was irrelevant, he had been mistaken to do so. Small wonder that Keynes's radical younger colleague Joan Robinson would refer to the IS-LM model as 'Bastard Keynesianism', or that, in his 1968 book, Leijonhufvud would draw a clear distinction between *Keynesian economics* and the *economics of Keynes*, and argue that macroeconomics would do well to abandon the former and begin to rebuild itself on a foundation drawn from the latter.

MONETARISM AND AFTER

Leijonhufvud's plea was to be ineffective. Instead, the *monetarist counter-revolution* would take centre stage, not least because by the 1970s inflation was emerging as the central problem facing market economies everywhere, and because monetarism was every bit as much devoted to the economics of inflation as the *General Theory* had been to the economics of depression. Even so, two other books of Keynes's, namely his (1923) *Tract on Monetary Reform* and (1940) *How to Pay for the War*, exerted a direct influence on monetarism's early evolution. In both of them, Keynes made a vigorous case for price-level stability as a necessary condition for the smooth functioning of a fully employed market economy and argued that if the money supply was expanded at a rate significantly in excess of the economy's potential rate of real growth, inflation would result. But he also explained that fiscally hard-pressed governments might nevertheless be driven to print money as a means of balancing their budgets. These arguments had considerable resonance when inflation became a pressing policy problem in the 1960s and 1970s, and the monetarists paid attention to these other books of Keynes's, particularly the *Tract*.

How to Pay for the War had also had an indirect influence on Milton Friedman's work in the 1940s. In it, Keynes argued that, with the onset of war, Britain's problem was no longer to find employment for surplus resources but to choose among alternative uses for scarce ones. The requirements of the war had created an *inflationary gap* between the economy's demand for goods and services and its capacity to produce them. Britain's 1941 budget was based on Keynes's analysis of how to bridge that gap without resort to the printing press, and its ideas made a considerable impression on Friedman, who, without being aware of their origins in Keynes's work, gave them great play in his first two articles on inflation (1942, 1943).

The eclipse of Keynes's (1936) ideas by monetarism in the 1960s and 1970s was only partly due to a change in the prevailing economic climate, for Friedman and Anna Schwartz's *Monetary History of the United States* (1963a) challenged some of them on their own ground, and persuasively so, too. In Keynes's view, the Depression in the United States had begun with a collapse of 'animal spirits' and had persisted because investment opportunities remained limited in a maturing economy; falling wages and prices had not prevented the economy's collapse, nor had, or could have had, expansionary monetary policy, because it could not drive the rate of interest low enough to revive investment: hence the case for fiscal policy as a means to sustained recovery. For Friedman and Schwartz, on the other hand, the Depression was mainly a matter of ill-conceived monetary policy: after an initial downturn, perhaps itself caused by a mild monetary tightening, adjustments to wages and prices had failed to restore output and employment because the quantity of money had then collapsed in the face of a series of preventable bank failures. Output had barely responded to expansionary monetary policy when it was tried, notably in 1932, because it had not been expansionary enough.[6]

This reinterpretation of the Great Depression was supported by copious empirical evidence, and it implied a deeply conservative message, quite contrary to that of the *General Theory*: namely, that the Depression provided no evidence that mechanisms inherent in a monetary economy required that it be subjected to continuous and rather large-scale government intervention. Such an economy was reliably self-regulating so long as monetary policy-makers refrained from creating chronic excess demands or supplies of money. In either circumstance, Say's Law might be violated – along the lines that Mill had hinted at in 1844, it might be noted – as friction-prone markets tried to eliminate the excesses in question, but there was no reason to follow Keynes in arguing that, in a monetary economy, the intertemporal co-ordination mechanism was chronically prone to failure.

This argument of Friedman and Schwartz's proved extremely influential, but monetarism was soon to cede its important place in macroeconomics to *new classical* economics (see e.g. Lucas and Sargent 1978), with whose advent the last vestiges of Keynes's economics would disappear from the area's mainstream. Initially, new classical economics seemed to be no more than a mathematically rigorous restatement of monetarism, but though it supported the same conservative policy stance, it also introduced two new and radical theoretical doctrines. First, the *rational expectations* idea had it that agents' expectations about the future should be treated 'as if' based on as much knowledge of the structure of the economy and the time series properties of the shocks impinging upon it as was available to the economist building the model used to analyze their behaviour. Second, the notion of *market clearing* required that such models should assume that supply and demand were kept continuously equal to one another in all markets.

Within neo-classical economics, therefore, fundamental uncertainty, failures of Say's Law, and the factors differentiating money and barter economies were ruled irrelevant by methodological fiat, and macroeconomics became completely detached from the ideas that had formed the subject of Keynes's *General Theory*, and unable, even unwilling, to discuss them. Ironically, it took on the very features that Keynes had so unfairly attributed to classical economics, prior to criticizing it. At the time of writing, neo-classical economics is under challenge from a body of work (see e.g. Michael Woodford 2003) whose main differentiating characteristic is the deployment of money wage and price stickiness postulates. This new body of work has therefore done nothing to move macroeconomics back towards analyzing the theoretical issues that were central to it when it emerged as a distinct sub-discipline; indeed, the universal acceptance of its self-adopted label – *New Keynesian economics* – suggests that contemporary macroeconomics has now forgotten what those issues were.

NOTES

I am grateful to Bradley Bateman, Roger Backhouse, Peter Howitt, Angela O'Mahony and Hans-Michael Trautwein for comments on earlier versions of this paper.

1   Here Keynes overstated his own originality. The concept of effective demand, and the term itself, was central to Ralph Hawtrey's (1913) discussions of cyclical fluctuations from 1913 onwards. He developed a special case of the analysis which Keynes would present as novel in 1936. On this, see David Laidler (1999).

2   The potential incompatibility of these two concepts of the natural rate gave rise to much discussion in the 1920s and 1930s. See Laidler (1999:

part 2) for a discussion of this matter, which is of marginal importance in the current context.

3   Keynes referred only to Kahn in the *General Theory*. Warming's paper appeared in the *Economic Journal*, of which Keynes was editor, so it is hard to believe that he was unaware of it, as Neville Cain (1979) pointed out.

4   Friedrich von Hayek (1931) and Lionel Robbins (1934) are key exponents of Austrian theory, which is discussed in more detail in Laidler (1999).

5   The best single account of the process whereby 'Keynesian Economics' came to be encapsulated in the so-called IS-LM model is Warren Young (1987). The discussion that follows here is partly based on Roger Backhouse and Laidler (2004).

6   Friedman and Schwartz's treatment of the Depression in the United States resembles that of Lauchlin Currie (1934), which was, as he acknowledged, influenced by Hawtrey's cycle theory.

4   Keynes as a Marshallian

For forty or fifty years, twentieth-century macroeconomics was predominantly 'Keynesian' – in one sense or another. That era ended some twenty or thirty years ago. The leading macroeconomists of today think of Keynesian economics as altogether superseded, and few of them have much respect for Keynes himself. A common judgement is that the lack of 'microfoundations' has been the crucial weakness of Keynes's theory and that it has therefore not stood the test of time.

In matters of 'micro' (as it came to be called much later), Keynes had his theory from Alfred Marshall. Marshall had been his teacher and, while he had his reservations about Marshall's successor, A. C. Pigou, Keynes remained very much in the Cambridge tradition and continued to hold Marshall in the highest regard. Marshall's reputation among modern economists went into eclipse some decades before that of Keynes. Their fates are linked. Modern neo-classical economics has developed along a path very different from the course that Marshall had charted, and the conceptual gap has eventually become so wide that neither he nor Keynes is well understood by young economists with 'modern' training (Leijonhufvud 1998).

To understand the meaning and significance of the statement that 'Keynes was a Marshallian', therefore, we need to delineate the contrast between the modern general equilibrium theory, which is the basic toolkit of today's macroeconomists, and Marshallian price theory. The ways in which the models are constructed differ at a quite basic level. Yet confusion between the two is common. This is in no small measure due to a terminological overlap. Both use such words as 'utility (or profit) maximization', 'equilibrium', 'competition', or 'price-taker' as technical terms, but, as we shall see, the *meanings* attached to them differ radically.

THE CLASSICAL TRADITION AND MODERN ECONOMICS

The term 'neo-classical' fits the three marginalist revolutionaries, William Jevons, Carl Menger and Léon Walras, rather ill, since they were all breaking with the classical tradition of Adam Smith, David Ricardo and John Stuart Mill. It does fit Marshall. He tried to solve the problems of that tradition and carry it forward. British classical theory sought to explain the *laws of motion* of society. Its basic behavioural propositions were couched in verbal differential equations: 'Population will grow as long as real wages are above subsistence', or 'Capitalists will accumulate as long as profit is positive.' Behaviour was seen as adaptive. It was assumed that agents maximize utility or profit, but these assumptions were understood as propositions about motivation, not about realizations. Classes or groups of people were thought to differ in the extent to which they acted on the basis of calculation. It was taken for granted that people frequently made mistakes but also that most would learn from their mistakes so that their behaviour would be 'rational' (and consequently more or less predictable) in settings with which they were familiar. Stable rules governing interactions were necessary to render the behaviour of others, and therefore the likely outcome of own effort, predictable to the individual. The institutional framework would also shape what people would learn from interacting with others and, therefore, the nature of the equilibrium to which the process would gravitate. 'Equilibrium' was understood as a state in which the pertinent 'law of motion' had ceased to operate.

Modern economics, in contrast, has concentrated on principles of efficient allocation. Its core is choice theory. The logic of choice is essentially timeless. In modern theory, it is formalized in terms of constrained optimization. When actually observed behaviour is interpreted as solutions to constrained optimization problems, *substantive rationality* is attributed to agents. This in turn means that decision-makers are assumed to know, at least probabilistically, their *true* opportunity sets in all their dimensions, so that they can evaluate all the utility-relevant outcomes of alternative courses of action. Applying this behaviour description to all agents requires that all decisions have to be consistent. Otherwise, some agents must fail to execute their optimal plans, and the theory does not leave room for such failures. Consistency of plans is the definition of equilibrium in this tradition. ('Equilibrium' is, however, a rather otiose term, since if no observed behaviour may be interpreted as a failure to optimize, 'disequilibria' are not possible.) In a temporal context, substantive optimization requires that agents know all future prices when formulating their transaction plans. In effect, all choices have to be reconciled before anyone's choice can be made! Modern economics dodges this logical conundrum by postulating a stochastic form of perfect foresight ('rational expectations').

Institutions do not fit naturally into these deductive structures. The existence of firms and the use of money, to take two prominent examples, are 'explained' by postulating transaction cost 'frictions' in markets. They are, in a sense, species of market failures. How markets actually work is not modelled, however.

MARSHALLIAN AND WALRASIAN CONSTRUCTIONS

Today's most familiar 'modern' models descend from Walras. The first stage in the construction of a Walrasian model poses the problem of an individual agent who faces a set of given prices and has to choose optimal quantities. The conceptual experiment is then repeated for different prices so as to generate the agent's net supply and demand schedules. At the second stage, these are aggregated across all agents, resulting in market excess demand schedules. At the third stage, the equilibrium condition that demand equal supply in all markets is imposed so as to find the price vector for which all the transaction plans are consistent in the aggregate.

The basic building-blocks of a Marshallian model are demand-price and supply-price schedules for individual agents. These are not loci of optimal points. The demand price of a household, for example, is the maximum price it would be willing to pay for a given quantity of the good in question. Obviously, any lower price would be preferred by the household. Similarly, the supply price would be the minimum price at which a supplier would be willing to provide the good, although any price higher than that would be preferred. Consequently, the Walrasian $q^d(p)$ and $q^s(p)$ functions and the Marshallian $p^d(q)$ and $p^s(q)$ functions must not be thought of as simply mathematical inverses of each other, although the now standard practice of drawing Walrasian price-into-quantity schedules in the quantity-into-price space of a Marshallian supply and demand diagram might suggest that it is legitimate to treat them as such.

The Marshallian constructs give rise to the routine rules governing the adaptation of agents to a constantly changing market environment. If his demand price exceeds the market price, the consumer will buy more; in the opposite case, he will buy less. If his supply price is below the market price, the producer will expand output; in the opposite case, he will cut back. To these, we should add similar routines for the middleman. If he encounters excess supply, he will reduce the price paid to the producer and the price offered the consumer; in the case of excess demand, he will raise prices. We shall refer to these basic behaviour postulates as 'Marshall's laws of motion' to emphasize that we are dealing with an adaptive dynamical system.

For a long time, teachers in the Marshallian tradition favoured a fish market in a port city as their example of how the market process worked. Each morning the fishing fleet returns to port with the night's catch, q_T. The entire catch is brought to a central market which operates, we may suppose, on double auction principles, that is to say, buyers and sellers search each other out, seeking to conclude pairwise trades at the best possible price. The price converges to the demand price for the landed catch, $p^*(q_T)$. This point-attractor of the price formation process – the market clearing price – is Marshall's temporary or market-day equilibrium.

The j-th boat owner observes the succession of market-day closing prices, averaging p^*_T. He has been bringing in a catch of $q_{T,j}$ on average at a marginal cost of $s_j(q_{T,j})$. His feedback rule is:

$$q_{T+1,j} = h_j[s_j(q_{T,j}) - p*_T] + q_{T,j} \tag{1}$$

With all firms following similar routines, the iteration in industry output, q_T, will (it is assumed) converge on the point-attractor q^*_T which is Marshall's short-period equilibrium. This defines one point on Marshall's industry supply schedule. To generate the rest of it, one has to imagine successively shifting the demand function and letting the market process find the point-attractor associated with each position of it. The model does not have a supply schedule constructed by aggregating the ex ante optimal outputs of all the firms.

In the short-period equilibrium, the law of motion of output has ceased to operate in the aggregate. The equilibrium concept is one of *constancy* of industry output, not the Walrasian *consistency* of the plans of all market participants. Having obtained this aggregate equilibrium, we turn next to the 'representative firm'. It has to be representative in the sense of having no incentive to expand or contract when industry output shows no tendency to change. In the competitive case, that would be when the cost incurred in producing the marginal unit of output equals the price received. Here the condition is stated in *ex post* (realized) terms, not in *ex ante* (planned) terms as in a Walrasian model. Marshall's quantities are in principle *observable*. In the atemporal formalisms of most undergraduate textbooks, however, the two versions of the optimality condition would be indistinguishable.

Yet the two types of construction are quite different. Walras builds from individual optimality to market equilibrium. Marshall obtains his (different concept of) equilibrium first and then backtracks to analyze the representative firm. Moreover, his optimality condition does not necessarily apply to any firm other than the representative one (which is a hypothetical one). The industry in (approximate) equilibrium will show a balanced mixture of expanding and contracting firms.

Competition in Marshall is a rivalrous process. The fishermen are price-takers, but they are not price-takers in the now common sense of being 'atomistic competitors' who know the market price prior to committing resources to production. They do not face 'perfectly elastic demand schedules' but find out what price their catches will fetch only when the catch of the whole fleet is brought to market. Marshallian competition does not require large numbers of firms producing perfect substitutes and the rest of the outlandish assumptions necessary to buttress the modern notion of 'perfect competition'. Many commentators on the *General Theory* have expressed surprise that Keynes made no use of Joan Robinson's imperfect competition. But as a Marshallian he was not trapped in perfect competition and felt no compulsion to escape into imperfect competition.

The capital stocks of firms are held constant in Marshall's short period. So investment belongs in the long period. The growing industry in Marshall discovers and exploits economies of scale in multiple dimensions. The structure of the system inevitably changes in the process, therefore. The individual firm is not likely to foresee exactly how it will change or what internal and external scale economies will be realized. The expansion of the industry is a collective trial-and-error process in which some will succeed and others fail. The path realized by particular firms will be unpredictable. The representative firm will continue to expand as long as positive quasi-rents are being earned. In the hypothetical case that the process plays itself out without major change in the overall environment, the industry should presumably arrive at the stationary equilibrium of the long period. Marshall gave as the equilibrium condition that past capital outlays compounded to the present should equal the discounted value of future net revenues. But he did not even attempt to provide a model of the short-period investment decision. Keynes needed to fill this gap and did so with his *marginal efficiency of capital* (MEC) construct.

Walrasian models of investment have a problem getting the optimal rate of change of the individual firm's capital stock to be determinate. A speed of adjustment variable (a rather alien feature in the overall scheme of things) has to be added in. A Marshallian construction is more straightforward. The demand price for a capital good is the present value of its expected future marginal revenue stream (expressed in *certainty equivalent* values). The higher the rate of investment in the present period, the larger the stock of capital which will compete in the future with a unit of capital acquired today. Consequently, demand-price schedules will slope downwards as functions of aggregate investment – assuming some knowledge about it, however imperfect, on the part of individual firms. Demand- and supply-price schedules are then juxtaposed, and one may imagine a double auction process (as in the fish market above) producing the short-period equilibrium. Since *ceteris paribus* demand prices are inversely related to the interest rate, the short-period equilibrium output of new capital goods will be higher the lower the rate. This relationship is Keynes's MEC schedule. It is clearly a Marshallian construct.

Keynes would have started out from a view of the uncertainties inherent in the growth process very much like Marshall's. As the author of the *Treatise on Probability* (1921), he would of course not consider the actuarial calculus as a solution to the firm's decision problem. In expressing the firm's expectations in certainty equivalents, he left room for both successes and failures, since certainty equivalents were subjective to the decision-maker and not derivable from objective frequency distributions.

Keynes went further than Marshall in one very important respect, however. Marshall over and over again laid great stress on what he called his 'continuity principle'. He made *Natura non facit saltum* the very motto of the *Principles* and invested it with a variety of more or less profound philosophical meanings. It seems probable that he also thought that continuity gave warrant to the assumption that his various adaptive processes would converge on their respective point-attractors and not give rise to complex dynamics of a kind for which the mathematics of his time provided no tools. Keynes broke with Marshall on continuity. His state of long-term expectations can shift abruptly and violently – so much so that the economy's capacity for gradual adaptation is overwhelmed.

SYSTEM STABILITY

Keynes started the construction of his *General Theory*, in chapter 3, by adapting this basic Marshallian apparatus to the economy as a whole. Output and employment are determined by *aggregate* demand price and supply price. These have the dimension of a flow of money expenditure or revenue: 'the aggregate supply price of the output of a given amount of employment is the expectation of proceeds which will just make it worth the while of entrepreneurs to give that employment' (JMK VII: 24). Aggregate output also obeys a typical Marshallian law of motion: 'if for a given value of N the expected proceeds are greater than the aggregate supply price ... there will be an incentive for entrepreneurs to increase employment'. (JMK VII: 25).

All students of Marshall would know, however, that the supply and demand apparatus was analytically useful only in so far as the determinants of the demand curve and those of the supply curve were independent of each other. Otherwise disturbances would shift both schedules together, in which case knowing their elasticities would not help determine the outcome. So the first objection against using demand and supply analysis to determine aggregate output that Keynes had to anticipate was that, for the economy as a whole, demand could not possibly be independent of supply. If there were not a measure of such independence, aggregate employment and output would of course be determined by the marginal productivity and marginal disutility of labour – as in classical (and now in new classical) theory.

Keynes firmly denied the proposition 'Supply creates its own Demand', which he chose to refer to as Say's Law (cf. Clower 2004). In modern theory, it is more generally known as Walras's Law. Much confusion has surrounded this 'law' (Clower and Leijonhufvud 1973) and the significance of Keynes's rejection of it. Keynesian economics (of a sort) was taught and practised for decades by people who for the most part did not understand what Keynes meant by rejecting it, or why it was crucial to his theory that the law was false. Yet it is because Supply does *not* create its own Demand that aggregate demand may need to be stabilized. The rationale for Keynesian stabilization policy, understood as aggregate demand management, is predicated on the rejection of Say's Law.

In general equilibrium theory, Walras's Law is taken to hold simply as a consequence of the aggregation of the budget constraints of individual agents. The budget constraint dictates that the market values of what an individual agent plans to demand and to supply be equal. The trading plan of each agent must have zero net value. What is true of each must be true of all. Consequently, the sum of the values of market excess demands across all markets must be zero. The validity of the 'law', understood in this way, is thus seen as a matter of quite trivial arithmetic.

Keynes, however, was concerned with the *motion* of the system. To him, therefore, the question became whether the excess demands, defined in this conventional way, would be 'effective' in driving adaptations in the economy towards the full-employment equilibrium. His answer was that not all planned or desired demands were always effective and that, consequently, it was possible to have effective excess supplies in some parts of the economy that were *not* matched by effective excess demands elsewhere.

Two types of such effective demand failures are keys to the *General Theory*. The first concerns the saving–investment nexus. Increased savings (reduced consumption) leads to an excess supply of consumer goods in the present but does so without signalling an excess demand for consumption in the future: 'An act of individual saving means – so to speak – a decision not to have dinner today. But it does *not* necessitate a decision to have dinner . . . or to consume any specified thing at any specified date' (JMK VII: 210). Hence Keynes's long-term expectations (the expectations of future returns to present investment) have a measure of autonomy that expectations about the return to investment lack in inter-temporal general equilibrium theory. Rather than being strictly linked to the inter-temporal plans of consumers, they are subject to what he called 'animal spirits' and can change abruptly, therefore.

The second type of effective demand failure is at the root of the Keynesian multiplier. Unemployed workers attempt to sell their labour in order to buy consumer goods. In so doing, they exert an excess supply in the labour market, but their corresponding excess demand for consumption goods is ineffective when not backed by ready purchasing power. The institutional structure, as Robert Clower (1967) characterized it, is one in which 'goods buy money and money buys goods, but goods do not buy goods'. At one stage in the working-out of the *General Theory*, Keynes used 'the monetary theory of production' as a working title (Pasinetti 1999). Firms work to maximize money profits, and labour works for money wages. In a later discarded draft of the *General Theory* (JMK XXIX: 76–87), Keynes considered the alternative institutional structure of a 'Co-operative Economy' in which labour services would be bartered directly for the employing firm's output. In this hypothetical setting, the second type of effective demand failure would not occur, and neither, therefore, could the system settle into an equilibrium with 'involuntary unemployment'. This kind of effective demand failure is thus the result of the institutional structure of a money economy.

The *combination* of the two effective demand failures is crucial. Neither one will by itself send the system into an unemployment equilibrium. If the economy were (somehow) to maintain itself at full employment while the interest rate was too high to co-ordinate saving and investment, the accumulating excess saving would eventually force the market interest rate into line with the Wicksellian 'natural rate'. Similarly, if saving out of full employment real income were not to exceed investment, flexibility of wages would suffice to guarantee full employment. The trouble arises when the two effective demand failures interact. When saving exceeds investment at full employment real income, output and employment will fall. This in turn will reduce consumption – the deviation from full employment is amplified through the consumption-'multiplier'. The contraction will proceed until the decline in incomes reduces saving to equality with investment. At this point, the flow supply of loanable funds (demand for securities) by the household sector no longer exceeds the demand for loanable funds (new issues) by the business sector. The excess demand for 'bonds' is zero. This removes the pressure on the out-of-line interest rate. At the same time, there is unemployment of labour, even though the money wage rate might be at the value that would clear the labour market in general equilibrium. There is no automatic tendency for the price that is 'wrong' (the interest rate) to change, while the price that is 'right' (the money wage rate) tends to move away from that level. A decline of money wages had been the 'classical' remedy for unemployment. In the case analyzed by Keynes, however, declining money wage rates will not restore equilibrium in the labour market, because the underlying problem is the inter-temporal co-ordination failure of full employment saving exceeding investment. Very flexible money wage rates would indeed make matters worse, in Keynes's view. A rapid deflation process would bring a cascade of defaults and 'derange' financial markets.

Before Keynes's 'revolutionary' work, the prevailing presumption among economists was that if only all agents in the economy – including workers – obeyed Marshall's 'laws of motion', the system would surely converge to a full-employment equilibrium. 'Frictions' might delay the process, but the eventual result was not in doubt. In today's macroeconomics, one should note, this presumption has been restored in full force. It is taken for granted that only labour market 'inflexibilities' of one sort or another – wage rigidity being the most prominent possibility – can account for unemployment exceeding its 'natural rate'.

The proposition that 'flexibility' is not only a necessary but even a sufficient condition for the attainment of equilibrium may perhaps seem plausible in an isolated market context. One should note, however, that in Marshall matters would not be so simple except for the assumption that market price responds far more quickly than industry output to changes in market conditions. If the two variables were to be 'equally flexible', their interaction would produce a non-linear process which does not inevitably settle down to the point-attractor of Marshall's short-period equilibrium. (The strange assumption that producers are informed of what the equilibrium price will be *before* making their production decisions ensures that this complication does not arise in Walrasian *tâtonnement* dynamics.) But Keynes's point was different, namely, that the proposition neglects the dynamic interaction among markets characteristic of a money-using economy. In such a system, the stability of the full-employment general equilibrium is not always guaranteed. Even if all agents obey Marshall's laws of motion, the economy may still home in on a state of large-scale unemployment. This unemployment is 'involuntary' in the sense that there has been *no intentional interference* with the working of markets.

Keynes's recognition of effective demand failures and of how they affect the dynamics of a system of multiple markets validates his claim to having advanced a more *General Theory* than that of his predecessors. The theory shows that the capability of a system of 'free markets' to co-ordinate activities has limits and indicates how co-ordination failures of a certain type can be overcome by economic policy. As such, it obviously had vast ideological and political implications. Decades later, it is clear that Keynes exaggerated the prevalence and magnitude of these effective demand failures. The capitalist system is not so bad at self-regulation as it seemed to him in the midst of the Great Depression. Traditional 'Keynesian' views against the reliance on 'free markets' and about the role of government in the economy have had to be modified accordingly. But this does not undermine Keynes's claim to greatness as an economic theorist, nor does it justify a retreat to economic doctrines that do not recognize the possibility of such major failures.

THE STATIC METHOD – AND ITS LIMITATIONS

The language of short and long runs is still loosely used in economics today, but modern intertemporal Walrasian theory has no counterpart to Marshall's hierarchy of market-day, short-period and long-period equilibria. Walrasian systems are always on equilibrium trajectories, all transactors realizing their potential optima. In the Marshallian system, all agents are constantly adapting, moving towards but seldom reaching their optima. The complex non-linear dynamics of a system where all of this is going on simultaneously neither Marshall nor anyone else could possibly handle in his time. Even today, despite much progress with complex systems, it remains beyond what can be done with analytical methods. Such systems can now be modelled on computers and their dynamic properties investigated experimentally, but this is of course an approach that could not even be imagined in Marshall's or Keynes's time.

Marshall tamed the complex dynamics of his theory by dealing separately with the various adjustment processes, while assuming that their adjustment speeds could be given a strong ranking such that the thus separated processes would converge on point-attractors without interfering with each other. These point-attractors are his three static equilibria. He was intensely conscious that this 'static method' was a crude and provisional way of dealing with his dynamic and 'organic' subject matter. Even when the context was simply that of a single market, the dynamics could not be thoroughly analyzed with the tools at his disposal. The static method was the best he could do.

Keynes's problem was infinitely worse. The scale and duration of unemployment in the midst of the Great Depression could not very well be explained in terms of labour markets that 'cleared' in any usual sense. But removing the supply-equal-demand equation for the labour market meant, of course, that one was dealing with a macrosystem that was *underdetermined* from the standpoint of standard equilibrium theorizing. The challenge for Keynes was to provide a reasonably disciplined way to analyze a general equilibrium system with one equation missing. He naturally sought to adapt Marshall's method to the problem, but this was not a straightforward matter. By the 1930s, the ranking of price- and output-adjustment speeds that Marshall had thought reasonable for competitive markets in his day hardly fitted the markets for manufactured brand-name goods produced under increasing returns to scale, for example. Moreover, different markets have different patterns of equilibrating adjustments and operate at different speeds. A system of multiple markets would make a complex, non-linear nightmare. It is far from obvious that Marshall's static method could make such a system tractable in a useful way. A Marshallian short-period macromodel would have to meet three requirements. First, one would have to define a suitable length of *period* so as to partition the endogenous variables into two groups depending on their speeds of adjustment, the slow-moving ones then to be treated as constants. Second, one would have to specify 'laws of motion' for the rapidly adjusting ones. Third, one would have to demonstrate that these interdependent 'laws of motion' could reasonably be supposed to bring the system rapidly to a well-defined point-attractor. The partitioning should be reasonably stable, so that it would not have to be altered every time a new question was to be asked of the model. The real world might not oblige the economist by conforming to these requirements!

The key assumption that Keynes made was to put the long-term rate of interest in the *ceteris paribus* pound: 'It may fluctuate for decades about a level which is chronically too high' (JMK VII: 204). It cannot, therefore, be relied upon to co-ordinate saving and investment. In the short run, the capital stock, the money wage rate and long-term expectations were taken as exogenous. All of them would vary over a sequence of short periods. Current investment would add to tomorrow's capital stock, current unemployment would lower tomorrow's wage, while the state of long-term expectations tomorrow might be influenced by totally exogenous events as well as by the current endogenous variables of the model.

Combining these assumptions about lag structure with appropriate 'laws of motion' to deduce the behaviour of the system was anything but a trivial matter. The system of beliefs that Keynes had formed – i.e. his *theory* – was of the economy as a complex dynamical system for which there was no usable formal representation, no analytically tractable set of differential equations. To find a manageable static model that would capture the essence of his theory, he had to reason through the dynamics 'verbally' while dealing with this system that was mathematically intractable! He did not get everything right, which is hardly surprising. He was really operating beyond the limits of what Marshall's method could accomplish.

Keynes's attempt to discredit the loanable funds theory of interest determination and to replace it with his own liquidity preference theory is particularly instructive. It shows both how easily the Marshallian method can be misunderstood and how it can go astray. Since, in his theory, saving and investment determined income, he reasoned that they could not also determine the rate of interest. Instead, money supply and money demand (liquidity preference) must determine the interest rate. These propositions do not make sense if understood as verbal statements about a simultaneous equation model, whether a Walrasian general equilibrium one (e.g. Hicks, 1939: 160ff) or one of the so-called IS-LM models that became standard in 'Keynesian' textbooks (e.g. Hansen 1953: ch. 7). They do make sense as alternative hypotheses about the Marshallian 'law of motion' for the interest rate. Then the loanable funds hypothesis is to be understood as the statement that the rate of interest will increase if, and only if, there is an excess demand for loans (excess supply of 'bonds') at the prevailing rate, while the liquidity preference hypothesis states that it will increase if, and only if, there is an excess demand for money. With reference to an adaptive dynamical system, Keynes's argument is not nonsensical, therefore. But it is wrong.

The issue is far from trivial. If the adjustment of the interest rate is not governed by the excess demand for credit, it cannot possibly co-ordinate the inter-temporal plans of producers and consumers. It is indeed crucial to Keynes's theory that there are conditions under which the interest rate mechanism will not work. Central bank policy or market expectations about the long-term rate of interest may prevent the interest rate from equating saving and investment at full employment. When this occurs (as it sometimes will), the system acquires characteristic Keynesian properties: (1) investment causes savings, but saving does not cause investment; (2) an increase in saving reduces income (the so-called 'Paradox of Thrift'); and (3) wage flexibility will not suffice to bring the economy to full employment. The trouble with the liquidity preference hypothesis of interest determination is that it implies that the price mechanism can *never* work to co-ordinate saving and investment – that it is *impossible* that it would.

This doctrine is not a good guide to the economy of our time. The capitalist economy is not perfectly self-regulating, but neither is it as totally incapable of 'automatism' as this theory suggests. And saving is not always and everywhere an anti-social act.

THE USE OF MATHEMATICS

Modern economists have poked a good deal of fun at Alfred Marshall over his frequent warnings against relying too much on mathematics in economic theory. As Robert Solow once remarked in the course of a lecture: 'Alfred Marshall seems to have thought that at each step of a mathematical deduction a little truth would leak out.' Keynes was roughly as sceptical as Marshall on the subject.

The attitude to mathematics in economics that Marshall and Keynes shared but that differs so starkly from that of most present-day economists reflects an underlying different conception of economic theory. Today, 'to theorize' means to deduce the properties of a model from a given set of primitive postulates about tastes and technologies. 'Theory' and 'model' are understood as synonymous terms. Marshall and Keynes, in contrast, were philosophical realists. Theory to them meant a set of beliefs about the world and about how best to understand it. The question would then be to what extent a particular set of mathematical tools could be used accurately to represent one's theoretical beliefs about the way the world worked. Both thought of the economy as a complex and evolving dynamical system. A mathematics for dealing rigorously with such a system was not available to them. Marshall's *static method*, with its presumed hierarchy of point-attractors, was a provisional way of coping with the dynamics, and the modelling of Marshallian statics with the aid of the calculus was predicated on its validity. However, even when dealing just with a single industry, Marshall felt it necessary to remind his readers that '. . . economic problems are imperfectly presented when they are treated as problems of statical equilibrium and not of organic growth' (*Principles*, p. 382). Consequently, whether mathematical derivations were to be trusted or not became a matter not of proof but of judgement. In dealing not just with an industry but with the entire economy, Keynes was operating beyond the limits of what reasonably might be asked of Marshall's method – and of the mathematics associated with it.

IS-LM

With the *General Theory*, Keynes thought he had found a static 'equilibrium' model that captured the essential properties of the dynamical macrosystem. John Hicks proposed a clever way of reducing a larger set of equations to two relationships between income and the interest rate that could be displayed in a simple two-dimensional diagram. One reduced form (IS) showed the possible combinations of income and the interest rate for which investment and saving would be equal, the other (LM) the combinations for which money demand and supply would be equal. The intersection of the two gave a representation of a Keynesian short-period equilibrium. This IS-LM construction seemed to Keynes at first, and to countless others later, an adequate formal representation of his theory. But that it was not. As mentioned above, it was, for example, not possible to use IS-LM to distinguish clearly between the liquidity preference and loanable funds hypotheses. (This, however, was just as well for Keynes!) More seriously, when used as the vehicle for defining the essential difference between Keynes and the Classics, IS-LM led inexorably to the fatuous conclusion that Keynes had explained unemployment by assuming money wages to be too high and rigid. Thus the saving–investment problem disappeared from the later Keynesian economics, which became identified with little else than the insistence that wages were inflexible.

Despite these critical deficiencies, IS-LM survived and prospered as the core not only of 'Keynesian' economics but also for some period of monetarism. The reason (albeit not identified as such) was that IS-LM did not obey Say's (Walras's) Law and, therefore, could be used to demonstrate many properties of Keynesian theory.

Hicks always did understand that Keynes's theory relied on Marshall's method and that its static equilibrium was a very provisional way of dealing with the adaptive dynamics of the macroeconomy. Over the years, he became increasingly uncomfortable with it.

> It is one of the major difficulties of the Keynes theory. . . that it works with a *period* which is taken to be one of equilibrium [of investment and saving out of current income] and which is nevertheless identified with the Marshallian 'short period', in which capital equipment . . . remains unchanged. The second seems to require that the period should not be too long, but the first requires that it should not be too short . . . It is not easy to see that there can be any length of time that will adequately satisfy both of these requirements.
>
> (Hicks 1965: 64–5)

Hicks also came to regard his own IS-LM model as flawed on similar grounds, namely, that the time required for the equilibration of IS and of LM could not be even approximately the same (Hicks 1983).

Eventually the IS-LM model came to be regarded as so seriously defective and beyond repair that it was abandoned altogether (although for reasons different from those stressed here). With its demise, Keynes's ideas lost all influence with younger cohorts of economists. The theory had come to be identified with the model, so that the deficiencies of the model became fatal to the theory. Few participants in these debates shared Hicks's understanding either of the difference between the theory and the model or of the horrendous difficulties in the way of making the static model do what the dynamic theory required.

KEYNES ECLIPSED: THE NEW CLASSICALS

As macroeconomics evolved in the post-Second World War period, it eventually buried Keynes under layers of 'Keynesian' economics, monetarism, neo-classical monetarism, real business-cycle theory, and 'New Keynesianism'. At certain junctures, the debates touched on matters pertinent to the Marshallian roots of Keynesian theory. A few examples will suffice.

1. In making the case that the effectiveness of monetary policy was underestimated in Keynesian economics, Friedman (1968) argued that the interest-elasticity of money demand was not a critical issue. An expansionary monetary policy

worked mainly through expectations of rising prices and nominal income. The liquidity effect on interest rates of monetary injection was a very short-run phenomenon of minor consequence. This argued in effect that the lag structure of the empirically valid model was different from what had been traditionally assumed. In the comparative statics of the nominal income model as modified by Friedman, a shift of LM brought with it at least a partial shift of IS also in the short run. The elasticities of the two reduced forms were more or less irrelevant. Generations of students had learned their macro by shifting one schedule while keeping the other fixed. But in Friedman's version, the model could no longer be handled like Marshall's scissors.

2. The rational expectations model of Lucas (1972) sharpened the Friedmanian challenge. In this model, the expectational link between IS and LM was completely rigid. The two necessarily had to shift together.

3. In demonstrating that the Phillips Curve should not be expected to be stable in the face of nominal shocks, Phelps (1967) and Friedman (1968) independently introduced the hypothesis of the 'natural rate of unemployment' or NAIRU (non-accelerating inflation rate of unemployment), understood as the proposition that the economy would converge on full employment as soon as wages had had time to adjust. In natural rate models, inflexibilities of wages or of other terms of the labour contract explain unemployment, a belief now shared by monetarists, New Keynesians and real business cycle adherents alike.

   In terms of Keynes's original theory, the NAIRU hypothesis would be true if, and only if, saving–investment equilibrium could be taken for granted. If saving out of full-employment income were to exceed investment, Keynes would have maintained, wage flexibility will not guarantee convergence to the natural rate. The NAIRU hypothesis was accepted by 'Keynesians' because they had already accepted wage inflexibility as the explanation of unemployment and had abandoned Keynes's intertemporal co-ordination problem.

   With the natural rate of unemployment, Say's (or Walras's) Law is, in effect, reinstated in macroeconomics. Supply once more creates its own demand. The full-employment equilibrium is stable, therefore, as long as prices respond to market excess demands and supplies. It was gradually realized that models with the natural rate property eliminate any rationale for stabilization policy, understood as aggregate demand management.

4. The Lucas critique (Lucas 1976) taught economists that demand and supply functions were not invariant to changes in government policy. This sent macrotheorists and econometricians 'beyond demand and supply curves' (Sargent 1982) in search of the 'deep parameters' of utility and production functions that might offer a firmer foundation for quantitative economics. Marshall, in contrast, would surely have thought of tastes and technology not as dependable constants but as constantly evolving, and Keynes would have noted that the general equilibrium theory underlying the new macroeconometrics presumes perfect co-ordination. This modern theory has relinquished the modular system architecture of Marshall and the co-ordination problems of Keynes in favour of the supremely coherent dynamic programme of a single 'representative agent'.

This representative agent will not be puzzled by paradoxes of saving; he will not suffer involuntary unemployment; and he is not likely to be gripped by financial panic or to get caught in the maelstrom of debt deflation. Macroeconomic theory has come a long way. One wonders sometimes whether it has been in the right direction.

CONCLUSIONS

The urgent, pressing, overwhelmingly important question in the 1930s was how to understand the Great Depression. Received economic theory provided no satisfactory answer. Keynes made two major departures from the economics that he had inherited in fashioning his own answer. The first was the breach with Marshall's continuity principle. Nature might jump, after all, and do so in such manner that a universe of gradient climbers could not keep up. The second was the discovery that the laws of motion, that seemed so obviously reliable in the case of a single market, did not guarantee convergence to full employment in an economy where the division of labour had evolved using and requiring the use of money. A more 'General Theory' was needed.

Keynes was a Marshallian in the deep sense, that when he broke with Marshall and went far beyond Marshall, their very differences presumed a shared system of thought. Keynes's claim to greatness as a theorist is based on his departures from Marshall.

5 Doctor Keynes: economic theory in a diagnostic science

THEORY AND PRACTICE

For the greater part of his professional life, John Maynard Keynes was known as a practical man: the author of topical tracts on current economic questions, an adviser to, and an emissary from, the British Treasury, a successful player of financial markets for himself and King's College Cambridge, a member of corporate boards and a portfolio manager for two insurance companies. He was, in this sense, a part-time academic. And although he had long been known to be a first-rate economist, it was only after the publication of the *General Theory of Employment, Interest and Money* in 1936 that he was able to secure his reputation as a first-rate economic theorist. Yet, of the ten volumes of books published in his lifetime, three (the *General Theory* and the two volumes of the *Treatise on Money*, volume I subtitled *The Pure Theory of Money* and volume II *The Applied Theory of Money*) feature 'theory' in their title. And if we note that three of the remaining volumes are clearly non-economic and two are as much political as economic, the proportion of his economic books self-consciously styled as theoretical rises to three-fifths. Even one of the remaining volumes, *A Tract on Monetary Reform*, contains a clearly theoretical core. If Keynes was indeed a theorist, what kind of a theorist was he?

In modern economics, *theory* has come to denote the particular field of economics that deals with formal representations of abstract economies divorced from particular applications – a synonym for mathematical economics. Theory may inform particular applications through *models* that particularize or instantiate theories under special assumptions. Accepting such a view, DeVroey (2004) argues that 'reasoning in prose is not a model *strictu sensu*, the arising of macroeconomics should be ascribed not to Keynes' *General Theory* but to the subsequent models that tried to translate Keynes' blurred message into a precise model'. Not only was Keynes not a theorist – not a producer of models – but the fact that he was not bars him from having founded macroeconomics, defined as a theoretical discipline.

There are, of course, many objections to De Vroey's characterization, not least that the *General Theory* is by no means devoid of formal, mathematical reasoning; yet it does capture the spirit of modern attitudes towards theory. Lucas (1981: 286) argued that the only reason the economists of the 1930s did not use the dynamic methods of the 1980s was that they lacked the mathematical machinery: 'To ask why [they] did not make use of the contingent-claim view of equilibrium is . . . like asking why Hannibal did not use tanks against the Romans instead of elephants.' We known from Keynes's deep appreciation of Ramsey's 'Mathematical Theory of Savings' that he was fully capable of understanding formalized theory and using it to good account (JMK VI: 144; JMK X: 335–6). Still, Keynes saw the limits to purely formal reasoning. As a matter of style: 'there are occasions for very exact methods of statement, such as are employed in Mr. Russell's *Principia Mathematica*. But there are advantages also in writing the English of Hume' (JMK VIII: 20). As a matter of substance:

It is a great fault of symbolic pseudo-mathematical methods of formalising a system of economic analysis . . . that they expressly assume strict independence between the factors involved and lose all their cogency and authority if this hypothesis is disallowed; whereas, in ordinary discourse, where we are not blindly manipulating but know all the time what we are doing and what the words mean, we can keep 'at the back of our heads' the necessary reserves and qualifications and the adjustments which we shall have to make later on, in a way in which we cannot keep complicated partial differentials 'at the back' of several pages of algebra which assume that they all vanish. Too large a proportion of recent 'mathematical' economics are merely concoctions, as imprecise as the initial assumptions they rest on, which allow the author to lose sight of the complexities and interdependencies of the real world in a maze of pretentious and unhelpful symbols.

(JMK VII: 297–8).

Just as striking as his commitment to English prose is the manner in which Keynes embeds his theoretical writings in topical policy debates. Stylistically, the distinction between Russell and Hume is a genuine distinction; yet it fails to get to the core difference between Keynes's theory and modern macroeconomics. Yes, some modern macroeconomics is abstract and academic; nonetheless, modern macroeconomists also serve as policy advisers and find their formal models of some service in that capacity. Still, the true difference between modern macroeconomic theory and Keynes's theory is, I believe, not unrelated to Keynes's perspective as a policy adviser.[1] Whereas modern theory serves as a simulacrum of the economy – stylized and abstract, to be sure – Keynes's theory is a diagnostic instrument in the service of Dr Keynes, consulting economic physician.[2]

MARSHALLIAN AND WALRASIAN METHODOLOGY

Keynes spent his intellectual childhood dangled, as it were, on Alfred Marshall's knee. His methodology is Marshallian in the sense of Milton Friedman's (1949, 1955) useful contrast with Walrasian methodology (Hoover 1988: 218–20; Hammond 1996: ch. 2).

Marshallian methodology sees economic theory as an 'economic organon' – 'not a body of concrete truth, but an engine for the discovery of concrete truth, similar to, say, the theory of mechanics', providing 'systematic and organized methods of reasoning' about factually based hypotheses concerning the 'manner of action of causes' (Marshall 1885: 159, 164, 171).

Walrasian methodology is named after the French economist Léon Walras (1834–1910), a pioneer of the theories of marginal utility and general equilibrium. Friedman, who, at the time he first drew the distinction, probably had only a second-hand knowledge of Walras's principal works, described Walrasian methodology as seeking abstractness, generality and a breadth of assumptions that would permit it to capture 'photographically' (Friedman's term) a systemic picture of the economy. Although Walras's theory of general equilibrium gave rise to the highly influential work of Gerard Debreu (1959), which long defined high mathematical theory in economics, Friedman's term is less directed at pure mathematical economics than at the approach that the prestige of such methods – even before Debreu – spawned among economists in more applied and empirical fields. As Friedman (1949: 83) puts it: 'we curtsy to Marshall but walk with Walras'. Koopmans's strongly a priori interpretation of the Cowles Commission programme provides a good example of the Walrasian approach (Koopmans 1950; Hood and Koopmans 1953; Hendry and Morgan 1995: ch. 43). The economy is viewed as a system, and theory is only as good as the completeness of its systematic grasp. While the models can be related to data along hypothetico-deductive lines, the emphasis is on the deduction from formal structures (essential to the approach to identification), with little feedback from data to theory.

The distinction between Walrasian and Marshallian methodology is not a distinction between general and partial equilibrium, if general equilibrium means a recognition of the complex interdependence of the various parts of the economy. Rather it is between a theory that is comprehensive and one that is purpose-built. It is necessary, according to Marshall (1885: 160) 'to sacrifice generality of form to some extent'. 'There is no use in waiting idly for [a unified social science]; we must do what we can with our present resources.' He goes on, 'common sense does not deal with a complex problem as a whole. Its first step is to break the problem into its several parts . . . the human mind has no other method of inquiry than this' (Marshall 1885: 164). The economist, Marshall (1885: 171) believes, 'must stand by the more laborious plan of interrogating the facts in order to learn the manner of action of causes singly and in combination'.

Where Friedman cast the Marshallian–Walrasian distinction as a contrast between concreteness and abstractness, I have elsewhere cast it in terms of different strategies (Hoover 2006). With the problem of microfoundations in mind, I contrasted a Walrasian engineering strategy with a Marshallian archaeological strategy. Both want to understand the structure of the economic building. For the Walrasian, it is a question of working it out, starting with the foundations. If we do not get them right, the superstructure will be shaky. For the Marshallian, the problem is that a systematic structure lies beneath the complexities of economic reality. To lay this structure bare, we must dig down to find the foundations, modifying and adapting our theoretical understanding as new facts accumulate, becoming ever more confident in our grasp of the superstructure, but never quite sure that we have reached the lowest level of the structure.

Keynes's attitude is similar to Marshall's, but Keynes is more a physician than archaeologist. Keynes's hands are soiled not by the dust of an economic Pompeii, but by the blood, sweat and ordure of the body economic. Like the body, the key mechanisms of the living economy are just as hidden and probably more complex than a buried city. And rather than a detached, academic interest, the study of economic physiology originates in the pressing need for diagnosis and cure.[3]

AN EXEMPLAR: *A TRACT ON MONETARY REFORM*

How does Keynes's Marshallian method play out in practice? And what is the role of theory in it? While Keynes's theory changes and develops across the three major economic works (the *Tract on Monetary Reform* (1923), the *Treatise on Money* (1930) and *The General Theory* (1936)), they display a consistent methodology and a similar structure. Of the three, the *Tract* was directed towards the broadest audience and employs the simplest theoretical structure, making it easier to see the role of theory in Keynes's methodological conception.

The opening two chapters of the *Tract* introduce the problem of price stability. Keynes sees the price fluctuations since the First World War as of a different order of magnitude than earlier fluctuations and as 'one of the most significant events in the economic history of the modern world' (JMK IV: 1). Characteristically, Keynes sets the stage with a data-rich description of the economic landscape. Perhaps more important, he engages in conceptual analysis, starting with a taxonomy of economic agents. Keynes lays out the costs of both inflation and deflation and its differential effects on investors (who later in the *General Theory* he prefers to call *rentiers*), businessmen and earners, concluding that inflation is 'unjust' and deflation 'inexpedient' (JMK IV: 36).

He also provides a preliminary sketch of the quantity theory of money. The quantity theory is one of the oldest theories in economics. Broadly, it states that the general level of prices in an economy is proportional to the stock of money. Keynes's initial discussion takes some sophisticated detours, including one on how the quantity theory would have to be modified to suit a hyperinflation. Anticipating the famous analysis of Cagan (1956), Keynes argued that the demand for money would fall during a period of extremely rapidly rising prices, as the inflation increased the cost of holding money measured by the accelerating fall in its purchasing power measured in the goods it could buy, encouraging people to avoid holding it whenever possible. In order to bring the supply and demand into alignment, the level of prices would have to rise more than in proportion to the stock of money.

Keynes sketches the political economy of inflation, laying the ultimate blame at the feet of an impecunious government and the political influence of the debtor class. The preliminary conceptual and data analysis sets up the main object of the subsequent theoretical analysis: how to secure, on average, a zero rate of expected inflation while minimizing the variability of the general price level.

The analytical core appears in chapter 3, 'The theory of money and the foreign exchanges'. Here Keynes says 'we must lay the theoretical foundations for the practical suggestions of the concluding chapters'. While some of the most interesting analysis concerns the foreign exchanges, we shall concentrate here on Keynes's use of the quantity theory. Unlike in his later works, in which Keynes aims at theoretical innovation, in the *Tract* he adopts what he regards as Marshall's account of the quantity theory. 'This theory,' he writes, 'is fundamental. Its correspondence to the facts is not open to question. Nevertheless, it is often misstated and misrepresented' (JMK IV: 61). His aim is to state it accurately in terms that are precisely defined.

The quantity equation in Keynes's notation can be written:

$$n = p(k + rk'),$$

where n is cash in circulation with the public; p is a cost-of-living index (measured as price per consumption unit); the public wishes to hold the equivalent of k units of consumption goods as cash and a further k' units as bank deposits; r is the customary bank-deposit reserve ratio (the fraction of deposits that banks must hold in cash), so that rk' is banks' holdings of reserves (JMK IV: 63). The characteristic neutrality property of the quantity theory (i.e. the proportionality of prices to money) is demonstrated on the assumption that cash (n) increases while the habits of the public and the banks $(k + rk')$ remain constant: to maintain equality in the quantity equation, prices must rise proportionately.

In keeping with other quantity theorists, such as David Hume and Irving Fisher, Keynes notes that neutrality is, at best, a long-run property.[4] In the short run it is a mistake to assume that k, k' and r are independent of n. Keynes's analysis of the short run follows a characteristic pattern. The object is the analysis of inflation and deflation. The ultimate causes are exhaustively considered, but the model is not extended to formalize the analysis. The quantity equation itself is the limit of formal analysis. Keynes uses it to provide a classificatory scheme for the various causes. Those that operate through changing cash fall under n; through changing credit conditions, under r; changing real balances (money demand), under k and k'. While k and k' are not directly controllable, they can be influenced by bank-rate policy, and remaining instabilities can be offset through the directly controllable n and r.

In the remainder of chapter 3 Keynes goes on to develop the theory of foreign exchange, but this is a good point to pause and take stock. The final chapters of the *Tract* use the theory of chapter 3 to reanalyze the problems identified in the first two chapters and to propose a set of policy recommendations to achieve the end of price stability. Taken as a whole, the *Tract* has the form of a diagnostic manual: a symptomatology, relevant physiology, illustrative case studies, and treatment and management options.

The analytical pattern of the *Tract* is exactly the same as that of the *Treatise on Money*. The *General Theory* is also conceived in the same functional pattern, though the book itself concentrates on the relevant physiology, leaving the other aspects at a casual and underdeveloped level. Keynes self-consciously adopted this more academic and detached form 'chiefly addressed to [his] fellow economists' since he believed that the failures of orthodox economics were not to be found 'in the superstructure, which has been erected with great care for logical consistency, but in a lack of clearness and of generality in the premises' (JMK VII: XXI).

Returning to the example of the *Tract*, the modern economist might be inclined to question whether Keynes's reformulated quantity equation qualifies as a theoretical contribution at all. It is a far cry from Debreu – or Walras, for that matter. But theory in economics has come to have a peculiar meaning. The *Oxford English Dictionary* lists a series of definitions that capture Keynes's conception. One defines *theory* as: 'A conception or mental scheme of something to be done, or of the method of doing it; a systematic statement of rules or principles to be followed.' His major theoretical works are certainly that.

A second runs:

A scheme or system of ideas or statements held as an explanation or account of a group of facts or phenomena; a hypothesis that has been confirmed or established by observation or experiment, and is propounded or accepted as accounting for the known facts; a statement of what are held to be the general laws, principles, or causes of something known or observed.

This fits Keynes's clearly casual analysis and explanatory intent: 'The moral' of his theoretical account of the quantity theory, Keynes writes, 'is that the price level is not mysterious, but is governed by a few, definite, analysable influences' (JMK IV: 68).

Perhaps the most apt definition runs: 'That department of an art or technical subject which consists in the knowledge or statement of the facts on which it depends, or the principles or methods, as distinguished from the *practice* of it.' One citation, for instance, contrasts *music theory*, the knowledge of harmony, counterpoint and so forth, with the art of playing. The *Tract*, like the *Treatise*, fits easily into this mould.

Even if we concede that Keynes has a theory, would not a modern critic be right to regard it as a thin gruel? That would be to misunderstand the function of theory in Keynes's diagnostic schema. The quantity equation in the *Tract* represents a key part of the complex economy, the *causal nexus* (to use Keynes's own phrase – JMK VII: 173) that connects money, prices and the real economy. Essentially, it is meant to capture and isolate a mechanism. Inputs come from outside this mechanism, and the variables of the quantity equation themselves exercise a causal influence over other variables outside the mechanism. But the equation captures the fundamental causal connections among n, p, k, k' and r. It serves as an accounting statement: whatever the complex of causes, their effects on the variables of the quantity equation must respect the identity; if any cause alters p, it must do so, not directly, but through its effect on n, k, k' or r. The theory is not a machine for prediction, but a tool for analysis. It provides a principled framework for systematically classifying the various symptoms of economic maladies, charting their likely courses and suggesting an appropriate regimen.[5]

THEORY AS A CAUSALLY ISOLATED SYSTEM

The diagnostic role of theory in Keynes's economics accounts for his ubiquitous use of causal language.[6] Causality is naturally a diagnostic concept (Hoover 2004a). English idiom says, 'I started the car', not 'I caused the car to start.' But if the car stalls, it is perfectly idiomatic to say, 'What caused it to stall?' Keynes underscores the importance of a causal account in the opening lines of chapter 10 of the *Treatise*:

The fundamental problem of monetary theory is not merely to establish identities or statical equations relating (e.g.) the turnover of monetary instruments to the turnover of things traded for money. The real task of such a theory is to treat the problem dynamically, analysing the different elements involved, in such a manner as to exhibit the causal process by which the price level is determined, and the method of transition from one position of equilibrium to another.

(JMK V: 120)

Keynes's strategy, as we saw in respect of the *Tract*, is to single out a causal nexus as the theoretical core of the analysis. But what qualifies a relationship to be an element of this nexus? Keynes's analytical practice can be clarified by Figure 5.1. Arrows represent causal influence running from inputs to outputs through the causal nexus or theoretical core. This fits the Marshallian strategy, as the theoretical core need not be the core of the whole economy, but only of that part relevant to the problem at hand.

The economy is complex, so the number of inputs (N) and outputs (M) may be very large. So too, in principle, may the number of elements of the causal core. Only four are shown in the figure, partly for expositional simplicity and partly because it illustrates Marshall's methodological view that the central elements must be chosen in a way that keeps their number tractable. Every possible linkage is shown among the four causal elements in the core, but the business of theory is to state the existence, nature and direction

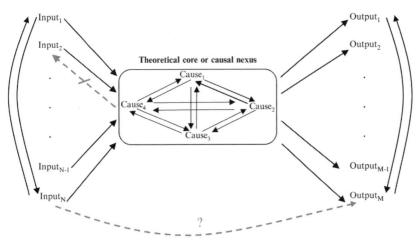

Figure 5.1. The causal structure of Keynes's economic theory.

of the linkages among causal variables, so not all these elements would be operative in a real theory.

The critical point is that the causal flow runs only in one direction from inputs to the core and from the core to outputs. In particular, a link such as the one shown as a dashed grey line from the causal nexus to Input₂ is ruled out. This reflects Keynes's strategy of laying out the core theory and then addressing the range of factors that influence its terms, each influencing the economy through the mediation of the core.

Can we rule out direct influences from inputs to outputs that do not go through the core as shown by the dashed grey link between Input_N and Output_M? Since Keynes does not offer us a methodological analysis, we can only infer from his practice. One piece of evidence to suggest that such links should be ruled out is Keynes's rejection of Fisher's account of the effect of inflation on interest rates (JMK VII: 142). Although Keynes accepts the fact of a correlation between interest rates and high inflation rates, he rejects Fisher's account because, unlike Fisher, he sees it as the product of a more intricate causal chain rather than as a direct linkage. Another piece of evidence is found in the sequence of more elaborate core theories that Keynes develops from the *Tract* through to the *General Theory*. In particular, the insight that Keynes believes separates the *General Theory* from his previous quantity-theoretic accounts is that the factors that determine prices also determine output, which leads him to widen his core theory to eliminate an unmediated linkage (JMK VII: xxii).

Keynes's analytical practice is not only Marshallian, it is also very much in the spirit of Simon's (2001; see also Boumans 2001) later account of *near-decomposability*. For Simon, a system is nearly decomposable when it can be divided into sub-systems such that the linkages among the elements within each sub-system are strong and the linkages between sub-systems are weak. One Marshallian element of Simon's conception is that, for many purposes, sub-systems can be analyzed as independent units, neglecting the other, weakly linked sub-systems. In practice, Simon frequently associates decomposability with a temporal hierarchy: the elements of a sub-system respond quickly to each other, but only slowly to those in other sub-systems; and, indeed, individual sub-systems can be treated as units relative to one another. For example, plate tectonics treats the continents as sub-systems that interact on a very long time-horizon; while another part of geology, hydrology, treats the interactions of water flows within continents on a much shorter horizon. Hydrology and plate tectonics lose little from mutual neglect.

That Keynes's thinking ran along these lines is evident in his treatment of aggregation and in his famous distinction between the economics of the individual producer and the economics of output as a whole – later enshrined in the division between microeconomics and macroeconomics (JMK VII: 293). For Keynes, as for Simon, time-horizon is a key distinction. It is often forgotten that Keynes's famous *bon mot*, '[i]n the long run we are all dead', was not offered as advice to live in the moment but as an aside in an analytical decomposition: 'But this *long run* is a misleading guide to current affairs. . . Economists set themselves too easy, too useless a task if in tempestuous seasons they can only tell us that when the storm is long past the ocean is flat again' (JMK IV: 65). The level of the ocean matters (coastal cities are lost to rising seas over centuries), but that process has nothing much to do with the immediate effects of, say, a tsunami. Keynes was alert to what we might now call the paradox of monetarism: in the long run, neutral money is the least important factor in the economy; while in the short run, non-neutral money may be the most important (e.g. JMK V: 83).

Keynes makes the point about decomposability less poetically but with more precision in the *General Theory*:

The division of the determinant of the economic system . . . must be made entirely on the basis of experience, so as to correspond on the one hand to the factors in which the changes seem to be slow or so little relevant as to have only a small and comparatively negligible short-term influence on our *quaesitum*; and on the other hand to those factors in which the changes are found in practice to exercise dominant influence on our *quaesitum* . . . Our final task might be to select those variables which can be deliberately controlled or managed by central authority in the kind of system in which we actually live.

(JMK VII: 247)

Echoes of Marshall; anticipations of Simon.

Keynes is unusually attentive to definitions and preliminary conceptual analysis. The *Treatise* opens with a chapter on the classification of money, and it contains a book of five chapters in sixty-three pages dealing with the problem of identifying the appropriate price index for money. The *General Theory* similarly devotes a book of four chapters in fifty-one pages to 'Definitions and ideas'. Keynes's focus on conceptual precision can be best understood as an attempt to articulate his theory in a manner that corresponds to the causal joints of the economy.[7] Referring to his own version of the quantity equation in the *Treatise*, Keynes observes:

they are mere identities; truisms which tell us nothing in themselves. In this respect they resemble all other versions of the quantity theory of money. Their only point is to analyse and arrange our material in what will turn out to be a useful way for tracing cause and effect, when we have vitalized them by the introduction of extraneous facts from the actual world.

(JMK V: 125; cf. 198)

Once again, Keynes anticipates the views of a later author. Nancy Cartwright (1989: ch. 2, section 2) tells the story of the Lamb dip, a phenomenon in which the intensity of a gas laser as a function of its frequency relative to resonance shows a double peak. The physicist Lamb was able to provide a mathematical analysis that permitted exact calculation of the effect, which he and others nevertheless regarded as inadequate until a causal account could be provided.

Keynes's account of liquidity preference in the *General Theory* proceeds from a similar motivation. Keynes taxes classical economics with maintaining simultaneously two different, and causally unconnected, theories of the interest rate in which in 'volume I dealing with the theory of value' it is determined by savings and investment and in 'volume II dealing with the theory of money' it is determined by the quantity of money (JMK VII: 182). Liquidity preference presents the interest rate as determined at the point that divides financial markets into two equally balanced groups – one expecting capital gains, the other capital losses. The interest rate, in turn, is a causal determinant of investment through comparison to the marginal efficiency of capital. Keynes argues that:

> the traditional analysis is faulty because it has failed to isolate correctly the independent variables of the system. Savings and investment are determinates of the system, not determinants. . . These determinants are, indeed, themselves complex and each is capable of being affected by prospective changes in the others. But they remain independent in the sense that their values cannot be inferred from one another.
>
> (JMK VII: 183–4)[8]

Some have regarded Hicks's (1946: ch. 12) demonstration of the equivalence of the liquidity preference theory with the earlier loanable funds theory of interest rates as showing that Keynes failed to understand simultaneity. But this misses the point: the Marshallian methodology and causal isolation require that while some relationships may be simultaneous, not every variable can be endogenous in any practically useful analysis. (The spirit of the modern vector-autoregression approach to econometrics, in which the only exogenous terms are random shocks, is quite contrary to Keynes's methodology.) Keynes, like Lamb, looks for an account in which not only does everything add up, but the causal forces are accurately mapped.

It is practically important to get the causal articulation right. Keynes argues that unclearness about 'the causal process through which a reduction in the quantity of money leads eventually to . . . lower . . . prices' encourages the policy-maker 'to contemplate deflation too light heartedly' (JMK V: 244).

A preference for causal articulation has a surprising implication for Keynes. One must sometimes prefer *qualitative* to *quantitative* investigation. Fisher's quantity equation, Keynes admits in the *Treatise*, is better suited to analyzing the available data (JMK V: 210). Where Keynes, following Cambridge tradition, always related the quantity of money to income, Fisher's famous quantity equation, $MV = PT$, relates money to the volume of transactions, which generally exceeds incomes by many orders of magnitude as businesses engage in many pounds' (or dollars') worth of monetary exchanges in the process of generating each pound or dollar of income. Although Keynes accepted that the alternatives to his 'fundamental equations', including not only Fisher's but also his own quantity equation from the *Tract*, are equally good as accounting identities, he came to believe that they fail to map the causes that truly animate the economy (JMK V: 198–9). The economy is sufficiently complex, and precise conceptual analysis demonstrates that it is difficult – or impossible – to capture key causes in statistical data: expectations, for example, are intrinsically unobservable. Qualitative analysis is often the best that we can do.

THEORY AND THE REAL WORLD

Keynes's modern reputation largely rests on the *General Theory*, and his opposition to Tinbergen's programme of econometric modelling is well known (JMK XIV: 306–18); it is thus easy to see him as divorced from data or, perhaps, even hostile to it. But the *Tract* is chock full of data, and Keynes introduces volume II of the *Treatise* as 'the applied theory and a quantitative study of the facts as they exist in the leading monetary systems of today' (JMK VI: 3).[9] How does Keynes imagine that theory is applied and how do facts relate to it?

The pure–applied distinction is not simply a distinction between theory that is quantified and adapted to particular economic organizations.[10] Rather, pure theory concerns the theoretical core or causal nexus of Keynes's theory, while applied theory concerns its linkages to the inputs and outputs shown in Figure 5.1. Much of volume II of the *Treatise* concerns the influence of such factors as bank rate, which do not appear in the theoretical core directly, on outcomes for the real economy, also not in the core, mediated through Keynes's fundamental equations.

Keynes's approach is not empiricist in the hypothetical-deductive mode; he does not subject his theory to direct tests. We might think of Keynes's theories as *synthetic a priori*. 'A priori' because they are largely based on common sense and background knowledge, which may implicitly include deductions from the mainstream economic theory of Marshall and other neo-classicals. 'Synthetic', not analytic, because, unlike Austrians (such as Menger 1950 and Mises 1966), Keynes does not regard economic theory as a branch of pure logic; rather, like Marshall, he regards it as an instrument of inquiry into facts about causes.

On the one hand, theory does not relate to data in the simple pattern of verification or falsification. Prior theory is critical to understanding the import of data. Malthus was, in Keynes's view, hard pressed to overthrow dominant Ricardian theory, despite its empirical inadequacies, in large measure because 'he failed to furnish an alternative [theoretical] construction' (JMK VII: 32). On the other hand, theory can be reasonably adjusted to fit the facts. For example, Keynes infers the smoothness of the aggregate liquidity preference function, not from prior theoretical considerations, but from the efficacy of open-market operations (JMK VII: 197).

Keynes's vision of the economy is that it is complex and our knowledge of it is bound to be incomplete and frequently qualitative only. Keynes's (XIV: 306–18) attack on Tinbergen's econometric business-cycle model was based in large measure on the presumed requirement of Tinbergen's (1939) statistics to capture a complete list of causes and for the relationships among the variables to be quantitatively stable – in his view an utter impossibility. Clearly, Keynes would have shown the same scepticism towards Tinbergen's successors, the Cowles Commission's econometric programme (Koopmans 1950; Hood and Koopmans 1953), and the 'Keynesian' efforts to use macroeconometric models to 'fine-tune' the economy.

Equally, Keynes would have dissented from the more recent vision of the goal of theory as providing a simulacrum for the economy. Lucas states the vision clearly: 'Our task . . . is to write a FORTRAN program that will accept specific economic policy rules as 'input' and will generate as 'output' statistics describing the operating characteristics of time series we care about, which are predicted to result from these policies' (Lucas 1981: 288).

Although Lucas's division of inputs, theoretical model and outputs echoes the categories used in Figure 5.1 to describe Keynes's own vision, there are essential differences. Lucas's programme can work only if it captures all the causally relevant factors, since he wants predictions or quantified operating characteristics of the economy. In effect, Lucas makes no distinction between causal relations that belong to the nexus and those that are outside it. It is as if the box representing the causal nexus were drawn around the entire causal system.

In contrast, Keynes, with his Marshallian methodology, does not assert that the causal nexus is complete – hence the causal connections among inputs and among outputs that do not run through the causal nexus. His theory can, even when applied quantitatively, at best suggest tendencies and influences that can provide guidance to the policy-maker, but not forecasts on which any confidence can be placed.

Keynes endorses '[t]he reasonable doubts of practical men [particularly Governor Strong], towards the idea that "the Federal Reserve System has the power to raise or lower the price level by some automatic method, by some magic mathematical formula"' (JMK VI: 305). More positively, Keynes offers a vision of the task of theory quite different from Lucas's: 'The object of our analysis is, not to provide a machine, or method of blind manipulation, which will furnish an infallible answer, but to provide ourselves with an organized and orderly method of thinking out particular problems . . .' (JMK VII: 297). In discussing the credit cycle, he observes that

[t]he possible varieties of the paths which a credit cycle can follow and its possible complications are so numerous that it is impracticable to outline all of them. One can describe the rules of chess and the nature of the game, work out the leading openings and play through a few characteristic end-games; but one cannot possibly catalogue all the games which can be played.

(JMK V: 253)

An effective economic theory is like a good chess manual, a source of guidance and wisdom to the practitioner, but not a mechanical algorithm for translating policy goals into policy actions, nor a crystal ball for foretelling their precise consequences.

The test of a theory as an element of a diagnostic manual is not found in a crucial experiment but in the ability of theory to make sense of the economic situation. Keynes proves the theory of the *Treatise* in the case studies of historical episodes in chapter 30 of volume II. Even in the more academic *General Theory*, he suggests that the marker of success is 'that our theory must be capable of explaining the phenomena of the trade cycle'.

This is the clue to Keynes's theoretical development from a Marshallian quantity-theorist to the aggregate-supply-and-demand analyst of the *General Theory*. There is no simple, statistical test; yet the theory must make sense of the data and offer a persuasive causal account of the actual development of the economy. While denying that the preconditions for formal statistical tests existed, he nevertheless preferred to examine his theories' ability to rationalize quantitative data where possible. Because he believed that many of the causally relevant conclusions of his theory were necessarily not quantitative, such examinations were not always possible. Yet that did not put the theories beyond test. In a telling aside, Keynes suggests that the doubts expressed by Federal Reserve Governor Strong about the efficacy of monetary control 'cannot be dispelled merely by pointing to the truisms of a quantity equation. In a sense they can only be dispelled by the prolonged success of an actual attempt at scientific control' (JMK VI: 309). Theories are tested, then, not only directly by economists but indirectly through the successes and failures of policy-makers. One of Keynes's goals for his theoretical analysis was to demonstrate that the prospects of success warranted the trial. The successive elaborations of Keynes's monetary theory were each motivated by his perception that the previous version had proved inadequate to the rationalization of the data or to the support of practical policy – a pragmatic, rather than academic, standard.

THE ECONOMIC THEORIST IN THE ECONOMY

Keynes's pragmatic, diagnostic conception of economic theory provides a different, and perhaps more satisfactory understanding, of the role of the economist in the economy. Returning to Keynes's chess analogy, we can think of the 'Keynesians' after the Second World War as seeing the economist as a chess master, who can stand above the board and move the pieces – at least within some limits. The perspective is overarching, if not omniscient. And, indeed, the ambition seemed to be a more comprehensive, predictive understanding of how the economic game would play out conditional on various moves – as if IBM's 'Big Blue' or its successor were to replace Keynes's chess manual.

The New Classical economists, particularly in the wake of Lucas's (1976) critique of econometric policy evaluation, argued that this vision was faulty, because the pieces were not ciphers but actors of the same species as the policy-makers. The new classical solution was, in effect, to endow each piece with the same information and perspective as the chess master. Yet the ambition was still a comprehensive, predictive understanding of the outcomes of the game. It was quickly pointed out that there are paradoxes in such an approach. If the pieces know as much as the chess master, who knows everything relevant up to a random error and can, therefore, predict the future (the rational-expectations hypothesis), then in what sense can the policy-maker truly be an advice-giver? Sargent (1984) saw this as a paradox of free will (cf. Craine and Hardouvelis 1983; LeRoy 1995). In the effort to respect the intentionality of the economic agent, the policy-maker himself has been reduced to a cipher.

Keynes's strategy is different. Neither the economist nor the economic agent possesses the practical omniscience of rational expectations. The chess player is just another player of the board – say, the king's bishop. Yes, he possesses a chess manual, but it is one that has been written, not from the overarching perspective of the chess master, but from the ground-level view of the bishop. Acquisition of economic knowledge occurs within the game. It is necessarily partial, bound by particular perspectives and subject to debate. Yes, Keynes and his fellow economists are the bishops. They argue and debate. They possess the arcane knowledge of the manuals of play; in that sense they know more than the other players. Their theories may be cast in an overarching perspective, but this is merely a projection from inside the game, and not the product of a standpoint that they somehow occupy above the game. The test of their theories is largely the success of their policy advice: does their side win the game? But tests of that sort can be run only if the economists can convince the kings, queens and even the pawns to follow their manual.

Seen this way, Keynes's understanding of the place of economic theory in the economy makes neither the mistake of the 'Keynesians' nor suffers from the paradoxes of the new classicals. And it suggests that Keynes's persistent efforts to cast his economic theory into a specific policy context and, more often than not, to expound it in forms that would be accessible to the policy-maker and the literate public arose not only out of a personal urge to practical action, but out of an understanding of the function and limitations of economic theory itself.

NOTES

1   I accept Clarke's (1988) thesis that the *Treatise on Money* was strongly formed by Keynes's contemporaneous experience as an adviser to the UK Treasury, while the *General Theory* was a more intellectually detached work. Nonetheless, I believe that without experience in practical policy-making, the *General Theory* would have been a very different book.

2   Keynes was not a doctor, even in the sense that most modern academics are. The degree of Doctor of Philosophy was uncommon in England in many subjects until after the Second World War, so that Keynes, like Marshall, Pigou, Hicks and many others, held only an MA degree, which involved no further study beyond the BA. Keynes also never held the title Professor. He was a long-serving fellow of King's College Cambridge.

3   Keynes himself, as well as expressing the view that '[i]f economists could manage to get themselves thought of as humble, competent people, on a level with dentists, that would be splendid' (JMK IX: 332), was no stranger to medical metaphors: e.g. JMK IV: 80; JMK VI: 130, 199ff.

4   It is here that Keynes delivers his quip about being dead in the long run.

5   Keynes's diagnostic use of the quantity theory bears a close kinship with Friedman and Schwartz's (1963a, b) analysis of the monetary history of the United States. This is hardly surprising, as Friedman was equally a disciple of Marshall (see Hoover 2006) and knew and approved of both the *Tract on Monetary Reform* and the *Treatise on Money*, despite his reputation as an anti-Keynesian, which was based largely on his objections to the policies advocated by followers of Keynes after the publication of the *General Theory*.

6   Some examples of Keynes's ubiquitous use of causal language are found in JMK IV: 129, 142; JMK V: 126, 139, 141, 163, 166, 201, 244, 231; JMK VII: 39, 57.

7   It does not weaken the point about the function of these definitions to
    recall that Keynes's *Treatise on Money* was severely criticized by
    Hayek and others because of its definitions.

8   Keynes's characterization of independence here anticipates Simon's
    (1953) definition of causal order with reference to recursive systems.

9   Bateman (1990) anticipates a key point of this essay: despite Keynes's
    critical assault on Tinbergen, Keynes was neither an opponent of
    empirical economics nor of econometrics in general.

10 See Backhouse (1998: 88–91) for a discussion of the difficulties of
    drawing a sharp distinction between economic theory and applied eco-
    nomics in Keynes's time, and Backhouse and Biddle (2000), especially
    pp. 1–7 for a discussion of Keynes's own view of the distinction.

6 Keynes and British economic policy

INTRODUCTION

Keynes's impact on economic policy has been the subject of widely contrasting interpretations. Most economists in the 1950s and 1960s, when unemployment rates of between 1 and 2 per cent came to be regarded as normal, credited Keynes (and their own profession) with providing the cure to the high unemployment that had marked the interwar years. Keynes's *General Theory of Employment, Interest and Money* (1936) was developed and refined by his followers – known as Keynesians – to guide governments in how to achieve the goals of full employment, stable prices and a sound external balance of payments (and thereby a stable, but adjustable, exchange rate). Keynesian economists believed that fiscal policy (variations in the levels of taxation and of government expenditure) was more effective than domestic monetary policy (variations in interest rates and in banks' reserves) in influencing demand for goods and services, as regards increasing employment. In the event, it was not difficult to maintain full employment during the long postwar boom.

In the 1970s some economists claimed that Keynes was responsible for high inflation, it being assumed that he was responsible for a bias towards budget deficits that increased demand beyond what the economy could supply. The key work setting out this view was James M. Buchanan and Richard E. Wagner's *Democracy in Deficit: The Political Legacy of Lord Keynes*. These two eminent American scholars argued that 'politicians naturally want to spend and to avoid taxing', and that Keynes, by persuading governments to abandon the pre-war doctrine of balanced budgets, in the interests of employment policy, had removed an essential discipline in political democracy (Buchanan and Wagner 1977: 183). In fact, as Robin Matthews had pointed out in 1968, British governments had varied budget current account *surpluses* to manage demand, and the net effect had been deflationary. In his view, in so far as postwar policy had contributed to full employment, it had done so by creating a stable environment in which businessmen had had the confidence to increase private investment above pre-war levels (Matthews 1968). On the other hand, the postwar period had seen a marked increase in capital expenditure by public authorities (including industries nationalized after the war), and there was room for discussion about what constituted a budget surplus or deficit. In 1978, John Burton produced figures, based on the public-sector borrowing requirement, that showed British budgets in deficit in every year except two from 1952 to 1976 (Buchanan, Wagner and Burton 1978: 32, 34). But pre-war budgets had aimed only at balancing central government's current account. Peter Clarke dispelled the myth about postwar budgets by producing figures on a consistent, pre-war basis, showing that the budget had been in surplus each year from 1948 until 1972, with the possible exception of 1965 (Clarke 1998: 190–212).

An alternative accusation against Keynesian economists was that they had taken Keynes's name in vain when advising that unemployment could be reduced below 3 per cent without producing demands for higher wages. In a notable speech at Preston in 1974, following the defeat of the Conservatives in the first general election that year, Sir Keith Joseph, one of Margaret Thatcher's mentors, began to argue publicly that policies leading to overfull employment had been a major cause of inflation, since a shortage of labour encouraged trade unions to demand, and employers to offer, higher wages. He observed that 'if we wish to fight the battles of the seventies with the weapons of the thirties we would do well to find out what was actually said and done in the thirties, not least by Keynes himself'. There was a lively debate among economists over the next few years about the significance of articles that Keynes had published in *The Times* in January and March 1937, when, according to Keynes, unemployment among workers covered by the national unemployment insurance scheme was 12.5 per cent (equivalent to 9.6 per cent of the labour force).[1] Keynes had urged that public investment should be postponed to offset a threatened slump, and Terence Hutchison claimed that the articles showed that Keynes's target for employment was far above that of the Keynesians (JMK XXI: 384–95, 404–9; Hutchison 1977; Peden 1980).

There are then, competing myths about Keynes and economic policy. His name has been used to support or condemn policies since his death in 1946. This chapter will focus on what Keynes said about monetary policy, public investment and fiscal policy in relation to unemployment and inflation. The next section provides some general context concerning Keynes's political philosophy, his contacts with policy-makers and the evolution of his economic thought. Subsequent sections deal with his advice in historical context, and the extent to which it shaped economic policy in his lifetime. A final section assesses the extent to which the historical Keynes differs from the myths constructed by Keynesians and their opponents.

KEYNES'S POLITICAL PHILOSOPHY AND ECONOMIC THOUGHT

For Keynes, politics was about a means to greater efficiency, freedom, economic security and justice rather than the attainment of an ideal form of government. Although a lifelong Liberal, he was prepared to advise governments of any political complexion (O'Donnell 1989). He believed in the persuasive power of argument, and famously claimed in the *General Theory* that 'the power of vested interests is vastly exaggerated compared with the gradual encroachment of ideas' (JMK VII: 383). While regarding capitalism and market forces as necessary to economic efficiency, he did not believe that individuals acting separately always produced the best results for society. He rejected the nineteenth-century doctrine of *laissez-faire* and argued for a wider agenda for the state to regulate matters where the individual was powerless to help himself. He came to believe that there was nothing inherent in the economic system to ensure full employment of capital and labour, and that the state must control the total levels of the community's savings and investment (JMK IX: 291–2; JMK VII: 377–8).

Keynes's political attitudes were reinforced by his experience as a civil servant and government adviser. He worked in the India Office from 1906 to 1909 and took an interest in India's currency system and its effect on prices, before returning to Cambridge to teach economics. In 1913 he was appointed to the Royal Commission on Indian Finance and Currency, and established his reputation as a financial expert with the publication of his first book, *Indian Currency and Finance*, in the same year. He was consulted by the Treasury during the financial crisis at the outbreak of the First World War and was a civil servant in the department from 1915 to 1919, dealing, among other things, with the sterling:dollar exchange rate. He was the Treasury's principal representative at the Paris peace conference until he resigned in protest over the reparations clauses of the Treaty of Versailles. He served Liberal chancellors (David Lloyd George and Reginald McKenna) and Conservative chancellors (Andrew Bonar Law and Austen Chamberlain), and after he returned to Cambridge he was consulted by three Conservative chancellors (Austen Chamberlain over the use of monetary policy to control inflation in 1919, Winston Churchill over the return to the Gold Standard in 1925 and Neville Chamberlain over budgetary policy in 1933), before being appointed as an adviser by a fourth, Sir (H.) Kingsley Wood, in 1940. Keynes's advice was also sought by a Labour prime minister, James Ramsay MacDonald, who made him a member of his Economic Advisory Council in 1930, and he was retained as an economic adviser by Labour's first postwar chancellor, Hugh Dalton. Keynes's links with the Bank of England were more distant; nevertheless, he was elected to the Bank's Court of Directors in 1941.

Keynes knew the leading Treasury officials, either from working with them during one or other of the wars, or from membership of the Tuesday Club, which was formed in 1917 to bring together City men, financial journalists, academic economists and civil servants. It was important for him to try to convert the Treasury to his views, since the department was responsible for the budget and controlled public expenditure, and also advised the chancellor on monetary policy (although the conduct of the latter was the responsibility of the Bank of England). Keynes also sought to influence public opinion by writing innumerable polemical newspaper articles and pamphlets, often being very critical of the civil servants and politicians who consulted him. Although he believed in rational argument, he also believed that 'words ought to be a little wild, for they are the assault of thoughts on the unthinking' (JMK XXI: 244). He was also aware that, if he was to get his ideas across to the average reader of a newspaper, he had to state his case boldly, without qualifications about practical problems. This approach did not always go down well with people responsible for policy.

A MANAGED CURRENCY VERSUS THE GOLD STANDARD, 1919–1939

The First World War was financed to a large extent by government borrowing from the Bank of England; the consequence was that money earned by the government's contractors found its way into the banking system, and increased the ability of banks to lend. During the war prices were kept in check to some extent by controls over investment and by rationing of consumer expenditure, but once these controls were abolished in 1919 an inflationary investment boom fed by bank credit quickly developed. In February 1920, the Chancellor, Austen Chamberlain, asked for Keynes's advice. Keynes replied that, with capital goods and labour fully employed, new credit pushed up prices, or lowered the exchange rate by encouraging imports. He advocated a sharp rise in interest rates to change businessmen's expectations and to discourage them from borrowing (Howson 1973). In the event, the advice was taken too slowly, and in too small doses, to check the boom: a severe slump followed in 1921, with falling prices and unprecedented unemployment (16.9 per cent of the insured labour force, or 12.2 per cent of the total labour force).

The Treasury and the Bank of England tried to achieve monetary stability by returning to the pre-war Gold Standard, whereby all major currencies had a fixed value in terms of gold and therefore had fixed exchange rates with each other. Keynes believed that it would be better to manage the currency to give priority to stability of domestic prices. He also argued that to revalue sterling by 10 per cent, as the Treasury and the Bank of England proposed to do, in order to return to the Gold Standard at the pre-war exchange rate of $4.86, would penalize export industries, since British prices had risen by more than American prices since 1914. Nevertheless, in 1925 the Chancellor, Winston Churchill, although impressed by Keynes's arguments, took the advice of Treasury officials and the Bank of England, with the consequence that sterling was overvalued

– although economic historians disagree on the extent and significance of this overvaluation (Moggridge 1972: 245–50; Dimsdale 1981; Redmond 1984; Taylor 1992; Barkai 1993; Wolcott 1993). Attempts by employers to make coal exports profitable again by cutting wage costs led to the General Strike of 1926. Contrary to Treasury officials' expectations, money wages remained stable from 1923, although prices were falling, and employers reacted by laying off labour.

Maintenance of a fixed exchange rate involved periodic adjustments of the Bank of England's discount rate – known as Bank rate – in response to external conditions, such as high New York interest rates during the stock exchange boom there in the late 1920s. Higher Bank rate tended to increase the interest rates at which banks would lend and hence tended to discourage business investment even when unemployment was higher than it had been before the war. Moreover, falling prices raised the value of money relative to fixed assets, and therefore the real rate of interest, leading businessmen to delay investment, even when nominal interest rates fell.

Once Britain had returned to the Gold Standard, Keynes was careful not to advocate a deliberate act of devaluation, as such an act by what was then the leading trading nation would be a severe shock to the international system. However, Britain was forced off the Gold Standard in September 1931, as exports fell, and the cost of unemployment benefit rose, in an international slump. Keynes's advice was sought at the end of the year by Sir Frederick Phillips, a Treasury official who was opposed to a return to the Gold Standard. Keynes and Phillips agreed that the Gold Standard had brought about a fall in prices, raising real wages, and therefore unemployment. Phillips favoured a policy that would restore prices to their 1929 level, which he did not think would provoke demands for higher money wages. Keynes recommended stabilizing sterling at about $3.40, which at current wage levels would make British exports cheaper, and imports dearer, than they had been when sterling was at $4.86. Phillips accepted this advice and devised the Exchange Equalization Account, which was to be used by the Bank of England to even out fluctuations in the exchange rate (Howson 1975: 82–9, 173–9; Howson 1980). The Treasury hoped to raise employment by helping the export industries, where unemployment was highest, but other countries also allowed their currencies to depreciate, or devalued them in terms of gold, so that Britain's competitive advantage was short-lived. The longer-term advantage of going off the Gold Standard was that it was no longer necessary to defend a fixed exchange rate by raising Bank rate, which was reduced from 6 per cent to 2 per cent in 1932 and kept at that level with a view to encouraging investment.

There remained fundamental disagreements between Keynes and the Treasury on monetary policy and its effectiveness. In his *Treatise on Money* in 1930 (JMK V and VI), and again in the *General Theory*, Keynes emphasized the importance of the long-term rate of interest rather than changes in short-term rates as an influence on investment (although a rise in the latter would tend to raise the long-term rate). In contrast, Ralph Hawtrey, the Treasury's only in-house economist in the interwar period, emphasized the importance of Bank rate, which, by influencing short-term rates of interest, also influenced investment through traders' willingness to hold stocks or place new orders. Keynes also argued that the Treasury's policy down to 1939 of funding the national debt – that is, of replacing short-term government bonds with longer-term ones – tended to reduce banks' reserves and their willingness to lend at lower interest rates, even after Bank rate had been reduced (Howson 1975: 95–106; Howson and Winch 1977: 144–5). Keynes's liquidity preference theory differed from earlier theories of the rate of interest by seeing it, not as the price that brought the demand for resources to invest into equilibrium with the readiness to abstain from consumption, but as the reward for parting with control over money for a stated period of time. According to Keynes, people held cash or assets, like Treasury bills, that could quickly be turned into cash, partly for current transactions, partly for security and partly because of uncertainty over future rates of interest. From this proposition he developed a theory of the term structure of interest rates. On the basis of this theory he argued that the monetary authorities – the Bank of England and the Treasury – could control interest rates by supplying demand for different types and maturities of securities, and by influencing expectations about long-term interest rates, if the monetary authorities were prepared to let the quantity of money to increase to meet requirements for current transactions, and to give up their attempts to control the market by funding the national debt (JMK VII: 165–72, 194–207). He also believed that monetary policy alone could not bring about recovery in the post-1929 slump, since businessmen were so pessimistic that they would respond to low interest rates only after the state had increased economic activity through public investment.

PUBLIC INVESTMENT AND FISCAL POLICY, 1924–1939

Keynes supported – and indeed helped to draft – the Liberal Party's proposals in 1928 and 1929 for expenditure of £251 million over two years on what were then called 'public works': principally roads, local authority housing and electrification through a national grid. The main barrier to such a policy was the 'Treasury view' that government borrowing to finance public expenditure would tend to crowd out private investment, with the result that there would be very little additional employment and no permanent additional employment. The Treasury view was based on the assumption that there would be no increase in bank credit, and that the government would be borrowing funds that would soon be used by private industry or invested abroad (and thereby, Treasury officials believed, encouraging British exports of capital goods). Treasury officials argued that if there were an increase in bank credit, prices would tend to rise and the exchange rate would tend to fall, forcing the Bank of England to raise Bank rate, and with it the price of borrowing, to stop an outflow of gold (Peden 2004: 57–61, 65–6). As a member of the Macmillan Committee on Finance and Industry, Keynes had the chance in May 1930 to debate the Treasury view with Sir Richard Hopkins, the most senior Treasury official in charge of financial policy and control of public expenditure, who was a witness before the committee. Hopkins, as an administrator, avoided discussion of economic theory, focusing instead on the practicality of Lloyd George's programme and the adverse effect that wasteful expenditure would have on business confidence – what Roger Middleton has called 'psychological crowding out' (Middleton 1985: 153–65, 171).

When Keynes had first advocated public works as a cure for unemployment in 1924, he too had believed that the supply of capital was limited, and his proposals had involved only a diversion of existing funds, such as idle balances in banks. He had suggested that the chancellor of the exchequer should cease to use the sinking fund in his budget, and budget surpluses, to redeem the national debt, and should instead promote productive capital expenditure of up to £100 million a year. By 1929 he had worked out a new theory of the connection between savings and investment, while writing the *Treatise on Money*. Previously it had been believed that savings and investment were kept in equilibrium by changes in interest rates. However, Keynes now argued that if the public increased its holdings of financial assets by more than the amount that businessmen wished to invest, prices would fall and businessmen would respond by reducing output and employment. So long as Bank rate had to be used to maintain the Gold Standard, interest rates might remain above the level at which Britain, as a mature economy, could find profitable domestic outlets for the whole of its savings. Unlike the Treasury, Keynes did not believe that investment abroad did much to promote exports. He advised that the Bank of England should expand credit, and that the government should promote loan-financed public works, by local authorities or public utilities, offering a sufficient rate of interest to ensure that the new credit was invested at home and not abroad. He believed that the cost of a public works programme would be offset by a reduction in the cost of unemployment relief and the increase in tax revenue from increased national income as a result of the additional work. He also believed that the initial public investment would encourage private investment through what he called the 'cumulative force of trade activity'. However, as yet he lacked a clear concept of the multiplier to measure this effect (Clarke 1988; Moggridge 1992: 463–4; Peden 1988: 27–8).

The multiplier is the ratio between the change in real national income and the initial change in expenditure that brought that change about. For example, public expenditure on roads will lead to an increase in the incomes of contractors and their suppliers and workers. The proportion of this income that is spent on British goods and services will increase the incomes of other people in the community. Keynes believed in 1933 that for every man employed directly, or at first remove in supplying equipment or materials, as a result of loan-financed public works, the equivalent of an extra job would be created indirectly over time. In other words, he believed that the multiplier was 2. However, in a series of newspaper articles entitled 'The means to prosperity', he argued that a multiplier of 1.5

would be sufficient to justify public investment that had a return on capital below the current rate of interest, if reductions in unemployment relief and additional tax receipts were taken into account (JMK IX: 335–66). Treasury officials were not convinced, especially when Keynes suggested that tax cuts leading to a budget deficit would also have a multiplier effect, eventually leading to higher revenue as a result of greater prosperity. They persuaded the Chancellor, Neville Chamberlain, that the only prudent course was to continue to aim at a balanced budget, albeit with a smaller sinking fund to repay the national debt than hitherto. Treasury officials believed that once budget deficits came to be seen as a means to prosperity, it would be impossible to control public expenditure, for the political popularity to be gained from spending would not be offset by the unpopularity of taxing (Middleton 1982; Peden 2004: 130–50, 153).

Keynes had more success in 1937, when his ideas for varying public investment to offset variations in private investment were accepted by an interdepartmental committee chaired by Phillips. The maximum variation was estimated at £50 million, but only after a year's delay while new projects were started, and what was contemplated fell far short of Lloyd George's proposal to increase public investment by £251 million over two years. The Treasury continued to believe that a lowering of interest rates would continue to be the principal means of warding off a depression (Howson and Winch 1977: 141–2; Peden 2004: 175). As already noted, by 1937 Keynes favoured postponing public investment where possible, even though unemployment was still high. He did so because the government had adopted a rearmament programme in 1936 that was to be financed by borrowing as soon as expenditure exceeded revenue – which happened in 1937 (Peden 1980). It has been estimated, on the basis of a multiplier of 1.6, that rearmament created just over a million jobs between 1935 and 1938 (Thomas 1983). However, the scale of borrowing for rearmament – £193 million in the financial years 1937/8 and 1938/9 – was sufficient to cause a deficit in the balance of payments on current account and a fall in the sterling: dollar exchange rate. Keynes had anticipated this adverse effect of budget deficits, which is why his proposals in 'The means to prosperity' included a suggestion designed to make it easier for all countries to expand public expenditure simultaneously without fears as to effects on their gold reserves. He proposed that there should be an international authority with the power to issue 'gold-notes', which would be held by central banks or treasuries as the equivalent of gold. Countries could obtain gold-notes in exchange for bonds bearing a nominal or low rate of interest up to a maximum quota that was intended to restore each country's reserves to the level of 1928. However, as Phillips anticipated, the proposal had little attraction to countries with substantial gold reserves, notably France and the United States, and international co-operation was not forthcoming (JMK IX: 355–64; Peden 2004: 150–2).

The Treasury still held to the Treasury view in 1939. Phillips agreed with Hawtrey in April 1939 that rearmament created employment only in so far as it was financed by an increase in bank credit, and not by borrowing funds that would otherwise have been invested in private enterprise. Phillips remarked: 'this is the famous or infamous "Treasury view", still a most bitter subject of contro-versy' (Peden 2004: 192). As Middleton has shown, the Treasury responded to the problem of financing rearmament by making 'the first attempts to actively manage demand – in a Keynesian sense – using the budget as an instrument of economic policy'. Taxes were not increased significantly in the 1939 budget because the Treasury was waiting for rearmament to bring the economy to full employ-ment. At full employment the yield of taxation would be higher, and a higher level of savings would make it easier for the government to borrow from the non-bank public – that is, without inflation (Mid-dleton 1985: 119–21). However, it is easy to exaggerate the signifi-cance of this change in Treasury thinking. No attempt was made to calculate national income or how savings might increase with national income, and Treasury officials had yet to be persuaded of the value of using the analytical framework of national income accounting that Keynes was to persuade them to adopt for the 1941 budget.

WAR FINANCE: MONETARY AND FISCAL POLICY 1939–1945

By the spring of 1939, the question of wartime financial policy was under active consideration. The Bank of England recommended that maximum rates of interest for government borrowing should be fixed at the outbreak of war and be held constant thereafter. A Treasury Committee on the Control of Savings and Investment, chaired by Phillips, considered how such a policy could be implemented. One of its members, Dennis Robertson, an economist who had worked with Keynes for many years, explained how Keynes's theory that government expenditure would increase national income, and thereby create the savings necessary to finance government expenditure without inflation, could be made to work. It would be necessary to control capital expenditure by local authorities and public utilities; to ration building materials; to control new issues on the stock market and to obtain the co-operation of the banks in limiting lending; and to require companies to lend undistributed profits to the government. Similar recommendations were made by the Economic Advisory Council's Committee on Economic Information, of which Keynes and Robertson were members, and on which Phillips was a Treasury observer. The Treasury Committee's report in August 1939 recommended that the monetary authorities should offer a range of short- and medium-term securities designed to meet the different needs and preferences of potential purchasers. To that extent the report represented an acceptance of Keynes's liquidity preference theory – but it did so in circumstances where there would be controls over investment (Howson 1988). During the war, and for some time afterwards, there were strict physical controls over the allocation of steel and other capital goods, making it possible to restrict private investment and to require that surplus savings be lent to the government. It also proved possible during the war to adhere to a 3 per cent ceiling for long-term borrowing (fifteen to twenty years), and 2.5 per cent for medium-term (five to ten years), but firms could not easily be persuaded to part with their money for long periods, with the result that one-third of the money borrowed within Britain during the war was in the form of potentially inflationary short-term borrowing or ways and means advances from the Bank of England.

The war greatly altered the circumstances in which professional economic advice was given in Whitehall. From December 1939, economists and statisticians were recruited to a new Central Economic Information Service (CEIS), which reported through the Offices of the War Cabinet. Churchill, who became prime minister in May 1940, encouraged the expansion of the CEIS, which was divided in December 1940 into the Economic Section and the Central Statistical Office. Most of the economists who entered

Whitehall during the war were young academics, who shared the same approach to economic analysis as Keynes (Cairncross and Watts 1989). Within the Treasury, Hawtrey had been due to retire in October 1939, and during the war he was employed principally in collecting material for a history of war finance, and had no influence on policy. In his place the Treasury took on economists who had been members of the Economic Advisory Council's Committee on Economic Information, Robertson and Hubert Henderson, and then, at the end of June 1940, Keynes.

Keynes had first offered advice on how to control inflation in articles in *The Times* in November 1939 and had then enlarged his ideas in a pamphlet, *How to Pay for the War*, in February 1940. He pointed out that the additional taxes imposed shortly after the outbreak of war in September would not offset the increase in purchasing power in the hands of the public that could be expected from greater employment and longer hours of work. Industrial output was being diverted from consumer goods to government orders for munitions. Keynes argued that, in these circumstances, attempts by workers to increase their consumption would only lead to inflation, and that the working class as a whole could ultimately enjoy an increase in real earnings only if they were prepared to accept his novel plan for compulsory savings, which he called 'deferred pay' and which were later renamed 'postwar credits'. Keynes thought that making post-war credits available to workers after the war would help to ward off a slump. There were then no official statistics of national income, but drawing on the best unofficial estimates available to him, Keynes used a national income accounting framework to set out where resources might be found for increased government expenditure. He arrived at a broad figure of £1,350 million as the amount by which consumption must be reduced. Voluntary savings, he thought, could be relied upon to produce £400 million, leaving another £950 million to be diverted from the public. Perhaps £400 million of this sum could be raised through the taxes already introduced in September, but £550 million would have to be found from new taxes and his plan for compulsory savings (JMK IX: 367–439; JMK XXII: 41–51).

Treasury officials, including Hopkins and Phillips, advised the Chancellor, Sir John Simon, in March 1940 not to adopt Keynes's plan. They thought that it would be difficult to administer, would discourage voluntary saving and would provoke strikes (Peden 2004: 216–22). Keynes tried again in July, when a new chancellor, Kingsley Wood, was due to present a budget to deal with an increasingly serious war situation, and when there was public pressure for drastic measures. Hopkins, acting on Robertson's advice, decided that the available national income data were not sufficiently accurate to back Keynes's proposals. However, from the summer of 1940 James Meade and Richard Stone in the CEIS were compiling better estimates of the components of national income. By January 1941, Keynes was able to produce a more convincing analysis of the additional sums that had to be found from taxation or savings if inflation were to be avoided. This time the opposition to his macroeconomic approach came not from officials but from Henderson, who thought that, in an economy dislocated by war, it was unreasonable to attempt a precise balance between aggregate purchasing power and aggregate supplies of goods and services. While agreeing that taxes should be increased, he preferred to look to price controls and rationing – both of which had been already introduced – to prevent profiteering. He thought that too severe taxation would provoke demands for higher wages, which would start a vicious spiral of increasing costs of production, leading to higher prices and more demands for wage increases. On the advice of his officials, Kingsley Wood made Keynes's macroeconomic analysis the focus of his budget speech, but the proposals for taxation and deferred postwar credits were tempered by what was considered to be likely to be acceptable to the public. Subsidies to keep down the cost of essential goods were used, with moderate success, to encourage wage restraint by trade unions. Keynes considered the 1941 budget to be a revolution in public finance, and indeed it set the pattern for subsequent budgets. The aspects of the 1941 budget where Keynes believed his influence to have been greatest were its logical structure and the limited acceptance of the principle of postwar credits (JMK XXII: 353–4; Moggridge 1992: 642–8; Peden 2000: 322–7; Skidelsky 2000: 81–9). The 1941 budget certainly marked the adoption of Keynes's macroeconomics in the context of controlling inflation, but its application to the political commitment to full employment came later in the war.

SHAPING THE POSTWAR WORLD: BRETTON WOODS, EMPLOYMENT POLICY AND CHEAP MONEY

One of the reasons why unemployment had been high between the wars had been the disruption of the international economy, caused partly by unstable exchange rates after the suspension of the Gold Standard by many countries in 1931, or by competitive devaluations. Keynes took a major part in Anglo-American negotiations from 1942 to 1944 leading to the establishment of the International Monetary Fund (IMF) and the World Bank, two institutions that were designed to provide a stable international monetary system after the war (Moggridge 1992: 721–55). He drafted a plan for what in 1941 he called an International Currency Union; subsequently modified and renamed an International Clearing Union, it provided the basis for Britain's proposals to the Americans. Keynes's objective was to make exchange rates stable but adjustable. He assumed that exchange controls imposed during the war would continue, giving central banks, including the Bank of England, effective control of all international payments, including capital movements, and he suggested that the transactions between central banks should be conducted through the Union. Member countries would be given an account, denominated in units called bancor, which would be accepted as the equivalent of gold, and the supply of which, unlike gold, would be absolutely elastic. Countries whose deficits on their balance of payments exceeded their accounts would be required to adjust their currencies downwards; those with persistent surpluses would be required to adjust their exchange rates upwards, by up to 5 per cent in both cases (JMK XXV: 21–40, 72–3, 140). The latter requirement was designed to remove the deflationary bias that had marked the operation of the Gold Standard in the interwar period, when deficit countries had had to deflate to protect their gold reserves, but the United States' monetary and tariff policies had acted to prevent gold inflows from increasing imports. Keynes recognized that the principal value of the plan for a Clearing Union was that it would encourage the United States government to commit itself to some kind of expansionist international monetary system. The American response, drafted by Harry White of the US Treasury, was for an international fund to stabilize exchange rates, and it was the White plan that provided the main basis of the

Bretton Woods agreements of July 1944. The agreements provided a much less expansionary bias to the postwar international monetary system than Keynes had hoped for. His idea of bancor was dropped in favour of the IMF holding quotas of gold and currencies of the members, an arrangement that would provide a much less elastic supply of international bank money. There was no obligation placed on countries with a balance-of-payments surplus to revalue their currencies upwards, and the strain of adjusting to disequilibrium was left, as under the Gold Standard, on countries in deficit. Nevertheless, Keynes successfully urged the British government to accept the Bretton Woods agreements. They represented an improvement on the interwar position and were in accordance with the views that he had developed then in favour of rules that would allow domestic economic policy a breathing space during short-run departures from external balance (Williamson 1983).

Planning for postwar employment policy began in the Economic Section in 1941, with Meade producing a series of papers on internal measures for the prevention of general unemployment. The major debates between the Keynesians in the Economic Section and more traditional officials in the Treasury took place after Sir William Beveridge's report recommending an enlarged system of social insurance was published in December 1942. Beveridge's plan was designed to be actuarially sound, provided the average level of unemployment did not exceed 8.5 per cent of the total labour force. Since unemployment had been well above that level for almost all of the interwar years, the Cabinet wanted to know whether it would be possible to keep unemployment down to that level before committing itself to the plan.

Meade argued that employment policy required maintenance of aggregate demand, together with increased mobility of labour and willingness of industry to relocate, and stability of prices and wages. Henderson, however, thought that Keynesian analysis was too abstract, and that the concept of the multiplier was too static. He ascribed most of Britain's interwar unemployment to disturbances in the international economy and the loss of export markets, and thought that an attempt to compensate for lost exports by expanding domestic demand could destroy confidence in sterling (Henderson 1955: 316–25). Treasury officials listened to Henderson as well as to Keynes.

As in the 1930s, the Treasury stressed the practical problems of using public investment to offset variations in private investment. As a group of leading officials concerned with employment policy noted on Keynes's support for the Economic Section's proposals: 'the difference of view is between economists assessing what they think is theoretically reasonable or possible, and people who have had long experience of guiding, stimulating and retarding works undertaken by public authorities. The economists tend to ignore the intractable time-lag' (Peden 2004: 310). As for the Economic Section's suggestion that budget deficits should be used to stimulate demand, Hopkins commented that there was a political danger of 'deficits becoming fashionable on many occasions and surpluses on none' (Peden 1983: 293). Keynes himself preferred balanced budgets for central government's current expenditure, with public investment programmes in a separate capital budget (Skidelsky 2000: 273–6; Wilson 1982). On the other hand, he was prepared to contemplate deficit finance for current expenditure, once investment fell to a much lower level than would occur for some years after the war (Booth 1983: 106, 114–16).

The outcome was the 1944 White Paper, *Employment Policy* (Cmd. 6527), which employed a Keynesian analysis of macroeconomic demand being the sum of private consumption, private investment, government expenditure, and the balance between exports and imports. However, it was pointed out that an expansion of internal demand would not be an appropriate remedy for loss of exports and might lead to inflation. A successful employment policy would depend on international collaboration to ensure expanding export markets, and also on British industry's ability to compete in these markets and in the home market. Public investment would be planned to offset fluctuations in private investment, but the term 'capital budget' was avoided, in case politicians were tempted to place in it current items that ought to be financed from taxation. As a second line of defence against unemployment, private consumption could be maintained, perhaps through variations in social insurance contributions or rates of taxation. It was made clear, however, that while the budget for central government current expenditure need not balance every year, it should balance over a longer period.

The White Paper also warned that stability of prices and wages was a condition of success for employment policy. The multiplier effect of demand management would be lower than Keynes believed possible if his assumption in the *General Theory* that workers would not resist moderate cuts in real wages (JMK VII: 14–15) was not justified. Keynes himself confessed in 1945 that he knew no solution to the wages problem in a full-employment economy (JMK XXVII: 385). In the event, a wage–price spiral was a feature of the postwar economy.

Whereas Keynes's comments on the bargaining power of trade unions were somewhat off-hand, he was successful in converting Treasury officials to his ideas on monetary policy. Hopkins set up a committee in February 1945 to enquire into the national debt. Wartime experience predisposed officials to accept Keynes's ideas based on his theory of liquidity preference. Hopkins referred explicitly to the *General Theory* when recommending the continuation, and even the reduction, of the prevailing low level of interest rates, with a view to stimulating investment in the long term and to reducing the burden on the budget. However, he also specified the conditions in which Keynes's theory might be expected to work. These were the continuation of direct controls over capital issues on the stock exchange; government allocation of goods, such as steel, needed for investment during the postwar reconstruction period; and permanent control over external capital movements. Hopkins's recommendations provided the basis for monetary policy during the period of the Labour government in 1945–51, while direct controls over investment were still effective (Howson 1993: 51–4, 322–9; Peden 2004: 334–44). Thereafter variations in interest rates were once more used to influence demand.

MYTHS ABOUT KEYNES IN HISTORICAL PERSPECTIVE

To what extent does Keynes deserve credit for full employment after the war? It is important not to place too much emphasis on the Keynesian technique of demand management. Keynes was well aware of the importance of the international environment, and while the international monetary system agreed on at Bretton Woods did not function smoothly at first after the war, the commitment to international collaboration that it implied helped to sustain greater growth in international trade than had been experienced in the interwar period. Keynes's macroeconomic approach to fiscal policy was adopted first to control inflation, and postwar demand management was, on balance, deflationary. Keynes aimed at stability of prices, and broadly prices were stable until the 1970s.

The association of Keynes with inflation arising from budget deficits is a myth. He did favour budget deficits to sustain consumption as a last resort in employment policy, but, contrary to his expectations, investment, both public and private, was sustained long after postwar reconstruction was complete. He believed that budgets would be balanced only if national income was stabilized and there was no mass unemployment (JMK XXVII: 366). The 1944 White Paper on employment policy was not a recipe for deficit finance.

The question of what level of unemployment Keynes regarded as an appropriate target for employment policy is more complex. While he thought that unemployment due to factors other than a lack of demand would be about 5 per cent in the circumstances of the 1930s, he did not regard these circumstances as immutable. He wrote in 1942 that the unemployment figure of 5 per cent (or 800,000 workers) used in his calculations of national income after the war was on the pessimistic side, and that, if everything that the state could do was done, unemployment would be at the sort of level experienced in wartime – 120,000 workers. The 1944 White Paper on employment policy made provision for microeconomic measures to deal with regional unemployment, which had been a feature of the interwar period. In 1944, Keynes commented on Beveridge's proposals in the latter's *Full Employment in a Free Society* that there was no harm in aiming at 3 per cent unemployment, but that it would be surprising if this target were achieved (JMK XXVII: 303, 381). Keynes did not attempt to estimate what level of unemployment could be achieved without stimulating a wage–price spiral, although during the war he had favoured an implicit bargain with trade unions by subsidising essential goods in return for wage restraint. Postwar Keynesian employment policy became increasingly associated with policies designed to stabilize wages and prices through national agreements with the trade unions and employers. The apparent failure of these policies in the 1970s helped to break down the Keynesian consensus.

NOTE

1 Unemployment has been measured in different ways at different times. Official figures in the interwar period were for workers covered by the national unemployment insurance scheme. Since workers not covered by the scheme, such as domestic servants and people in the professions, were those least likely to be unemployed, the effect was to give a higher percentage figure than if unemployment had been measured as a percentage of the total labour force. Moreover, Keynes's figure of 12.5 per cent appears not to have been seasonally adjusted for the effects of winter on out-door workers; the annual average official figure for 1937 was 10.8 per cent.

7 Keynes and Cambridge

... a tall man with an odd face and a restless eye, walking fast with a slight stoop up the aisle in Hall and holding on to the selvedge of his gown with both hands in front of him; pacing the Back Lawn with a companion in the summer; or hurrying across the Court with his black brief-case on the way to London.

H. G. Durnford, *John Maynard Keynes*, Cambridge: King's College, 1949: 16

... a kind and even simple heart under that immensely impressive armour of intellect.

V. Woolf, *Moments of Being.* 2nd edn. London: Hogarth Press, 1985: 198

He was the greatest genius I ever met. His personal magnetism for young men, including myself, was unequalled. His charm, artistry and personality are such as I have never met in anyone else. He combined the scientist, artist and human moralist and man of affairs in a unique manner.

Meade 1990: 251

PREFACE

Keynes's involvement with Cambridge was so deep and had so many dimensions that to write about it is a daunting task. This chapter approaches it from three directions. The first – and probably the simplest – is to provide a concise account of what Keynes did in Cambridge, summarizing those parts of his biography relevant to this topic (pp. 119–24). The second line leads to the issue of how Keynes was perceived by those close to him in Cambridge (pp. 124–29). The number involved is too large to be dealt with in one paper, and I shall confine my considerations to those colleagues and pupils he was most in contact with. The sources on which this section is based are mainly correspondence and later recollections mainly by economists who were in Cambridge during Keynes's lifetime. Finally, I address a more general, but also more difficult, question, namely what Keynes meant to Cambridge economics, which he endowed with impetus, and of which he is still considered the leading player (pp. 129–32). It also addresses the issue of the so-called Keynesian tradition in economics, as synonymous with public expenditure and the welfare state.

KEYNES AT CAMBRIDGE

The early years of Keynes's adult life were not spent in Cambridge – from 1897 to 1902 he was at Eton – so we can take 1902, when he entered King's College as an undergraduate, as the beginning of our story. Thanks to his biographers (Harrod 1951; Skidelsky 1983; Moggridge 1992) we know quite a lot about this period of apprenticeship, which ended with his designation as twelfth wrangler[1] in the Mathematical Tripos of 1905. Academically and socially he was extremely successful, active in many clubs, discussion groups and student societies.[2] A keen player of golf and bridge with a passion for buying books, he made himself equally popular with his contemporaries and his elders.

He made friends with Lytton Strachey, who, together with Leonard Woolf and other Apostles, formed the Cambridge nucleus of the Bloomsbury Group, which kept close ties with Cambridge long after Keynes's death.[3] As a freshman he fell in love with a young Trinity man and nephew to Beatrice Webb, Arthur Hobhouse, the first of his male affairs. For the following seventeen years Keynes embraced and acted out the Apostles credo that 'love of young men was a higher form of love' (Skidelsky 1983: 128).

The focus of his undergraduate years were the many societies and clubs to which he belonged, and life at King's, rather than whole-hearted dedication to his chosen academic subject, mathematics; so, not unsurprisingly, when he had a fourth year to spend at King's he gave up mathematics and turned to economics. Barely a month after the Tripos, he started work on Marshall's *Principles*.

In the autumn of 1905, he started attending Marshall's lectures and, having decided to prepare for the Civil Service examination rather than pursue an academic career, continued attending them in the Lent term. Marshall's teaching left an indelible mark on him, opening up to him the career of the academic economist once he put his mind to becoming one.

At the India Office, where he started work in the autumn of 1906, he had plenty of spare time: he found he could get through a lot of office work in a few hours, which left him the remaining hours to write a dissertation for election at King's. His work on probability won him a Fellowship not on the first assay, but on the second, in December 1907. Two major events were to befall him in the following year: his love affair with Duncan Grant, who gave him access to the world of art, and his acceptance of a lectureship in economics at Cambridge, offered to him by the newly appointed Professor of Political Economy – A. C. Pigou – but preordained by his predecessor, Marshall, who initially volunteered to pay for it out of his own pocket.[4] During these pre-First World War years he plunged into activities that would shape his commitment to Cambridge: the Political Economy Club, the Faculty Board, the Council of the Senate, the *Economic Journal* and the various College Committees.[5] However, the First World War, his preoccupations in the Treasury and his involvement in the Bloomsbury circle shifted the pendulum of his life: 'Cambridge remained the focus for his intellectual – and much of his social life, but it was no longer such a focus of his other activities as it had been before 1914' (Moggridge 1992: 352).

From his return to Cambridge after the First World War until his death in 1946, there was just one long spell when Keynes was a full-time Cambridge man: between 1919 and 1937 (when he was affected by the heart disease that was to seal his doom). Throughout this period, his life followed a regular pattern: 'he was in Cambridge in term time from Thursday evening till Tuesday afternoon. Mid-week would be spent in London. Vacations were divided between London, foreign travel and Sussex' (Skidelsky 1992: 4). However, after his marriage to Lydia Lopokova in 1925, his social life no longer revolved exclusively around the Bloomsbury circle, and in Cambridge he would still spend most of the time as a single don.

In term time, every day of the week followed a set pattern for him. On Saturday mornings (and sometimes on Mondays too) there was the College Council, or the Governing Body, which often met for four or five hours. On Saturday afternoons, in the company of Piero Sraffa, an Italian who had come to Cambridge, he hunted down old books in second-hand bookshops and on the stalls in Market Place (Kahn 1984: 171). On Sunday mornings he would go over the *Economic Journal* business matters with Austin Robinson, who gives us a vivid picture of his collaboration, from 1934, as review editor 'seated among the Sunday papers and the proofs of the Journal at the foot of Keynes's bed in his room at King's' (Robinson 1990: 166). And then there was lunch or tea at his parents' house in Harvey Road. And of course there was lecturing, supervising, attending University business, the work for the Royal Economic Society, managing College economic and academic affairs[6] and, every other Monday in term time, attending the Political Economy Club.

This seminar ('Keynes's Club') was the focal point of economic debates in Cambridge. According to Lorie Tarshis, who was a student there in 1935: 'Kahn [was] invariably present with a sprinkling of other faculty members . . . Sometimes academics from outside Cambridge attended too . . . there was a contingent of students, a very few research students amongst them and perhaps ten or twelve undergraduates.' A paper was read by Keynes or a distinguished visitor, and students whose slips had been drawn were expected to stand up and comment on it; see also Plumptre 1947: 393; Moggridge 1992: 189; Skidelsky 1992: 5.

After the students had made their remarks, we all were served tea and fruit cake. Then Keynes asked each of the Faculty members and distinguished visitors present whether he wished to speak. And after that Keynes stood up . . . Sometimes – I guess usually – the paper and the discussion that followed it were merely the springboard from which, after gentle criticism and encouragement for the students who had participated, he jumped into any or many related topics – with a wit, a grace and an imagination that were a joy to experience.

(Patinkin and Leith 1977: 50–1)

We also have a vivid account by Keynes's 'favourite pupil' (JMK to Lydia Lopokova, 29 April 1928, JMK papers: PP/45/190:4) of how he conducted supervision, usually with four students 'round the open fire', talking to them and encouraging them to talk (Kahn 1984: 171; see also Plumptre 1947). His lectures were extremely popular, attended by people who went there for the pleasure of listening to Keynes delivering his latest discoveries and ideas.

Keynes occupied an unusual position within the Faculty of Economics at Cambridge, instituted thanks to the efforts of Marshall, who had won the battle to have a separate Tripos in Economics in 1903. Though one of Cambridge's dominant figures, Keynes was not the Professor. Indeed, after he resigned from his University lectureship in 1920, he held no University teaching position beyond his Fellowship at King's. His lectures reflected his intellectual pursuits, and after 1929 he usually delivered them from notes on the proof pages of the book he was writing. Some of the lecture notes survive, and some, such as those relating to the making of the *General Theory*, have been collated from students' notes and published (Rymes 1989), allowing us to trace the turns of his mind and the unfolding of his ideas, as it were, in their making.

Keynes was extremely influential in many decisions relating to academic appointments, regulations and projects. To all these activities he brought a personal concern for the people he befriended and, naturally, most of them relied on him for advice and support. He stepped in to prevent Joan Robinson's proposal to give a course on money for two terms from being turned down (JMK to C. R. Fay, 5 March 1935, JMK papers: UA/14.2). He invented two occupations for Sraffa when in 1931 he resigned from his lectureship and threatened to leave Cambridge, namely the editorship of Ricardo's *Works and Correspondence* and the post of Assistant Director of Research (Marcuzzo 2005). At the end of 1938, he was persuaded to set up a the Cambridge Research Scheme of the National Institute of Economic and Social Research into Prime Costs, Proceeds and Output – which was later to become the core of the Department of Applied Economics – to provide the Polish economist Michal Kalecki with a job in Cambridge.

He was mindful of the high standards in economic teaching and research set by Marshall, and watchful that the Cambridge tradition be kept up. Once he complained to Pigou:

I am just at the end of the Tripos examining. The general standard is lower than anything I have previously struck for Part II . . . The appalling ignorance of even the more intelligent candidates must be partly, I think, due to the breakdown of the curriculum last year through illness and leave of absence. And Hicks's teaching of the Principles has, I think, definitely confused the men and put them further back than as if they had had no such instruction.

(JMK to A. C. Pigou, 15 June 1939, JMK papers: EJ/1/6/5–7)

On another occasion he complained to Kahn about the standards of Kalecki's first results of his research into prime costs, proceeds and output: 'I see evidence of great industry, but what may turn out to be a total lack of flair for this kind of inquiry' (JMK to R. F. Kahn, July 1939, RFK papers: 5/1/142–44).

His concern for the welfare of his college led him to stretch the Bursar's activities beyond what was usually done by the holder of this position, extending the scope of outlets for college money. As a consequence of his endeavours, investment activities for the college ranged from farming and property transactions to securities, currencies and commodities. (Keynes's personal investments covered the same range of assets, but on a smaller scale and in a different composition.) He was no risk-averse investor, although he thought that 'it is safer to be a speculator than an investor in the sense that . . . a speculator is one who runs risks of which he is aware and an investor is one who runs risks of which he is unaware' (JMK XII: 109). His policy – as he once explained to Kahn - 'assumes the ability to pick specialities which have, on the average, prospects of raising enormously more than an index of market leaders . . . which means buying them on their instrinsic value when, for one reason or another, they are unfashionable or appear very vulnerable on a short view' (JMK XII: 100–1). Throughout the 1937–8 Stock Exchange crisis, Keynes believed – perhaps too optimistically – that his philosophy helped in keeping the value of both college investment and his own relatively stable.[7]

Keynes was Secretary of the Royal Economic Society from 1913 to 1945, and, according to Austin Robinson, '[he] ran it, and reported what he had done and what he proposed to do. The meetings served to validate his actions' (Robinson 1990: 166). Last, but not least, he left his mark on the Cambridge city landscape with the Arts

Theatre, which he built in 1935, personally overseeing all the minute details of its making and operation.

During the last ten years of his life he spent rather less time in Cambridge: he had been seriously ill since 1937, working for the Treasury since 1940, and, throughout the period, living mostly in London or in his Tilton farmhouse, except for spells in the United States. His previous schedule had to be altered, and for months during his illness all matters – especially college finances and University business – had to be handed over to Kahn. However, he was eager to be in touch with his college, although ready to slacken his ties with University life. In 1942, Joan Robinson had informed Keynes that there was a proposal for him to succeed Pigou to Marshall's Chair of Political Economy at Cambridge; Keynes refused to take such a possibility into consideration, judging that he would not be able to stay in Cambridge permanently after the war (Joan Robinson to J. M. Keynes, 9 December 1942, JMK papers: UA/5/6:19–20). And in March 1944 he wrote to Kahn, 'I . . . have no intention of staying in government service any longer than I can. There is much of College business which I actually enjoy and would miss, if I were without it' (JMK to RFK, 9 March 1944, Kahn papers: 13/57:485).

Unfortunately, he had only two years to live, most of them spent in a desperate effort to preserve Britain's interests and to design a new international economic order. He was never to return to his Cambridge life.

KEYNES AND THE CAMBRIDGE ECONOMISTS

There is a controversy amongst economists as to whether there is continuity in Keynes's thought between his two major works, the *Treatise on Probability* (JMK VIII) of 1921 and the *General Theory of Employment, Interest and Money* (JMK VII) of 1936.[8] These were fifteen years apart, and during this period Keynes produced at least one other landmark contribution, the *Treatise on Money* (JMK V–VI) of 1930, besides the *Tract on Monetary Reform* (JMK IV) of 1923 and the two collections *Essays in Persuasion* (JMK IX) of 1931 and *Essays in Biography* (JMK X) of 1933, which epitomize his many and varied qualities – cleverness, scholarship and literary flair. Philosophically and methodologically he remained faithful to the approach to human behaviour resting on the two pillars of expectations and conventions, his conception of probability offering the clue to 'actions to be judged on the basis of their *likely* consequences' (Clarke 1998: 18). This approach also provided the key to understanding how opinions are formed and how they can be transformed through the joint effects of persuasion and artfully designed institutions. As he put it in a letter to T. S. Eliot: 'the main task is producing first the intellectual conviction and then intellectually to devise the means' (JMK XXVII: 384).

Keynes gave form and finish to his ideas by submitting them to others. It was characteristic of him to make abrupt switches in strategy as he approached problems, while following a main line many consider constant, his interlocutors providing the sounding-board and fleshing out his ideas emotionally. This is why 'criticism and conversation' were so important to him. In a passage in the Preface to the *General Theory* he wrote: 'It is astonishing what foolish things one can temporarily believe *if one thinks too long alone*, particularly in economics (along with the other moral sciences), where it is often impossible to bring one's ideas to a conclusive test either formal or experimental' (JMK VII: xxiii, italics added).

Who were Keynes's interlocutors among the Cambridge economists?[9] The earliest were undoubtedly his father, John Neville Keynes, and his teacher, Alfred Marshall. Then there were his pupils, G. F. Shove, D. H. Robertson and, above all, R. F. Kahn (with Joan Robinson self-appointed in the role), the extant correspondence with them amounting to about 2,140 letters. Then there were A. C. Pigou and Piero Sraffa – closer contemporaries of his – and correspondence with them accounts for another extant 370 letters. The correspondence between this group of Cambridge economists, totalling about 2,885 letters during Keynes's lifetime, has been the object of a study in its own right (Marcuzzo and Rosselli 2005). Here I can give only the gist of it by pointing out the influence that Keynes exercised over his interlocutors, in turn to be influenced by them, in promoting research, shaping academic institutions and fostering new ideas about economics.

In a letter to Roy Harrod, 30 August 1936, six months after the *General Theory* was published, Keynes wrote: 'I have no companions, it seems, in my own generation, either of the earliest teachers

or of the earliest pupils; yet I cannot in thought help being somewhat bound to them, – which they find exceedingly irritating' (JMK
XIV: 85). Sraffa, neither a teacher nor a pupil, nor indeed strictly a
contemporary, but with whose name the Cambridge approach to
economics is also associated, was not to be the fellow economist
with whom Keynes could share the honour of having changed the
course of economics for much of the remaining century. Sraffa's
agenda was the demolition of the Marshallian supply and demand
apparatus (and marginal analysis), and a return to classical political
economy, which included Marx. Keynes did not live long enough to
see the project disclosed to the world, but he would have never
endorsed it. No matter how highly he regarded Sraffa or how
strongly he felt the need to have him in Cambridge, he was reluctant
to abandon his Marshallian tools, and he was allergic to Marx. On
the other hand, no matter how much Sraffa felt for Keynes (both
personally and intellectually), he considered him a 'bourgeois intellectual' whose 'mentality' prevented him from appreciating Marx
and understanding the working-class issues (P. Sraffa to R. Palme
Dutt, 19 April 1932, in Marcuzzo 2005). Thus Sraffa remained
'secretly sceptical of the new ideas' (Robinson 1978: xii), as Joan
Robinson had observed then and afterwards,[10] isolating himself
from the Keynesian revolution and, in turn, depriving it of his own
contributions. Since the late 1960s, many attempts have been made
to argue for or against the compatibility of the approaches adopted
by Keynes and Sraffa, but whether distinct or complementary, the
two names represent the hallmark of Cambridge economics in the
post-Marshallian era.

The making of the *General Theory* and its aftermath marked the
watershed in Cambridge economics, drawing a dividing line
between those who understood and accepted it and those who
defended the tradition. Initially, Keynes was exposed to the critical
contribution coming from his 'inner circle', in particular Sraffa and
Kahn, who were instrumental in persuading him that the *Treatise*
approach had severe limitations, forcing him onto a new track.
Interestingly enough, criticism from 'outside' – such as observations
by Hayek or Robertson – did not get the same hearing, outsiders not
being attuned to Keynes's attack on 'previously held views'. Even as
close a follower and admirer as Harrod had trouble in understanding
the 'new' relationship between saving and investment as late as

1934 (Besomi 2000), and in 1935 he was still defending the 'classical' interest rate theory. Keynes himself fudged the issue, having convinced himself that there was a fundamental continuity between the *Treatise* and the *General Theory*. Throughout the process that led him from the former to the latter book, he repeatedly claimed that the *Treatise* analysis was in fact compatible with that of the *General Theory* and that he had made the new argument only 'much more accurate and instructive' (JMK VII: 77).

When the book appeared, a line was drawn in Cambridge (and elsewhere, for that matter) between those who felt themselves in total agreement with Keynes and those who felt either misrepresented or alienated. Kahn, and Joan and Austin Robinson belonged to the former category, Pigou and Robertson to the latter. Sraffa remained silent. What were the issues at stake?

First of all, it was a matter of method. Robertson addressed the problems of economic fluctuations and cycles in terms of a succession of periods. At the beginning of every period there is a given level of the main economic variables, which is the result of the past levels and, more generally, of what happened in the previous periods. On the contrary, in Keynes's short-period approach the current level of saving is a function of current income, without any reference to the past level of savings, and the effect of the multiplier on income was supposed to be instantaneous. Secondly, there was the question of the rate of interest. Robertson considered the rate of interest as the price bringing the demand and supply of loanable funds into equilibrium, unlike Keynes's theory of liquidity preference, where it is seen as the price necessary to bring demand for money in line with the available supply. Given this difference, he was unable to accept Keynes's message about the inevitability of persistent states of underemployment (Sanfilippo 2005), and in turn Keynes found himself parting company with Robertson. As he wrote to him: 'You are, so to speak, bent on creeping back into your mother's womb; whilst I am shaking myself like a dog on a dry land' (JMK XIV: 164–5).

In the case of Pigou, Keynes took a more decisive distance, albeit more on the plane of theory than of policies. He sided with Marshall's methodological approach rather than Pigou's and found an ally in G. F. Shove as a severe critic of Pigou's method of analysis. Keynes's emphasis on the virtue of the relative imprecision of economics contrasts sharply with the formal mathematization that Pigou subscribed to and Shove opposed.

In the 1930s, the main point of disagreement between Keynes and Pigou was whether a cut in money wages would cure unemployment. In October 1937, Pigou presented his argument, based on the quantity theory of money, that 'if a cut in wages leaves employment unchanged, money income has no ground for change' (JMK XIV: 256–7). Keynes's reply left no room for conciliation of the two approaches: '. . .I maintain that, if there is a cut in wages, unemployment being unchanged, there is a ground for a change in money income' (JMK XIV: 257). On the same day, a disheartened Keynes wrote to Kahn: 'As in the case of Dennis [Robertson], when it comes to practice, there is really extremely little between us. Why do they insist on maintaining theories from which their own practical conclusions cannot possibly follow?' (JMK XIV: 259).

On the other hand, he felt he had made himself understood to Kahn and, to some extent, to Joan Robinson, and with them he felt truly attuned. In March 1934, after 'a stiff week's supervision from R. F. K.' (JMK XIII: 422), Keynes reported enthusiastically to Joan Robinson that '[Kahn] is a marvellous critic and suggester and improver – there never was anyone in the history of the world to whom it was so helpful to submit one's stuff' (ibid.). In December 1935, three days before the final version of his book was delivered to the printer, he also acknowledged his debt to her: 'I owe you a great deal of gratitude for taking so much trouble over my proofs . . . In the final proof reading [the book] seemed so flat and stale. But you have cheered me and so does Kahn, who has been here for Christmas' (J. M. Keynes to J. Robinson, 27 December 1935, JVR papers: vii/240/9–10).

Was the dividing line generational, Kahn and Robinson being younger, enthusiastic and prone to become his proselytes? Or was it a matter of Keynes being perceived by Pigou and Robertson – the defenders of the Marshallian tradition – as a heretic and iconoclast in rejecting the 'classical school' as futile and basically wrong?

Actually, Kahn and Joan Robinson were always manoeuvring to bring people round to seeing and possibly accepting Keynes's point of view. Although Kahn and Robinson shared many opinions and views, both their impact on him and his on them took different forms, partly because they were not equally close to him and partly because of their personalities. Kahn was a travelling companion in the making of the *General Theory* (Marcuzzo 2002), a close helper in running college life and constantly consulted by Keynes in his doings in University affairs and economic matters. Theoretically, he was the torch-bearer of Keynesian liquidity preference and monetary theory against the resurgence of quantity theory well into the high years of monetarism. Joan Robinson was the born proselytizer who later went to the front line in the fight against what she herself dubbed 'bastard Keynesism', the reinstatement of rigidity in money prices and wages in preventing full employment, neglecting the role of uncertainty, expectations and time.

The fascination of Keynes's intellect and flair for creating consensus resulted in a sense of exclusion experienced by all who were deprived of proximity simply by not being at Cambridge. This implied that all sought special relations with Keynes, which meant being in constant contact with his ideas. Keynes, in the same way that Marshall had been in his time, *was* economics in Cambridge.

KEYNES AND CAMBRIDGE ECONOMICS

The *Economic Journal*, where Keynes 'made the overwhelming majority of editorial decisions himself' (Moggridge 1990: 146), provided the forum for what Keynes considered good economic reasoning and arguments. He was open-minded, but with exacting standards: 'I feel much clearer, however, about the de-merit of the articles I reject', he wrote in 1934, 'than I do about the merit of those which are included' (Moggridge 1990: 149).

On more than one occasion he summed up in explicit terms what a good economist should be. One extensive quotation may suffice to illustrate the point:

Economics is a science of thinking in terms of models joined to the art of choosing models which are relevant to the contemporary world. It is compelled to do this, because unlike the typical natural science, the material to which it is applied is, in too many respects, not homogeneous through time. The object of a model is to segregate the semi-permanent or relatively constant factors from those which are transitory or fluctuating so as to develop a logical way of thinking about the latter, and of understanding the time sequences to which they give rise in particular cases. Good economists are scarce because the gift for using 'vigilant observation' to choose good models, although it does not require a highly specialised intellectual technique, appears to be a very rare one.

(JMK XIV: 297)

There is in fact a Cambridge school or, better, Cambridge tradition in economics that has its source of inspiration in Marshall but its main focus in Keynes, the author of its *pièce de resistance*. He brought to it a style of doing economics together with the ingredients that would have it widely held to be synonymous with Keynesian economics.

The premise of Keynesian economics, as we find it in the *General Theory*, is that 'we cannot hope to make completely accurate generalisations' (JMK VII: 254) because the economic system is not ruled by 'natural forces' that economists can discover and order in a neat pattern of causes and effects. The implication of this assumption is that the task of economics is rather to 'select those variables which can be deliberately controlled and managed by central authority in the kind of system in which we actually live' (JMK VII: 254). As regards the contents of the Keynesian theory, we have in the first place rejection of the 'classical' conclusion that market forces are at work to bring the economic system to the full employment of resources. Letting individuals pursue self-interest does not – contrary to the Smithian parable of 'the butcher, the brewer and the baker' – produce a social good, but unemployment and waste of resources. Hence Keynes's argument against *laissez-faire*: aggregate economic behaviour does not have the same outcome as individual economic behaviour, so what is good for the individual may not be good for the whole.

The goal is to change the environment within which individuals operate, so that moral and rational motives become the spring of action of the collectivity as a whole (JMK XVII: 453). In this Keynes saw the main task of economic policy, 'managing' rather than 'transmuting' human nature, very much in the spirit of Marshall,[11] although pursued with other means and tools. In the last chapter of the *General Theory*, he concluded that it is 'wise and prudent statesmanship to allow the game to be played, *subject to rules and limitations*' (JMK VII: 374, italics added).

Keynes's approach, based on the categories of knowledge, ignorance and rational belief, is chosen as the appropriate method for a 'moral science' such as economics that deals with complexity and judgement. It is largely at odds with the developments of Keynesian economics, which cut the knot of complexity by endorsing a mechanistic description of the working of the economic system (Fitzgibbons 2000).

Moreover, Keynes brought new arguments and strength to the tradition of thought that Marshall and Pigou upheld, in favour of some state intervention against exclusive reliance on market mechanism, tracing the implications of individual behaviour for the welfare of society, admitting failures and suggesting ways of improving the working of the system for the collectivity as a whole. Following in their footprints, but on the basis of a different economic theory, Keynes devised forms of intervention that led to his being portrayed as the father of the welfare state and deficit spending (Buchanan and Wagner 1977).

To evaluate this claim in relation to Keynes's writings is beyond the scope of this chapter. All that can be done here is to summarize his main views. The structure of the welfare state rests on three pillars: (a) on fiscal policy, (b) social security and (c) full employment. Keynes was fully committed to (c), and partially committed to (a) and (b). Government expenditure was to be finalized to provide enough investment to counter-weight a decline in private investment and an insufficient level of consumption to generate the level of aggregate demand necessary to maintain full employment. Skidelsky is probably right in saying that 'Keynes was never a passionate social reformer' (Skidelsky 2000: 265), and certainly he was at least closer to being a liberal than a champion of pervasive state intervention in society.

First, he was not in favour of high taxes to pay for social benefits and pensions, the costs of which ought to be borne by employers: 'Should not the employer', he wrote, 'meet the total cost of providing him with a wealthy worker? If the unemployed were allowed to starve what would employers do when the demand for employment, seasonally or cyclically, increased again? Why should the general taxpayer pay for a pool of available dock labour?' (JMK XXVII: 224).

Secondly, he was in favour of making the state accountable to the taxpayer for the goods and services provided, associating 'as closely as possible the cost of particular services with the sources out of which they are provided', since he believed that 'this is the only way by which to preserve sound accounting, to measure efficiency, to maintain economy and to keep the public properly aware of what things cost' (JMK XXVII: 225).

Although Keynes's disbelief in the smooth working of market forces came long before[12] the *General Theory*, the case for intervention is made there forcefully in the case of aggregate demand failure. However, the policy message in the *General Theory* is to sustain the level of investment – more 'stabilizing business confidence' (Bateman 1996: 148) than debt-financed public works. His reliance on 'socializing investment' rather than fiscal policy aimed at smoothing out consumption levels over the cycle[13] shows his concern for the size of the deficit and the importance attributed to market incentives to bring about the desired level of employment. 'If the State is able to determine the aggregate amount of resources devoted to augmenting the instruments [of production] and the basic rate of reward to those who own them,' he wrote in the *General Theory*, 'it will have accomplished all that is necessary' (JMK VII: 378). And he was not in full agreement with the other so-called father-founder of the welfare state, William Beveridge, on the recipe for attaining full employment, by 'managing' consumption: 'I entirely fail to understand how you can avoid making public investment a counterweight to fluctuations in private investment' (JMK XXVII: 371).

Thus, the implication that Keynes was in favour of large and growing public expenditure such as we have experienced since the Second World War as a consequence of so-called Keynesian policies is untenable.[14] His 'vision' of the future of capitalist society rested on the belief that freedom from economic constraints[15] would allow the vast majority of the population to pursue happiness and enjoyment in their lives. 'It is not any fear of a failure of physical productivity to provide an adequate material standard of life that fills me with foreboding,' he remarked, addressing the House of Lords in February 1943. 'The real problems of the future are first of all the maintenance of peace, of international co-operation and amity, and beyond that the profound moral and social problems of how to organize material abundance to yield up the fruits of a good life' (JMK XXVII: 261).

CONCLUSIONS

Keynes died on Easter Sunday, 21 April 1946. The words chosen to be read at the memorial service held in Westminster Abbey came from Blake's *Jerusalem*:

I will not cease from mental fight,
Nor shall my sword sleep in my hand,
Till we have built Jerusalem
In England's green and pleasant land.

These words – as Skidelsky noted – are appropriate to remember him as 'striving to realise a utopia beyond the economics of industrialism' (Skidelsky 2000: 478) and effectively to evoke his perennial 'mental fight' against received views. In this, and indeed in some other respects,[16] he equalled the other star that illuminated Cambridge, Isaac Newton. In his last note, drafted two weeks before he died, Keynes wrote that Newton's garden, close to his room in Trinity College, was 'his laboratory' (JMK X: 376). Cambridge was Keynes's 'laboratory', with its emotional and intellectual interactions, the shared set of values and lifestyles, the common pursuit of truth and well-doing. It is indeed a shame that his ashes were not deposited in the crypt at King's, as he had wished and had instructed in his will.[17]

NOTES

I wish to thank D. Besomi, A. Carabelli, C. Goodwin, D. Moggridge, N. Naldi, T. Raffaelli, F. Ranchetti, A. Roncaglia, A. Rosselli, E. Sanfilippo, A. Simonazzi and F. Vianello for comments to an earlier draft and to the editors of this volume, B. Bateman and R. Backhouse, for their suggestions. None of the persons implicated are of course responsible for remaining errors or omissions. Permission to quote from the papers of J. M. Keynes (JMK), R. F. Kahn (RFK) and J. Robinson (JVR) is gratefully acknowledged to the Provost and Fellows of King's College, Cambridge.

1 In Cambridge those who took the Mathematics Tripos were arranged in order, rather than classified, and one was designated senior wrangler, second wrangler, third wrangler and so on. Marshall was second wrangler in 1865.

2 Skidelsky (1983: 106–25) and Moggridge (1992: 52–81) mention the following: Baskerville Club, University Liberal Club, Decemviri,

Moral Science Club, Knave Club and Pitt Club Apennine Society, Richmond Shakespeare Society, Cambridge Union or Debating Society, Oscar Browning's Political Society, Lowes Dickinson's Discussion Society and, for Keynes, the most important of all, the Conversazione Society or Apostles.

3 On Keynes's involvement with the Bloomsbury Group, see chapter 12 of the present volume.

4 Pigou then paid it until Keynes became University lecturer in 1920.

5 He was member of three committees: Estates, Building and Fellowship.

6 Keynes became Second Bursar in November 1919 and, from 1924 until his death in 1946, First Bursar.

7 Keynes's net assets fell from £506,522 to £181,547, and those of the college (the 'Chest') from 680 to 443 (1920 = 100); see JMK XII: 11–13. I am grateful to D. Moggridge for pointing this out to me.

8 See Davis (1994b) for a good review of the opposite views on the continuity issue and, more recently, Runde and Mizuhara (2003).

9 Economists were indeed not his only interlocutors. In Cambridge, philosophers like Moore, Ramsey, Russell and Wittgenstein played an important role. Unfortunately, the evidence is not there of a similar intellectual intercourse as with the economists, both in terms of quantity and content of extant letters. Much is therefore indirect evidence, which nevertheless is very important to understand Keynes's frame of mind. On this, see Raffaelli, chapter 9 of the present volume.

10 She once wrote to Kahn, 'Do you think Kalecki will induce Piero to take the General Theory seriously?' (J. Robinson to R. F. Kahn, 20 March 1937, RFK papers: 13/90/2/165–6).

11 For the purposes relevant here, it will suffice to offer two quotations from the *Principles* and *Industry and Trade*, respectively: 'the human will, guided by careful thought, can so modify circumstances as largely to modify character; and thus to bring about new conditions of life still more favourable to character; and therefore to the economic, as well as the moral, well-being of the masses of the people' (Marshall 1920: 48). 'A chief purpose of every study of human action should be to suggest the probable outcome of present tendencies; and thus to indicate, tacitly if not expressly, such modifications of those tendencies as might further the well-being of mankind' (Marshall 1923: 7).

12 'Keynes challenged laissez-faire as a *policy* well before he had developed a critique of the orthodox economic *theory* of the self-adjusting tendencies of the free market' (Meade 1990: 21).

13 'The discussion of post-war fiscal policy brought out Keynes's aversion to the use of personal taxation as an instrument of counter-cyclical policy' (Dimsdale 1988: 334–5).

14 'It is simply unreasonable to claim that [the] growth in government is the *logical* consequence of Keynes's views on the functions of government, as distinct from those of his followers' (Peacock 1993: 28).

15 'As a liberal, Keynes viewed unemployment as the key economic problem; once that was solved, market capitalism would be restored as the efficient allocator' (Durbin 1988: 41).

16 Newton also 'became one of the greatest and most efficient of our civil servants. He was a very successful investor of funds . . . and died as a rich man' (JMK X: 371).

17 His executor, Geoffrey Keynes, 'forgot about that instruction and scattered them on the Downs' (Moggridge 1992: 836).

8   Keynes and his correspondence[1]

INTRODUCTION

By almost any standard, Maynard Keynes was a massive correspondent. The *Collected Writings* contain full transcriptions or excerpts from over 2,000 unpublished letters and 202 published letters to newspapers. Added to those are 413 minutes and 364 memoranda or comments. The *Collected Writings* are far from complete. Maria Cristina Marcuzzo in this volume (chapter 7) notes that there are 2,140 published and unpublished letters to Gerald Shove, Dennis Robertson, Richard Kahn and Joan Robinson, as well as a further 370 to A. C. Pigou and Piero Sraffa. One could add the long non-professional runs of letters, most notably to his parents, Lytton Strachey, Duncan Grant, Vanessa Bell and Lydia Lopokova.

The mass of this surviving correspondence owes much to the fact that Keynes rarely threw anything away. From an early stage in his professional career he had a secretary whose carbon copies remained in his papers. He also spent almost twelve years in the Treasury, which, despite the disruptions of its being blitzed in 1940, was remarkably efficient at keeping paper, even if significant amounts of 1914–19 material ended up in Keynes's own papers. Even out of the Treasury he generated correspondence and reactions from Treasury officials.[2] Finally, some of the recipients of his letters were themselves pack rats.

This mass of material has fed the Keynes industry, although its use has been uneven. There has, inevitably, been heavier use of the Keynes Papers in King's College Cambridge, which have the advantage of being available elsewhere on microfilm, than, say, his papers in the National Archives or his correspondence with his publishers, the last of which reveals the risks of depending on the Cambridge collection alone.

For the purposes of this discussion I would like to look at the light that Keynes's correspondence can throw on two aspects of his activities: his management of his own intellectual property and his wartime collaboration with Dennis Robertson.

KEYNES'S MANAGEMENT OF HIS INTELLECTUAL PROPERTY

Keynes's management of his intellectual property had at least two aspects. The first were his own publishing arrangements. As far as his 'professional' economic articles are concerned, the story is simple. While he was editor of the *Economic Journal* (1911–45), his only publications in other English-language journals, other than seven replies to critics (of which only two were over a page in length), were three: his November 1914 invited contribution to the *Quarterly Journal of Economics*, 'The City of London and the Bank of England, August 1914', (JMK XI: 278–98); his 1936 Jevons centenary allocution to the Royal Statistical Society which appeared in the Society's *Journal* (JMK X: 109–50); and his 1937 presidential address to the Eugenics Society which appeared in that Society's *Review* (JMK XIV: 124–33).[3] His practice with his journalism depended on the stage of his career and his connections. There were his numerous contributions to the *Nation and Athenaeum* and the *New Statesman and Nation*, which were unusual for a chair. Otherwise, as a generalization one could say that before he had 'given up writing as a means of income' (JMK XXVIII: 339) in the 1930s and concentrated on *The Times*, he was fairly catholic in his choice of outlets.

For his books and pamphlets, Keynes used five English-language publishers during his career: Cambridge University Press, Harcourt Brace, the Hogarth Press, Macmillan and the New Republic.[4] Although he signed his first contract with Cambridge, he published only his last book with them: the edition of *An Abstract of A Treatise on Human Nature, 1740: A Pamphlet Hitherto Unknown by David Hume* (1938), which he produced with Piero Sraffa. He published three pamphlets with the Hogarth Press run by Leonard Woolf: 'The economic consequences of Mr. Churchill' (1925); 'A short view of Russia' (1925); and 'The end of laissez faire' (1926).

The first of these, with its demand for 10,000 copies at short notice which obviously disrupted her life, Virginia Woolf recorded in her diary, and she briefly mentioned both the first and last in her letters (Bell 1980: 35, 38; Nicolson and Trautman 1977, 194–5, 282). The New Republic published a combined American edition of the last two of these three pamphlets. Macmillan's American house published *A Treatise on Probability*. Otherwise, Harcourt Brace acted as his American publishers. In Britain, except for his 1929 pamphlet with Hubert Henderson 'Can Lloyd George do it?', which was published by the *Nation and Athenaeum*, Keynes used Macmillan, who published the *Economic Journal* and other Royal Economic Society publications.

Keynes had known Daniel Macmillan at Eton and began reviewing manuscripts for the firm in August 1910. He replied cautiously when Macmillan suggested he try his hand at a textbook – declining the idea of a textbook but mentioning the possibility of turning the lectures on Indian trade and finance that he would be giving the following year in Cambridge and London into a small book (BL ADD.MS 55201, f.2). There matters rested until the autumn of 1912, when Cambridge University Press, with whom Keynes had contracted for *A Treatise on Probability* in 1910, tried to revise its terms for what it now realized would be a longer book. Keynes asked to be released from the contract and took *Probability* and a project tentatively entitled 'Monetary affairs of India' to Macmillan on a half-profits basis. *Indian Currency and Finance* appeared on 6 June 1913, the day after Keynes's thirtieth birthday and a month after he had attended his first meeting as a member of the Royal Commission on Indian Finance and Currency.

Keynes's relationship with Macmillan changed dramatically with the *Economic Consequences of the Peace*. Keynes had resigned from the Treasury over the Treaty of Versailles on 5 June 1919. He began writing the book at Charleston, Vanessa Bell and Duncan Grant's Sussex farmhouse, on 23 June. Three days later he offered it to Dan Macmillan, who accepted on the firm's 'usual terms' on 28 June, agreeing to ask the New York office how many copies they would take. Macmillan was clearly thinking in terms of a print run of 1,000 copies, but Keynes had in mind a much more substantial figure of 5,000. George Macmillan, standing in for the holidaying Dan, agreed to obtain an estimate for 5,000, while expressing the opinion that it was probably not worth printing an American edition and briskly telling Keynes that if he didn't like Macmillan's American arrangements, he could go elsewhere (KCKP, EC3, Daniel Macmillan to Keynes, 28 July 1919; George Macmillan to Keynes, 8, 12 and 15 August 1919 (also at BL, AAD.MS. 55556, ff.68, 144–5, 228–9)). With George Macmillan's figures to hand, Keynes calculated the possible profits on a printing of 5,000 in various bindings and at various prices.[5] As a result of his calculations, the author–publisher arrangement was transformed. Keynes would hereafter publish on commission: he would pay the costs of production; Macmillan would receive a commission of 10 per cent on those costs (printing, paper, binding, advertising and so on), as well as 10 per cent of the net amount received from sales. Keynes would keep the rest. Desultory discussions continued with William Macmillan on an American edition, but the intervention of Felix Frankfurter, Professor of Law at Harvard (with whom Keynes dined in London on 25 August), and the American journalist Walter Lippmann ended them (KCKP, EC3, William Macmillan to Keynes, 21 and 25 August 1919). On 2 October 1919, Harcourt Brace agreed to produce and publish the book on a royalty basis (KCKP, EC5$_1$). The book sold 60,000 copies in Britain and the United States in its first two months – but it was just as well that Keynes received $6,947.37 from Harcourt Brace in March 1920 and $5,025 in September. As a result of disastrous speculations in May 1920, he needed *advances* on his profits to help bail himself out.[6]

Keynes's post-1919 arrangement with Macmillan meant he had more control over production, pricing and publicity. In March 1921, for example, he revised the 1912 arrangement with Macmillan covering *Probability*, partly because he wished to set a price lower than Macmillan's 'profit-maximizing' one and partly because he wanted to circulate for comment galley proofs without worrying about the cost of corrections (KCKP, TP1$_2$, Keynes to Daniel Macmillan, 19 March 1921). His arrangement with Macmillan meant that his most significant work, *The General Theory of Employment, Interest and Money*, could appear at a price of 5s for 404 pages, well below the price of such books as Joan Robinson's *The Economics of Imperfect Competition* (12s 6d for 352 pages) or Lionel Robbins's *The Great Depression* (8s 6d for 238 pages). It also had unintended consequences: in the Second World War, Keynes had to insure the stocks of his books against war risks (KCKP, BP$_1$, Messrs Macmillan to Keynes, 8 December 1939).

On the one occasion after 1919 when he did publish with Macmillan on a royalty basis – *How to Pay for the War* (1940) – Macmillan's timidity made him long for his usual terms:

The main question, however, which arises out of your letter of the 16th February is your printing order. I am sure that so small an order as 5,000 copies is a serious risk. I shall reckon the pamphlet a failure if less than 20,000 copies are sold, and am hoping for something well in excess of that. I have never written any book on economics, however highbrow, which has sold less than 5,000 copies, nor any pamphlet which has sold less than 12,000;[7] though these have had vastly less advance publicity than this one. . . I should be prepared, if necessary to give away 5,000 copies myself rather than have so little circulation for it. . . The suggestion at one time was that I should have this printed as a *New Statesman* pamphlet. We should never have dreamed, in such a case, of an initial order of only 5,000 copies; and, in the case of a Penguin Special, which was another suggestion which had been made the initial printing would, I think, have been 50,000. . .

All of the above brings to a head still more definitely than before the question of terms. Obviously I cannot ask your firm to run risks or spend money on the above scale. It looks to me as though it would be wise, after all, for us to return to the arrangement which I originally discussed with Mr Harold Macmillan, by which you publish on my behalf on commission. I am quite prepared to lose £500 on the book rather than jeopardise its free and prompt circulation or cut down unduly the amount spent on publicity. I was always a little anxious that any other arrangement might stand in the way of my, as I am afraid, excessively uncommercial ideas.

(BL, ADD.MS 55204, ff.90–1 Keynes to Roland Heath, 18 February 1940)

Macmillan stuck to the original terms but raised its printing order to 11,500. It followed with a reprint of 15,000 copies on publication and, later, with what was virtually a second edition, even if it was not called one (KCKP, HP7, Roland Heath to Keynes, 19 February and 4 March 1940; Harold Macmillan to Keynes, 19 March 1940).[8]

Keynes's arrangements with Macmillan had implications for his American publishing. Under American law, in order to obtain copyright for a British author, a complete copy of the British edition had to be deposited in Washington within thirty days of publication in England, and an American edition printed from type set in the

United States had to be on the market within thirty days of that deposit (KCKP, EC5, A. Harcourt to Keynes, 2 September 1919). If, however, an author was willing to violate the manufacturing condition of the American copyright law and forgo copyright protection, the initial British print run could be increased – and average per copy costs of production reduced – by shipping sheets or bound volumes to the American publisher. Keynes's first initiative resulted in shipping bound volumes of *A Treatise on Probability* for distribution by Macmillan's American house (KCKP, TP$_{12}$, Keynes to Daniel Macmillan, 16 April, 17 and 22 May and 1 June 1921; Daniel Macmillan to Keynes, 12 April, 12, 20 and 25 May 1921; BL, ADD. MS 44202, Keynes to Daniel Macmillan, 5 October 1927).[9] It is clear from the correspondence that he did not find the experience satisfactory, and he did not use Macmillan's American house again. He began to ship sheets to Harcourt Brace in New York with *A Treatise on Money* (1930). He subsequently sent sheets for *Essays in Persuasion* (1931), *Essays in Biography* (1933) and the *General Theory* (1936).[10] He was aware he would not have copyright protection, but as he told Alfred Harcourt over the *Treatise on Money*: 'I should imagine that the chances of a pirated edition for a big book of this kind would be very remote indeed, in which case it seems rather wasteful to set up the whole thing twice, let alone the chances of misprints creeping in' (KCKP, TM3, 26 September 1928). The book, which has never been pirated, eventually ran to over 750 pages and appeared in two volumes.

Although Keynes had copyright for almost all the individual items in *Essays in Persuasion*, Alfred Harcourt warned him that violating the manufacturing condition would probably mean he would lose copyright protection even in those items. Harcourt, nonetheless, regarded the question as 'academic' (KCKP, P1, Keynes to Alfred Harcourt, 8 October 1931; Alfred Harcourt to Keynes, 20 October 1931). Keynes in reply took a swipe at American law:

I am interested to hear what you report about copyright. It sounds to me a most peculiar state of law. But I know there is no form of rapine which the American law and American courts are not prepared to ensue towards foreign authors. However you are right as to my final decision. I do not rate high the risk of a pirated edition and consider the economies of joint production outweigh this risk.

(KCKP, P1, Keynes to Alfred Harcourt, 31 October 1931)

One result of this arrangement was that, as Harcourt Brace normally reprinted photographically, later American issues of these books do not always carry the corrections Keynes inserted in subsequent English printings.[11]

Keynes's relationship with his publishers was unusual in many dimensions, especially in his departure from the customary half-profits, or more modern royalty, arrangement.[12] With the author bearing the risk, many other aspects of the author–publisher relationship change: with no need to allocate the costs of proof corrections, in Keynes's pre-xerox days galley proofs could circulate as drafts subject to revision;[13] the author could control the price and, if he believed that demand was price-elastic, reduce it significantly to increase sales; and, in the interest of deliberately reducing unit costs, deliberately forgo copyright protection in cases where print runs were long enough for most publishers to meet the American manufacturing condition. But the (bestselling) author has to be willing to bear the risks and to take the time to see to all the details. Whether it were raising pigs at his Sussex farm, Tilton, managing the Cambridge Arts Theatre, or dealing with his publishers, Keynes revelled in the details.[14]

Keynes's management of his intellectual property extended beyond his arrangements with his publishers. As any other author in his field, he was concerned with the reception of his ideas among economists and policy-makers. By 1939, he was particularly skilled at using all his connections, as the campaign surrounding *How to Pay for the War* demonstrated (JMK XXII: chs. 2 and 4; Moggridge 1992: ch. 24).

Moreover, in managing his intellectual property as an economist, Keynes had one potential asset: his editorship of the *Economic Journal*. Editorship might also be a constraint, as Friedrich Hayek found in the case of *Economica* when he and Lionel Robbins had asked A. C. Pigou to review the *General Theory* (Howson 2001). But Keynes was not inhibited from using his position to comment on articles published by others in the *same* issue, immediately after the paper in question.[15] He sometimes recognized a need to be fair, remarking to Dennis Robertson on a submission by Evan Durbin: 'Where . . . I want your help is in the much longer passage dealing with Hayek. Here I am simply left feeling like Sidgwick examining the Hegelian candidate. I can see that it is nonsense, but is it the right nonsense?' (KCKP, GTE/1, 26 October 1933).

He also recognized a need to *appear* to be fair, remarking again to Dennis Robertson:

I would be grateful if you could let me have . . . [your criticisms of the *General Theory*] for the *E.J.* The number of contributions sent me, which deal with different aspects of my book, is embarrassing me as editor, and it is difficult to decide how many it is right and reasonable to print. But it would help the position a good deal if I could have a critique from you; at any rate it might do a little to protect me from the charge of making the *E.J.* a propagandist organ!

(JMK XIV: 88)

A. C. Pigou also raised the issue in June 1939:

I agree . . . as you are so much the centre of controversy there must be difficulty in choosing articles for the *Economic Journal*. But you certainly print as much anti-you as pro-you. And, as you said, when I spoke about the *E.J.* once before,[16] since such a lot of economists are working round the same sort of stuff, it's inevitable that there should be a lot of articles about it.

(JMK XIV: 320, n.1)

The line was a very fine one. In 1937, while Keynes was recovering from his heart attack, at Ruthin Castle in North Wales, in place of what would have been his presidential address to the Royal Economic Society, A. C. Pigou submitted an article called 'Real and money wages in relation to unemployment'. The convention for the *Journal* was to print presidential addresses as the lead article in the relevant issue, as was Pigou's 'Presidential address' in June 1939. Keynes rarely used referees even for normal articles, but presidential addresses would never be refereed. Although the paper did not mention Keynes by name, it was an attack on one of the central pillars of the *General Theory*.[17] When the article came in, Keynes had just been moved from Cambridge to Ruthin, and he did not read it until it was in page proof. His initial reaction was somewhat confused. He told Austin Robinson on 7 August:

I don't feel at all happy about printing it without giving him [Pigou] an opportunity of reconsidering it . . . As there is plenty of time, would you withhold from Clay's the order to print until I have heard from Kahn, to whom I have sent my comments, and have heard from you after reading the enclosed [comment], which, if it is right, I should send in reply to the December *Journal*. I feel a scruple in not sending him some notes of my criticism, not necessarily in the exact form enclosed, before the printing of it is irrevocable . . . Will you let me have your candid reactions?

(JMK XIV: 234–5)

In sending his comment to Kahn, he was more explicit as to procedure:

If I have made a mistake, or have misunderstood the whole point at issue, reply at your leisure. But if you are completely and without hesitation convinced that my points are correct, send me a telegram. I should then be inclined to try and get in touch with him [Pigou] and send him a copy of my comment forthwith, since there is still time, if he were to wish to withdraw it, to reprint the whole *Journal* merely at the cost of what the Prof. calls coin. For if I am right, it seems to me that it would be unfair to him and to the whole tribe of economists if, in a state of sickness, the President of the Royal Economic Society were to print such stuff. On the other hand, if you think my scruple about letting the thing go to press is absurd, say that.

(JMK XIV: 238–9)

On 14 August, Keynes cabled Austin Robinson to print Pigou's article. Keynes did not send his draft comment to Pigou immediately. Instead, in consultation with Kahn, he revised it and did not circulate it to Robertson and Pigou until 12 October.

By that stage a third player had come on the scene. On 27 September Nicholas Kaldor, then a lecturer at LSE, submitted his own criticism to the *Journal*. Kaldor also sent a copy of his comment to Dennis Robertson, who passed it on to Pigou. Keynes, having told Kaldor of his intention to comment on the article himself, sent the revised draft of his comments on 6 October, but oddly, given the conventions of scholarly journals, did not send a copy of Kaldor's comment to Pigou. But then neither did Kaldor.

After Robertson had seen Pigou on 9 October, he circulated a note he had given Pigou to Kaldor and Keynes. Pigou himself entered the discussion just over a week later. By the end of the month, the comments by Keynes and Kaldor had reached their final form and Pigou had agreed to reply to the comments in the March 1938 issue of the *Journal*.[18] The reply, at one stage almost 10,000 words long, emerged as a brief note at the end of December.

In the course of this multi-sided discussion, several interesting results emerged. Keynes, at Kahn's insistence, attempted to prevent the discussion being what Kahn saw in Keynes's first draft reply – just 'the usual "new stuff *versus* old" sort of argument' (KCKP, GTE$_{14}$, 30 August). As Kahn emphasized on 22 October:

It is of the *highest* importance to make it abundantly clear so that the casual reader will recognise, that as far as Pigou is concerned the issue is not one of schools of thought but of the most *crashing* and *stupid* errors of statement and reasoning, such as nobody would deny once his eyes were opened. Your reply ought to be that such argument is ruled out of court.

(JMK XIV: 260)

For the same reason, Kahn insisted the reply to Pigou stand alone. However, despite Keynes and Kahn's search for fundamental error, they did not succeed in finding one convincing enough for Robertson, Pigou or Kaldor. Instead it was the Kaldor line of argument that proved telling with Robertson and Pigou – a line of argument that Kahn believed (without having read it!) 'darkens counsel' and 'thoroughly muddled and merely fogs the issue'. He was miffed that Kaldor would be favoured with publication when 'we could all of us write replies to Pigou if you wanted them' (JMK XIV: 260), ultimately forcing Keynes to emphasize that:

I am quite clear that I must print Kaldor's article, and cannot possibly use my editorial discretion to suppress it. In fact, no one else has sent me any comment on Pigou.
The most useful opportunity for the rest of you will be after the Professor's reply in March. My present intention is not to say any more myself, but to leave to you any further stage in the controversy.

(JMK XIV: 262)

There was no further discussion of the issues raised by Pigou after March 1938. As a result, there was no role for Kahn, or for that matter Joan Robinson, to play in the evolving literature. Discussion reverted to the theory of the rate of interest which Keynes and Dennis Robertson pursued until the summer of 1938, and which Keynes's disciples took up again with Robertson after the end of the war.

The episode shows how in one case Keynes's attempt to manage his intellectual property misfired. His hostile search for intellectual inconsistencies, 'a good illustration of Bertrand Russell's *dictum* that from two inconsistent propositions *any* proposition can be made to follow' (JMK XIV: 234), in Pigou's paper resulted in a reply that did not convince Pigou, Dennis Robertson or Nicholas Kaldor. On the other hand, Kaldor's 'somewhat "charitable" interpretation' (JMK XIV: 244) was more successful with Pigou. Perhaps it is not surprising that Keynes relied less on Kahn's advice after this episode than before.

Keynes's efforts to manage his intellectual property after the publication of the *General Theory* have been touched on in other studies. Some imply, with no supporting evidence, that Keynes's famous February 1937 *Quarterly Journal of Economics* paper, 'The general theory of employment', was written 'as a counterweight to the IS-LM approach endorsed by [James] Meade, [Roy] Harrod and [John] Hicks'.[19] There are, it seems to me, two problems with this line of argument. The first is chronological. The *Quarterly Journal* paper appeared in February 1937. It was thus written before the end of 1936. Keynes did not 'catch up' on his reading and go through Hicks's seminal paper, 'Mr. Keynes and the classics', until late March 1937, although he might have 'sniffed' it after Hicks sent it to him in October 1936 (JMK XIV: 77, 79). The second is the praise that Keynes bestowed on the three papers, going so far with Harrod as to suggest that 'I should like to read your paper instead' of his own in Stockholm in September 1936 (JMK XIV: 84). Given this praise, it would seem most unlikely that Keynes would, as Young suggests, turn and attack these views, especially without explicit attribution.

THE WARTIME CORRESPONDENCE BETWEEN KEYNES AND ROBERTSON

As a second example of the uses of correspondence, I would like to take the wartime correspondence between Keynes and Dennis Robertson, almost all of which is in the National Archives.[20] Dennis Robertson had been Keynes's student before 1914. From 1919 to 1938, he was Keynes's Cambridge colleague. For the first decade they had enjoyed a fruitful collaboration as Robertson produced *Money* (1922, 1928) and *Banking Policy and the Price-level* (1926) and Keynes worked towards the publication of *A Treatise on Money* (1930). However, although Robertson would have liked 'to subscribe to the fundamental analysis' of the *Treatise*, as he reported to Keynes, 'the more I've studied it, the more obstacles I find in the way of doing so' (JMK XIII: 211). Robertson was even more unhappy with the *General Theory* and the new, younger generation of Keynes's collaborators, Richard Kahn and, particularly, Joan Robinson. The break with Keynes over matters of theory deeply distressed him. He was also shattered by the death of his mother in 1935. In May 1937, as he told Hubert Henderson, when discussing the vacant Price Chair in International Economics at the Royal Institute of International Affairs:

So far as I can see, I am (i) more tempted to leave Cambridge than I should have thought it likely a few years ago, because I have a sensation that I *shall* there find myself increasingly on a shelf. I don't think this is just pique, – it *is* a fact that (e.g.) research students who come there to work on the trade cycle are now asking – probably quite rightly – to work with Kahn and Mrs. Robinson, not with me!
But (ii) extremely doubtful whether . . . I am constitutionally capable of turning out anything which could plausibly be called a work of research. . . I've more or less got reconciled to the idea all that I can do is (a) to produce short articles etc. which may or may not be stimulating (b) to take such parts as come my way in practical enquiries.
(Nuffield College Oxford, Henderson Papers, Box 22b, 27 May 1937)

Robertson eventually declined the offer of the chair, a decision with which Keynes agreed. He took professional advice about his psychological state in the summer of 1937. But things did not get better, and 'a sudden cri-de-coeur' to Lionel Robbins while he was examining in Cambridge resulted in his leaving Cambridge in December 1938 for the Cassel Professorship with special reference to currency and banking at LSE (Robbins Papers, Correspondence with Economists, to Lionel Robbins, 18 September 1938; for further details see Moggridge 1992: 597–603).

Robertson taught two terms at LSE before he entered the Treasury on the outbreak of war in September 1939 as an adviser–assistant to Sir Frederick Phillips on the Finance side. Although he worried to some extent about domestic issues – and in 1944 wrote a draft of what became the White Paper on *Employment Policy* (NA T230/68, J. M. Fleming to Robertson, 21 February 1944; CAB124/214,

Norman Brook to Robertson, 31 January 1944 and Robertson to Norman Brook, 1 March 1944) – his main concern was on the international side, in particular Britain's balance of payments position. Keynes did not join the Treasury until July 1940, when he was appointed a member of the Chancellor of the Exchequer's Consultative Council and given a room in the Treasury. Once in the building, he inevitably became involved in policy-making, but his first forays largely related to domestic affairs, most notably budgetary policy. This was peripheral to Robertson's remit, although he had been asked for his views on Keynes's national accounts basis for discussions of war finance before the outbreak of hostilities (Howson and Winch 1977: 150). Their only substantial discussion before the 1941 Budget concerned the national income White Paper (JMK XXII: 338–48).

Keynes became more and more involved in external financial policy in the course of 1941. Initially, his concern was primarily with lend-lease, which took him to Washington between May and July 1941. After his return, he maintained his watching brief on lend-lease, but he also gradually became involved in planning for the postwar world, first with his proposals for an International Clearing Union, which by January 1942 was in its fourth draft and on its way to being the Treasury 'plan' for the postwar world.

Lend-lease matters saw the two economists involved with their Treasury colleagues in discussing the shape of the agenda for the Anglo-American talks promised in Article VII of the master lend-lease agreement. Here the initial draft was Keynes's, but it was Robertson's comments and redraft that eventually went to the top of the file, even if the talks themselves took another year to get off the ground (NA T160/1159; F18003/01, Robertson to Hopkins and others, 16 June 1942; Keynes to Robertson and others, 17 June 1942; Robertson to Hopkins and others, 20 June 1942; Robertson to Hopkins, 24 July 1942). Again, when the Treasury worried about Britain's growing gold and dollar balances and possible policies to reduce American pressure to keep the reserves low, Keynes's early memorandum (JMK XXIII: 243–52) was the subject of extensive comment from Robertson (NA T247/64, 15 September 1942), which clearly influenced the next stage of Keynes's thinking (JMK XXIII: 252–62).

Robertson welcomed Keynes's Clearing Union plan, as it supplanted other proposals. He wrote to Keynes on the second draft, which had moved it to the centre of subsequent discussions:

I sat up last night reading your revised 'proposals' with great excitement, – and with a growing hope that the spirit of Burke and Adam Smith is on earth again to prevent the affairs of a Great Empire from being settled by a gang of bank-clerks who have tasted blood. . .
And then with a growing hope that we shall choose the right things and not the wrong ones to have such rows with the Americans as we must have.

(JMK XXIV: 66)

With subsequent drafts, he was full of improving suggestions. If not so prolific with suggestions or letters as Roy Harrod, he ensured that Keynes took seriously some of Harrod's suggestions, such as the importance of the scarce-currency clause which entered American drafts of the Stabilization Fund in February 1943 (JMK XIV: 226–32). However, Robertson really came into his own when he was sent to the United States in May 1943 to support Sir Frederick Phillips, who had represented the Treasury in Washington since 1940. Robertson's subtle mind was well-suited to support Keynes's attempts to understand fully the American Stabilization Fund and to begin devising a strategy that would result in a compromise on an institution which looked like the one the Americans had proposed but would not be antithetical to British interests. The result was a substantial correspondence (JMK XXV: 258–63, 285–92, 294–304, 308–16). Keynes's exchanges with Robertson provided a good basis for the subsequent Anglo-American postwar economic talks in Washington, where Robertson joined the British team of Keynes, James Meade, Redvers Opie, Lionel Robbins, Lucius Thompson-McCausland and Sir David Waley. To his disgruntlement, he was not able to come back to London with the delegation (TCC, Robertson to Edgar Jones, 6 November 1943). He was fed up with the Treasury and longed to 'get *out*' (TCC, Robertson to Edgar Jones, 15 August 1943). But it would be another year before he returned to academic life – and then not to LSE but to Cambridge, as Pigou's successor as Professor of Political Economy.

In the interim were the meetings at Atlantic City and the Bretton Woods conference. Robertson was again a member of the British delegation, and he made his views known in advance as to what parts of the British negotiating strategy seemed sensible and likely to succeed and what would not (NA T247/28, to JMK, 8 June 1944). Robertson and Keynes bore the main burden of the negotiating (Howson and Moggridge 1990: 171). Robertson's close friendship with E. M. Bernstein eased matters (*ibid.*: 175, 180, 184). After it was all over Keynes remarked to Sir Richard Hopkins on 22 July:

If anyone is picked out I think it would have to be Dennis, whose help has been absolutely indispensable. He alone had the intellectual subtlety and patience of mind and tenacity of character to grasp and hold on to all details and fight them through Bernstein (who adores Dennis), so that I, frequently occupied otherwise, could feel completely happy about the situation.

(JMK XXVI: 109)

Unfortunately, the good feelings at the end of Bretton Woods were soon dissipated. On 31 July, Robertson sent Keynes a paper entitled 'A note on the International Monetary Fund (an essay in rabbinics)', the subtitle reflecting Keynes's (and presumably Robertson's) bemused attitude to the able Jewish officials in the American Treasury responsible for much of the drafting of the Fund's Articles of Agreement (JMK XXVI: 114–17; see also Howson and Moggridge 1990: 133).

Robertson's paper concerned the obligations of a member of the Fund to maintain currency convertibility. Discussion centred on two provisions of the Articles – Article VIII, Section 2(a), 'Avoidance of Restrictions on Current Payments', and Article VIII, Section 4, 'Convertibility of Foreign-Held Balances'. The first stated that members might 'impose restrictions on the making of payments and transfers for current international transactions' in three sets of circumstances: (a) during the transition, (b) if the scarce-currency clause was invoked and (c) with the approval of the Fund. The second dealt with the circumstances under which overseas balances would be convertible. These conditions, which excluded balances accumulated before the end of the transition, stated that such balances would be convertible if they had been recently acquired as a result of current transactions or if their conversion was 'needed for making payments for current transactions'. This raised a potential difficulty: would a member be able unilaterally to suspend convertibility if it was ineligible to obtain resources from the Fund either because it had exhausted its borrowing rights or because the withdrawal was regarded as a capital movement and the country was therefore ineligible for Fund assistance under Article IV, Section 1? Robertson's initial elucidation, which was too narrow and did not raise the full extent of the difficulty that he had discovered, suggested that the obligation for conversion under Section 2(a) would exist even if a country could not use the Fund's resources and even if it was not bound by the convertibility obligation under Section 4 (Gold 1981: 2; Pressnell 1987: ch.7, §6).

By then Keynes was in Ottawa negotiating changes in Canada's wartime financial assistance to Britain.[21] He welcomed Robertson's paper as 'an excuse for using a day . . . to divert the mind to something interesting away from the barren fields and wastelands of financial diplomacy' (JMK XXVI: 117) and replied with 'A note on a note on the I.M.F. (an essay in metarabbinics)' (JMK XXVI: 118–22). He denied that Section 2(a) created an obligation of convertibility. According to him, all that was involved was 'an obligation not to kill convertibility': there was 'no obligation "officiously to keep it alive"' (JMK XXVI: 118). If a non-resident holder of sterling earned in a current transaction wished to dispose of it within the appropriate margins around parity, he could not be forbidden from doing so, but there was no obligation on the part of the British authorities to provide him with foreign exchange. A member was required to provide foreign exchange for a currency, subject to the qualifications of Article VIII, Section 4, only to another central bank; so the foreign individual was completely at the mercy of his central bank. If this were not the case, Britain would lose the benefit of the qualifications it had fought for in Section 3, according to which it was obliged to convert under the Section only if it could use the Fund's resources to do so.

Keynes's distinction between the rights of individuals and of central banks went back to the presuppositions of the first draft of the Clearing Union almost three years before (JMK XXV: 33). As he put it to Robertson on 14 August:

I think the Americans were always rather confused as to whether they wanted central banks to support private markets in exchanges, or whether they wanted to concentrate transactions in the hands of the respective central banks. In my view the former is mere conservatism and cuts right

across the philosophy of the Fund. With the other alternative, the general
structure of the Fund begins to make sense.

(JMK XXVI: 173)

Robertson returned to the discussion on 29 August with some of
the history of the drafting of the relevant clauses and a brief rebuttal
of Keynes's position (JMK XXVI: 124–7).

On 17 September, Keynes raised the issue in wider Treasury
circles in London, circulating a note which he also sent to members
of the Bretton Woods delegation. At the outset he emphasized the
importance of the discussion:

I have now carefully re-examined the text and am of the opinion that, on all
the main points which have been raised as doubtful, the strict interpretation is what I intended and thought it to be, and that, therefore, all is well.
I am however, disturbed that Professor Robertson takes a different view. If
Professor Robertson's interpretation is correct, then in my opinion, *the
draft is not one which the Chancellor is justified in commending to the
House of Commons.*

(JMK XXVI: 134, emphasis added)

He proceeded to state his side of the argument as well as Robertson's. He showed signs of annoyance: he 'did not become aware of
this difference between Professor Robertson (who was the British
Delegate representing us on the Committee which dealt with this
clause) and myself until the Conference was over' (JMK XXVI:
137).

Keynes's paper received several replies, with the only firm support for his position coming from W. E. Beckett, the legal adviser at
Bretton Woods. As a result, Keynes asked the Chancellor for permission to raise the point orally with Harry White while he was in
Washington for the forthcoming Stage II negotiations and to take advantage of the provision that such 'drafting errors' could be corrected
by the secretariat as envisaged at Bretton Woods.

Robertson's problem refused to go away. Edward Bernstein and
Ansel Luxford, the legal adviser to the American delegation at
Bretton Woods, according to Keynes 'knew all about . . . and strongly
supported, in substance, the interpretation sprung on us (or, at any
rate, on me) after our return [*sic*] by Professor Robertson'. Harry
White attached little importance to the point and intimated that if
Keynes had raised it at Bretton Woods he would have compromised,

but he disputed Keynes's interpretation of the clause. Nor could he see any way to alter it (JMK XXVI: 148–9).

This put the ball firmly back into the British court. Keynes had to decide whether the issue was of vital importance. He thought it was; so he proposed that the Chancellor write to Henry Morgenthau, the American Secretary of the Treasury, pointing out the problem and suggesting that he would inform Parliament that Britain's adherence to the Bretton Woods Agreements was conditional on clarification through one of two possible redrafts. On 10 January 1945, Keynes was told to draft the letter.

Keynes's original memorandum and draft letter took the discussion outside Whitehall because he had sent copies to Dennis Robertson, who had returned to Cambridge in October 1944 as Pigou's successor. The subsequent discussion cleared up matters in some respects but muddied them in others. The elucidation came in the recognition, pressed home by Robertson, that the text in the Final Act did not represent a drafting slip (JMK XXVI: 160, 124–5, 170, 171–2). The clauses had been the object of intense discussion at Bretton Woods, where the initial British draft had put the section on balances first and the one on current transactions second. Along with the original phrasing, this suggested that the former qualified the latter. The Americans and Canadians had strongly disagreed with this, and when the Americans had tried to add a sentence ruling out such an interpretation, Robertson had resisted. The British then tried to get the qualification into the text; after a heated discussion with Louis Rasminsky of the Canadian delegation, to which Keynes had been summoned, this had ended in an impasse and even a possible breaking-point in the negotiations. The compromise embodied in the Final Act then reversed the order of the clauses from the original British draft and ensured that the section governing current transactions was not dependent on that concerning balances.

When the compromise was agreed, Robertson attempted to obtain Keynes's approval. According to recollections after the event, Robertson had not been able to see Keynes and had to depend on Sir Wilfrid Eady to clear the agreement. Eady recollected:

You, I think, were tied up at the time with some other anxiety. The crucial question is, when I gave you Dennis Robertson's note of 11th July, did you tell me that Dennis and the Americans and the Canadians could go to hell, or did you say 'Oh, all right then'. You think you said the former. Dennis thinks you said the latter. And I cut the inglorious figure of being completely blank, except that I do know that whatever you said became a directive.

(JMK XXVI: 170)

Robertson regretted that after receiving Keynes's assent through Eady he did not check with him to be certain that he understood its implications (JMK XXVI: 160). Lionel Robbins remembered hearing from Robertson that his difficulties with the Americans had been removed and that Eady had secured the necessary approvals (JMK XXVI: 171). By January 1945, all Keynes could remember was 'Eady coming to me about some drafting point near the end, but no consciousness that it was this one. If it was, we neither of us, I fancy, understood it' (JMK XXVI: 174).

That did not end matters. A letter did go to Secretary Morgenthau; the United States refused to provide a written response and tried to suppress the existence of the letter or, successfully in the end, get it redrafted so as not to suggest that the drafting of the Articles of Agreement had been deficient through haste. By the time the Secretary replied in June 1945, it was too late to do anything: the Bretton Woods enabling legislation had passed the House of Representatives and amendments would require new legislation. In his reply, the Chancellor virtually closed the matter.

All of this soured Keynes's improved relations with Dennis Robertson. It is clear from the correspondence that the fact that it was Robertson rather than some outsider who raised the problem so soon after Bretton Woods didn't help. Nor did subsequent misunderstandings as to who said what and when. Nor did Robertson's subsequent tendency to find benefits in his version, even if Keynes agreed with their importance in normal circumstances (JMK XXVI: 164–6). It was an unfortunate conclusion to over a generation of fruitful collaboration. Robertson was badly hurt by it. At least Keynes did not tell his younger Cambridge colleagues of the affair, for given their later reactions it would have made Robertson's life as Professor even more difficult.[22]

CONCLUSIONS

The two examples discussed above give some indication of how Keynes's correspondence can affect our view of Keynes, his activities and his ideas. In two of the cases, the exchanges with Pigou over real and money wages and the drafting at Bretton Woods, Keynes was unsuccessful in achieving his ends. However, they are just examples. The extent of Keynes's surviving correspondence has allowed scholars to develop a biographical literature on Keynes that is different from that for any other economist.[23] We know more about Keynes because we can construct biographical narratives about Keynes's life. Such narratives serve an important scholarly purpose in allowing us to understand Keynes's economics more clearly and appreciate it more fully. Personal knowledge is an advantage in understanding an economist's ideas. As George Stigler put it:

> Even though Jones and I have always spoken English and may even have gone to the same graduate school, each of us thinks somewhat differently; we each have a different order in which we think and probably a different pace in expressing ideas. Family members use words which have special meanings for them . . . So it is with every person, and that is why intimate association makes communication between people efficient and accurate. If I had known David Ricardo, I would be better able to understand his written words. That would be a help, because to this day the meanings of his theories are much debated.
>
> (Stigler 1988: 36–7)

The usefulness of Keynes's correspondence in developing such an understanding of Keynes varies. Along with the existence of students' lecture notes, a large number of drafts and two sets of galley proofs circulated for discussion, the very rich correspondence has been at the heart of several attempts to tell of the creation of the *General Theory* (Patinkin 1976; Dimand 1988; Clarke 1988; Felix 1995). Its usefulness for other of Keynes's books is more variable. Even where we have almost as rich a set of drafts, as in the case of *Economic Consequences of the Peace*, the correspondence lets us down – at least before publication. The same richness of drafts but paucity of correspondence is true of Keynes's philosophical development, but here the paucity of correspondence characterizes the years after publication of the *Treatise on Probability* as well; so that discussion of Keynes's philosophical development and its relationship to his economics has been inevitably more speculative (Carabelli 1988; O'Donnell 1989; Bateman and Davis 1991; Davis 1994; Bateman 1996; Runde and Mizuhara 2003). There is nothing even on the scale of Keynes's correspondence with Ludwig Wittgenstein (von Wright 1974). The vast riches of the Second World War correspondence and related materials has allowed the creation of a vivid picture of Keynes's operations within wartime government, including his classic conflict-of-interest situation as chairman-designate of the Arts Council of Great Britain and chairman of its largest beneficiary, the Royal Opera (Moggridge 2005). Those creating biographical narratives of Keynes's forebears and contemporaries, both economists and non-economists, have inevitably found valuable material (Holroyd 1971; Presley 1978; Spalding 1983; Durbin 1985; Deutscher 1990; Groenewegen 1995; Spalding 1997; Fletcher 2000). Indeed, the one thing we can be certain of is that in the future, as in the past, Keynes's correspondence will be turned to by all manner of students of British life and thought in the first half of the twentieth century.

NOTES

1   TCC – Trinity College Cambridge, Robertson Papers; BL – British Library; NA – National Archives. Unpublished Keynes papers are cited with the permission of the Provost and Scholars of King's College, Cambridge; Robbins papers with the permission of Christopher Johnson; and crown copyright material with the permission of the National Archives.

2   For a sample, see Peden 2004.

3   Before he took over the *Journal*, there was a 1911 paper on index numbers in the *Statistical Journal* (JMK XI: 159–73) and a 1910 paper on 'Great Britain's Foreign Investments' in the *New Quarterly* (JMK XV: 44–59). The rest were in the *Journal*.

4   He also dealt with Nisbet and Cambridge University Press over the Cambridge Economic Handbooks that he edited. Little correspondence remains in the Keynes Papers, and Nisbet's records have been destroyed.

5   Charging 7s 6d for a full cloth-bound volume and selling 4,800 copies would, Keynes estimated, net him £765; a stiff paper-bound volume selling at 6s would net £600.

6   Alfred Harcourt to Keynes, 12 March 1920; royalty statement, September 1920 KCKP, EC5₁, Keynes to Daniel Macmillan, 29 May 1920 (BL, ADD.MS. 55201, ff. 92–130). At one point Keynes was technically bankrupt (JMK XII: 5–6). In addition to the £1,500 resulting from the

letter of 29 May, Macmillan had paid Keynes £1,000 in April. Keynes asked Dan Macmillan for a further £500 on 19 November (BL, ADD.MS 55201, f. 109), but was refused by Maurice Macmillan even though the amount to his credit was £486 9s 7d (note to file 22 November 1920, BL, ADD.MS 55201, f. 110; KCKP, EC3, Maurice Macmillan to Keynes, 22 November 1920.

7   These last two figures had been altered in the letter sent, from the originally typed 10,000 and 14,000.

8   Keynes's remarks to Roland Heath on the 'second' edition are of some interest:

> I notice, however, that although the various misprints have been corrected, there is no indication that the text is a second edition, a reprint or in any way revised. This seems to me rather troublesome, as there is no means of discovering whether a copy in anyone's hands is the corrected or uncorrected version. Also I am a bit shocked *bibliographically* at this action! Surely when a revised text is issued, there should be some indication that this is so. I know there are cases to the contrary. Locke played the same trick in respect of the second edition of his pamphlet on education, and was only caught out by bibliographers two or three years ago. But this is not a practice to be encouraged.
>
> (KCKP, HP7, Keynes to Roland Heath, 4 April 1940, also at BL, ADD.MS 55204, f. 132)

One result is that the rarer, red-covered, corrected version of *How to Pay for the War* consistently sells for less than the more common, green-covered, uncorrected version.

9   The arrangement saw Macmillan in New York taking 400 bound copies at half the UK published price.

10 In the case of *A Treatise on Money* this took his total first print run to 8,000 copies (3,000 for the United States). With the *General Theory*, the print run was 12,000 (5,000 for the United States) (BL, ADD.MS 55202, f. 170, Keynes to Harold Macmillan, 22 June 1929; BL, ADD.MS 55203, f. 150, Keynes to Dan Macmillan, 6 November 1935).

11 With the *General Theory*, the case is confused. Keynes initially supplied Harcourt Brace with English-printed sheets but ceased to do so after the outbreak of the Second World War when paper became unavailable. When Harcourt Brace began reprinting, they used a copy of the first printing as the basis of their text, a practice which has persisted.

12 There are at least two exceptions among economists — Léon Walras and Philip Wicksteed. For all Walras's books from 1874 onwards, the name of L. Corbaz et Cie. of Geneva appeared on the title page along with those of one or two booksellers such as Guillaumin et Cie. of Paris and H. Georg of Basel. However, Corbaz, a commercial printer and stationer, merely acted as banker and business agent. Walras paid all

the expenses and supplied the books to the booksellers on a sale or return basis at a 50 per cent profit margin. Unlike Keynes's, it was not an arrangement of choice. Nor was it a profitable arrangement for Walras: in 1891 when he closed his accounts on a number of publications, including the first edition of his *Eléments d'économie politique pure*, he *owed* Corbaz 1,803 francs (Jaffé 1983: 84–5). In the case of Wicksteed's *The Co-ordination of the Laws of Distribution* (1894), the publisher was Macmillan. Sales were few: his daughter remembered him giving most of his copies away and him saying that 'only four copies had been sold – two of them to his prospective sons-in-law' (Robbins Papers, Rebecca Wicksteed to Lionel Robbins, 7 September 1930).

13   In the case of *A Treatise on Money* the revision meant an expansion from one to two volumes with an extensive re-writing and reorganisation of the earlier chapters.

14   In the case of the Arts Theatre this meant running the box office, pricing wine in the restaurant and reading plays such as Auden and Isherwood's *The Ascent of the F6* and *On the Frontier* in manuscript and seeing them through to production. For the use of Keynes's resulting correspondence in a discussion of London theatre in the 1930s, see Sidnell 1986.

15   Good examples are 'A Reply to Sir William Beveridge' (JMK XIX: 125–37) which immediately followed the author's 'Population policy and unemployment' (December 1922); and 'A Comment on Professor Cannan's Article' (JMK XI: 411–19) which immediately followed the author's 'Limitation of currency or limitation of credit' (March 1924).

16   The reference is to their June–July 1938 exchange of letters (JMK XXIX: 173–8).

17   Richard Kahn believed that Joan Robinson's *Essays in the Theory of Employment* had been the stimulus and implied that Dennis Robertson had drawn the relevant passage from 'Certain Proposed Remedies for Unemployment' (pp. 56–7) to Pigou's attention (JMK XIV: 266). At the conclusion of his article, Pigou had stated: 'I should like to add that this article has passed through a number of stages, at each of which Mr D. H. Robertson has patiently eliminated mistakes' (Pigou 1937: 422).

18   At one stage Keynes planned to incorporate his comment on Pigou into a longer article dealing with the criticisms of Ohlin, Pigou and Robertson, the last, as he told Robertson 'to taunt you into producing a theory of the rate of interest which is capable of being criticised' (JMK XIV: 254). However, on Kahn's advice, he decided to keep the Pigou piece separate and to limit his article, 'The ex ante theory of interest' (JMK XIV: 215–23) to Ohlin's views alone (JMK XIV: 255, 260–1).

Kaldor's revisions to his comment brought the first use of IS–LM into the literature.

19 Peter Clarke (1988: 302) citing Warren Young (1987: 9–10, 178).

20 The pre-war correspondence has been discussed in Moggridge 1992, Presley 1992, Fletcher 2000 and Sanfilippo 2005.

21 For an extract from one of his lively background letters to the Chancellor of the Exchequer on this visit see JMK XXIV: 69–76.

22 See Kahn in Thirlwall (ed.) 1976: 21–3. For a more malign construction of the incident, which might well have been the reaction of the younger generation, see *ibid.*: 59.

23 A similarly rich, if more dispersed, hoard, with almost 4,000 items for the interwar period, probably exists for Roy Harrod.

9 Keynes and philosophers

CAMBRIDGE PHILOSOPHERS AND EARLY BELIEFS

In 1903, Cambridge saw the launching of three seminal works that would exercise a powerful impact on twentieth-century philosophy: G. E. Moore's *Principia Ethica* and *Refutation of Idealism*, and Bertrand Russell's *Principles of Mathematics*. It was natural for a sophisticated and ambitious freshman in mathematics, the son of a lecturer in moral science, to plunge into animated philosophical debates. Keynes attended Moore's lectures on ethics and McTaggart's on metaphysics, also becoming an active member of the Apostles Society, of which the three elder philosophers were leading figures. While still an undergraduate student, Keynes wrote papers on ethics, aesthetics and metaphysics and in 1907 completed the fellowship dissertation, later expanded into *A Treatise on Probability*.

It is generally agreed that *Principia Ethica* was 'the book' the young Keynes 'grew up under', as he himself recollected in the autobiographical *Memoir* read in 1938 at a meeting of Bloomsbury, the London group that was heir to the Cambridge Apostles. On that occasion, he gave a lively and passionate picture of the Moorian dispensation of love, beauty and truth, conceived as Platonic ideas and representing the greatest incarnation of the good, embodied in subjective mental states of personal affection and aesthetic enjoyment. This 'religion', Keynes said, fitted 'the undisturbed individualism which was the extraordinary achievement of the early Edwardian days' (JMK X: 444). Speaking of the book's 'exciting, exhilarating influence, the beginning of a renaissance, the opening of a new heaven on a new earth' (JMK X: 435), he genuinely revived the immediate emotive response experienced by the young Apostles on reading it, their 'amazing feeling' that they, and only they, knew 'the rudiments of a true theory of ethics' (Harrod 1951: 114). Thirty-five years later, Keynes still stood by Moore's 'Ideal': '[this religion] remains nearer the truth than any other that I know . . . It is still my religion under the surface' (JMK X: 442). Keynes's unwavering conception of economics as instrumental to the good life, classic as it is from Aristotle to Marshall, was certainly nurtured by this Apostolic religion.

Moore's devastating attack against the 'naturalistic fallacy' – the pretension of reducing ethics to something else – is a landmark in modern moral philosophy. More ephemeral was his belief that the meaning of good is as self-evident as that of yellow and likewise accessible by direct acquaintance (Moore 1903: 7–21). In early twentieth-century Cambridge, however, this naïve epistemology was acclaimed as a breakthrough: Russell maintained that logical notions are indefinable entities, apprehended by intuitive acquaintance, and Keynes took a similar stance on probability relations. By 1938, this epistemology had long become obsolete (Davis 1994a) and Keynes was able to make fun of his former mentor: 'Moore had a nightmare once in which he could not distinguish propositions from tables. But even when he was awake, he could not distinguish love and beauty and truth from the furniture' (JMK X: 444).

A complementary trait of Cambridge philosophy was logical and analytical preciseness – verging on 'scholasticism' – aimed at deducing all complex propositions, by argument, from their simplest elements, known by acquaintance. *Principia Ethica* – 'a triumph of lucidity', according to Russell – seemed to have accomplished the aspiration of bringing ethics under the scrutiny of philosophical analysis, sweeping away the conundrums of metaphysics, but it befell *Principles of Mathematics* to set the yardstick of analytical rigour in philosophical reasoning. An incipient divide is perceivable in the two philosophers' attitude towards ordinary language, which Moore took as his frame of reference, while Russell aimed to construct an ideal language, free of any ambiguity. This discrepancy would later expand into the gap distancing analytical philosophy from logical positivism, but this was not yet the issue of the day, and Keynes could show confidence both in ordinary usage and in the effort to doctor it by means of logical clarification. To highlight the revolt of his own generation and tease the younger members of

Bloomsbury, attracted by the sirens of Marxian and Freudian rebellion, Keynes qualified himself and his fellow Apostles as 'immoralists', who took no notice of Moore's chapter on the worldly consequences of human action and 'the duty of the individual to obey general rules' (JMK X: 446). But this recollection is rather misleading: Keynes's early papers bear witness to careful consideration and final rejection of Moore's conclusion that one is never entitled to break with general rules of conduct. In the chapter 'Ethics in relation to conduct', Moore argued that knowledge, being largely incomplete, can never guarantee the good results of actions, however well pondered they are, and added that resorting to probability does not improve the lot of individual judgement. At most, we can 'only pretend to calculate the effects of actions within what may be called an "immediate" future', but, for a choice based on this knowledge to be rational, 'we must certainly have some reason to believe that no consequences of our action in a further future will generally be such as to reverse the balance of good that is probable in the future which we can foresee' (Moore 1903: 152). Since even the probability, not only the certainty, that the foreseeable good results of any action will not be offset by unforeseeable distant evils is beyond proof, Moore concluded that we must fall back on customary rules of conduct, based on the experience that they *generally* – that is, in terms of frequency, probably – produce better effects than other courses of action. The test of time speaks in their favour, on probability grounds, against the pretensions of individual judgement.

Moore's theory of conduct risked thwarting the Apostles' enthusiasm at his revelation: how was the excitement generated by the feeling of exclusive possession of the true theory of ethics to be reconciled with passive obedience to customary norms? In a paper named after the supposedly neglected chapter (KCKP, UA/19/2), Keynes blames Moore's conservative conclusion on the implicit acceptance of a wrong theory of probability – the then dominant frequency theory – according to which 'a statement of probability is a statement respecting a series the *majority* of whose terms are known to obey a certain law'. Whereas in Moore's theory probability judgements 'can be confirmed or refuted by future events', Keynes grounds their validity in themselves: 'a statement of probability always has reference to the available evidence and cannot be refuted or confirmed by subsequent events'. Probability, Keynes argues, is a logical relation between a proposition and a given set of premises; new evidence does not make it false, but gives rise to a new probability relation. But how do we know these relations, and how reliable is our knowledge? After some oscillation, as illustrated by the 1905 notes 'Miscellanea ethica' (KCKP, UA/21), Keynes discovered that Moore's conservatism could be defeated by turning his own weapons against his practical ethics: if probability relations are known by direct acquaintance, like Moore's good, they fulfil the role of rational guides to action, notwithstanding the utter darkness of the remote future (Bateman, 1996). Keynes would make the final reckoning with Moore's application of probability to conduct in chapter 26 of *A Treatise on Probability*, in a few pages already present in the fellowship dissertation: 'Mr. Moore's argument must be derived from the empirical or frequency theory of probability, according to which we must know for certain what will happen *generally* (whatever that may mean) before we can assert a probability.' Keynes stated, contrariwise, that 'the results of our endeavours are very uncertain, but we have a genuine probability, even when the evidence upon which it is founded is slight' (JMK VIII: 342).

'The curious connexion between "probable" and "ought"', revealed by *Principia Ethica*, influenced Keynes's decision to work on probability: 'the large part played by considerations of probability in [Moore's] theory of right conduct was an important contributory cause to my spending all the leisure of many years on the study of that subject' (JMK X: 445).

Interestingly enough, Keynes's contemporaneous analysis of *The Political Doctrines of Edmund Burke* (KCKP, UA/20/3) overlaps with that of Moore's ethics. To face radical uncertainty about the distant future, Burke also relied on custom and tradition. In his reaction, Keynes accuses him of 'timidity' and rejects the idea that traditional ethical rules are untouchable and do not require amendment. In politics, however, he subscribes to Burke's criterion of 'expediency', which makes room for individual evaluation of circumstantial evidence. As Fitzgibbons (1988: 62) suggests, Keynes combined Moore's religion with Burke's rules for political action, taking from the former the view that high ideals do exist in heaven and from the latter a constructive attitude towards the role of reason in worldly affairs, notwithstanding our limited powers of prediction.

These are not the typical problems of someone unconcerned with politics and society, as Keynes would have his younger audience believe, and were to play a major role in his economic research.[1]

Keynes's early reflection also addressed Moore's 'principle of organic unity', according to which the value of a whole is different from the sum of the value of its parts. Uncontroversial in aesthetics – a painting is more than the sum of its parts – the principle is much more doubtful in ethics. Moore argued for its tenability on the ground that the same mental state can be part of different states of affairs and that this combination confers an intrinsic value on the whole, independently of that of its elements. This would imply that ethics is concerned not only with subjective mental states, but also with external objects and circumstances. To prevent this intrusion from disturbing the straightforward application of Moore's acquaintance with goodness, Keynes first elaborated the distinction between 'good' states of mind and 'fit' objects, which aimed to simplify ethics proper by relegating the principle of organic unity to the theory of fitness ('Miscellanea ethica'). The distinction formed the ontological basis of a planned treatise on ethics, and for a while organic unities were banished, till they were reinstated as partially applying to goodness ('The principle of organic unity', KCKP: UA/35; Davis, 1994a: 77–8; Bateman 1996: 8). Keynes's partial acceptance of organic unities should not be confused with the outright organicism of Idealist philosophy; on the contrary, his main concern was to limit the principle, so that human action could be subject to probability judgements. In the *Treatise* he notes that if goodness were 'always *organic*' this would have the same intimidating effect on the individual as ignorance of the remote future: probability statements always relate to partial systems, and their reliability rests on the assumption 'that the goodness of a part is *favourably* relevant to the goodness of the whole'. Though organic unities are readmitted, their range is severely limited: 'the units whose goodness we must regard as organic and indivisible are not always larger than those the goodness of which we can perceive and judge directly' (JMK VIII: 342–3). Keynes soon realized the tremendous impact of the principle, even in this limited capacity, on the pure theory of economics, since utility belongs to the class of qualities that obey the principle inasmuch as its units cannot be summed up ('Miscellanea ethica'). It is plausible that the later

Keynes, no longer concerned with its conservative implications, became better disposed towards the principle. However, his scattered remarks go no further than to call on it again to support rejection of the Utilitarian calculus (JMK X: 262), which presumes no organicism at all. This in no way amounts to full-blown acceptance of organicist philosophy.

A Treatise on Probability develops the basic ideas of the fellowship dissertation. Nearly completed in 1911, set up in type by August 1914, the book was published in 1921. Triggered by juvenile ethical concerns, Keynes's interest in probability widened and deepened as he closely examined all the relevant literature on the subject. As reviewers noticed, this thorough investigation of probability is 'essentially philosophical' (Broad 1922: 72): 'where Keynes says "the Theory of Probability", others would say Logic' (Ramsey 1926, 1978: 87). In the first chapters, devoted to the philosophical foundations, Keynes disposes of the frequency theory, according to which probabilities are limit-values of series of events. This theory – typical of 'an era when statistical regularities were rampant' (Hacking 1990: 127) – 'is too narrow to justify its claim to present a complete theory of probability' (JMK VIII: 119). Though valuable in many contexts, as in games of chance, it cannot rationally justify the decisions on which it rests (for instance, choice of the relevant series). Moreover, since frequencies relate to statistical regularities and do not allow the attribution of probability values to single events, the frequency theory, as Keynes laments, would make probability useless as the guide of life (JMK VIII: 104). Keynes's concept of probability is wider and corresponds to 'degree of rational belief' in statements on the occurrence of events which do not necessarily belong to any regular series. Conceiving of probability as a new branch of logic, Keynes revives Leibniz's plan to extend logic beyond the traditional boundaries of formal implication to embrace probable inference. Since the emergence of probability, in the Renaissance, these two interpretations – the logical-epistemological and the frequency interpretation – had stood side by side, with classical scholars ready to identify the two 'without hesitation or justification' (Lorraine 1988: 126). Keynes was one of the first to stress their opposition, and his rehabilitation of the logical theory initiated a new trend which would gain momentum with the spread of logical positivism (Weinberg 1936; Hacking 1975: 134).

An implication of Keynes's logical theory is that whereas frequencies relate to events, or (better) series of events, logical probabilities are only attributable to propositions. Furthermore, while other logical properties – such as truth and falsehood – belong to propositions taken in isolation, probability denotes the relationship between a proposition and the evidence embodied in the premises: 'No proposition is in itself either probable or improbable, just as no place can be intrinsically distant' (JMK VIII: 7). Keynes's peculiar notation for the probability-relation, a/h, emphasizes that we cannot speak of the probability of proposition a unless we refer it to some other proposition, or set of propositions, h. The importance he attaches to this notation (JMK VIII: 130) provides an instance of the analytical and philosophical clarification he aimed at. Like other aspects of Keynes's theory, especially those concerning the axioms and theorems of the probability calculus, this notation was inspired by his teacher and friend W. E. Johnson (Broad 1922: 74).

Keynes's probability-relation is a primary notion 'which cannot be explained or defined in terms of other logical notions' (JMK VIII: 8, 56–7). Ruling out any chance that the relation may be known by argument, he falls back on Moore's naïve epistemology: all probabilistic knowledge rests on 'direct acquaintance' with probability-relations, as self-evident as the notion of yellow (JMK VIII: 13). Keynes presents the probability-relation as a new primitive idea, to be added to Russell's elementary logical notions. Though unable to detect how direct acquaintance works,[2] both authors grounded on its very existence their belief that logical knowledge is neither analytical nor empirical. Their basic agreement is attested by Russell's explicit acknowledgement of indebtedness on probability and induction (Russell 1914) and confirmed by his favourable review of *Treatise on Probability* (Russell 1922).

In Russell's eyes, Keynes was a powerful ally of empirical rationalism. Both conceived of logic as more fundamental than mathematics, and Keynes does not contradict this conception when raising issues that severely undermine the hope 'of gradually bringing the moral sciences under the sway of mathematical reasoning' (JMK VIII: 349). First, he 'masterfully' (Hacking 1975: 73) argues that probabilities cannot always be measured, a price his theory has to pay to encompass ordinal as well as cardinal probability. He even goes on to state that in many cases probabilities are incomparable and cannot be arranged in order of magnitude. When this happens – for instance, when 'the barometer is high, but the clouds are black' – it is impossible to reduce such conflicting evidence to unity, and 'it will be rational to allow caprice to determine us' on whether to take an umbrella (JMK VIII: 32). Most readers noticed the novelty of this position and voiced their criticism: frequentists tended to restrict the concept to cases in which probability can be expressed by the limit of the numerical ratio between favourable and equiprobable cases; logicists, such as Jeffreys and Carnap, who shared Keynes's main conception, tried to remedy the inconveniencies generated by non-numerical probabilities; subjectivists à la Ramsey, whose theory was formulated in the 1920s, assumed that all probabilistic beliefs could be assigned betting quotients, which are numerical (JNK VIII: editor's foreword).

A second problem arises with the concept of 'weight', which Keynes derived from German sources (von Kries and Meinong), though Johnson himself was not alien to the notion. By definition, a probability judgement 'has more *weight* than another if it is based upon a greater amount of relevant evidence' (JMK VIII: 84), since 'to say that a new piece of evidence is "relevant" is the same thing as to say that it increases the "weight" of the argument' (JMK VIII: 78). Weight is another objective, unanalyzable property, independent of probability, as proved by the fact that they vary in opposite directions whenever new relevant evidence, which by definition adds to the weight, reduces the probability of a proposition. Weight bears on the application of probability to practice, since, before making a decision, we have to assess not only the probability of a proposition, but also its reliability: 'in deciding on a course of action, it seems plausible to suppose that we ought to take account of the weight as well as the probability of different expectations' (JMK VIII: 83). 'Uncertain as to how much importance to attach' to weight (JMK VIII: 77), Keynes gives a positive answer to the 'perplexing' question of whether a greater body of evidence tilts the balance in favour of a course of action (JMK VIII: 345). At first dismissive of the 'practical significance' of weight, he recognized its role by the time he wrote the *General Theory*, where weight is the only concept rescued from the early book. The fact that key economic evaluations are based on slight evidence – that is, have low weight – explains why they are unstable and exposed to the sudden loss of confidence that triggers business depressions (JMK VII: 148, 240).

Third, though not yet distinguishing risk from uncertainty, as he would in 1937, he insists on the irreducibility of risk to the numerical calculus (JMK VIII: 346–9). The difficulties of measuring probabilities, of combining this measure with that of weight and taking risk into account, challenge the pretension that human action is always guided by 'mathematical expectation' (JMK VIII: 344–5). If we add the problem of multiplying the probability of the outcomes by their utility, or goodness, which is partly organic, such a pretension is completely overturned.

Carabelli (1988) places great emphasis on Keynes's non-measurable and incommensurable probabilities and the discredit they throw on the concept of mathematical expectation, as if his approach were personal and unique. She does not consider that Keynes's denial of the possibility of reducing the moral sciences to mathematical treatment was reinforced by studying with Marshall, whose annoyance at the tendency to excessive formalization is proverbial (Pigou 1925: 419). Moreover, interesting as they are, especially in view of Keynes's later economic work, limitations on the possibility of applying the mathematical calculus to human beliefs do not form the core of *A Treatise on Probability*, whose aim is to prove, after Russell, that logic is more general than mathematics and provides the foundations of rational thought.

Keynes's extended logic retains the axioms of the probability calculus, valid beyond the restricted area of numerical probability. The special conditions for the latter to hold coincide with those for applying the principle of indifference, the new name that Keynes awards to the principle of non-sufficient reason in order to stress that it is based on knowledge – of indifference – rather than mere ignorance. Careless uses of the principle abound, and its application must be confined to cases in which a set of equiprobable atomic propositions can safely be identified. To be considered equiprobable, the alternatives must be indivisible, exhaustive and symmetric regarding relevant evidence. Symmetry implies prior direct intuition of there being 'no known reason for preferring one of a set of alternatives to any other' (JMK VIII: 57). This judgement of indifference, in turn, depends upon judging the relevance or irrelevance of the available evidence. The faces of a coin can be said to be equiprobable if all relevant knowledge (e.g. weight, surface) is symmetrical and the rest (e.g. direction of sunray, colour) can be dismissed as irrelevant. Once equiprobability is established, the initial probabilities of the alternatives can be given cardinal numbers, and the numerical calculus holds.

Similarly restrictive conditions are necessary to vindicate the principle of induction, another of Keynes's outspoken aims, in the tradition of Bacon and Mill, but without their quest for certainty: 'By far the most important types of . . . arguments' which are 'rational but not conclusive' – and therefore fall under the heading of probability – are 'those which are based on the methods of induction and analogy' (JMK VIII: 241). The validity of induction, as of all probability judgements, is a question of logic, not of experience, and, being relative to the available evidence, cannot be tested by the acquisition of new evidence (JMK VIII: 245–6). Of the two parts of inductive reasoning, Keynes emphasizes the role of analogy as distinct from pure induction. 'Reasoning by analogy' consciously aims to show the irrelevance of similarities other than those included in inductive generalizations or to widen the range of dissimilarity between the instances still fulfilling the law. Pure induction – that is, increase in the number of cases – is valuable only in so far as it '*may* diminish the unessential resemblances between the instances' (JMK VIII: 259). In the footsteps of Bacon and Mill, Keynes maintains that induction is an active process of the mind, not a blind enumeration of cases.

So far, Keynes had reached no conclusion regarding the probability of inductive inferences, but merely shown how to increase a given probability value taken as the starting-point. To demonstrate the validity of inductive generalizations, even on probability grounds, they must be assigned some definite initial probability, and this must be 'derived from some other source' than induction itself (JMK VIII: 263–5). In games of chance, the task is performed by the principle of indifference, but we cannot assume that alternative inductive hypotheses – such as different natural laws capable of explaining the same empirical data – are indivisible, exhaustive and symmetrical, as we can with the two faces of a coin. To assign numerical probabilities to natural laws, Keynes resorted to the hypothesis that they are generated by a set of indivisible, exhaustive and symmetrical properties. This 'principle of limited independent variety' postulates, *ad hoc*, that the universe consists of legal atoms, and that the number of properties of material objects is limited. If natural phenomena were always organic, indecomposable into atomic units, the number of potential laws would be unlimited, and none of them could be assigned a definite initial probability. This postulate runs parallel to the assumption that, in the moral world, goodness is not always 'organic'.

The principle of limited independent variety is more powerful, but less evident, than the principles of causality and uniformity of nature, which are known by acquaintance (JMK VIII: 293) but are insufficient to vindicate inductive reasoning. Unable to prove the principle of limited independent variety, Keynes sketches a half-baked defence of its most relevant consequence – the validity of induction – on probability grounds: once we accept the unwarranted assumption that induction has some definite a priori probability, experience of repeated success is sufficient to strengthen its trustworthiness. At most, we can say that the world seems to be so constituted as to confirm the inductive hypothesis; but while Keynes clearly states the conditions for the validity of induction, the epistemology on which its acceptance is based remains 'wrapped in mystery' (Broad 1922) and 'raises some of the most difficult and most debated problems of philosophy' (Russell 1914: 38). Keynes himself concludes that the principle of induction lurks 'darkly present to our minds, even though it still eludes the peering eyes of philosophy' (JMK VIII: 294). His analysis of induction confirms that he regarded all logical reasoning as depending on prior direct judgements of probability, relevance, symmetry, similarity or applicability of the inductive method. They formed the subject of the still infant science of epistemology, 'an unexplored field where no certain opinion is discoverable' (JMK VIII: 292).

Statistical inference represents a particular type of inductive reasoning, likewise dependent on considerations of analogy (JMK VIII: 402). Here too, uncharted applications of the principle of indifference, such as that displayed by Laplace's law of succession, lead to false conclusions, and analysis of the circumstances and logical clarity alone can avoid the dangers of 'mathematical charlatanry'

(JMK VIII: 401). Keynes's scepticism on statistics – again reminiscent of Marshall's and of their joint polemics against Pearson – anticipates his scornful 1939 remarks on Tinbergen's econometric models (JMK XIV: 306ff).

In spite of the underlying naïve epistemology, Keynes's book can be considered, without exaggeration, a milestone of twentieth-century philosophy of probability and induction. Nicod, Weinberg and Carnap took it as their starting-point. Though the frequency theory survived Keynes's critique, he contributed to surveying the wider concept of rational belief, which the subjectivist approach, later adopted by Ramsey and De Finetti, restricted to that of logical consistency. On induction, the received opinion is that Keynes perceptively focused on the need for initial a priori probabilities, but did not succeed in solving the problem, which Popper's *Logik der Forschung* was soon to declare insoluble, even on Keynes's probabilistic terms.

RAMSEY AND WITTGENSTEIN

Ten years after publication of the *Treatise*, Keynes had the opportunity to reconsider its main tenets in reviewing Ramsey's *Foundations of Mathematics*, issued soon after the premature death of this brilliant philosopher and personal friend. The review contains the most relevant statement of Keynes's post-1921 philosophical views and is worth quoting *in extenso*:

Ramsey argues, as against the view which I put forward, that probability is concerned not with objective relations between propositions but (in some sense) with degrees of belief, and he succeeds in showing that the calculus of probabilities simply amounts to a set of rules for ensuring that the system of degrees of belief which we hold shall be a consistent system. Thus the calculus of probability belongs to formal logic. But the basis of our degrees of belief – or the a priori probabilities, as they used to be called – is part of our human outfit, perhaps given to us by natural selection, analogous to our perceptions and our memories rather than to formal logic. So far I yield to Ramsey – I think he is right. But in attempting to distinguish 'rational' degrees of belief from belief in general he was not yet, I think, quite successful. It is not getting to the bottom of the principle of induction merely to say it is a useful mental habit.

(JMK X: 338–9)

Ramsey is a key figure in the development of twentieth-century philosophy. His pragmatist approach contributed to the abandonment of the logicist programme of Neopositivism. Elaborating the idea that the meaning of a sentence is defined 'by reference to the actions to which asserting it would lead' (Ramsey 1927: 57), he may have induced Wittgenstein, with whom he was in close contact, to embrace the view that meaning depends on use. In 1922 Ramsey published a very critical review of the *Treatise*, vindicating the frequency theory against Keynes's assault. Though confident that Ramsey's 'very damaging' criticisms were wrong, Keynes acknowledged that things could not be cleared up 'until a big advance has been made in the treatment of Probability in relation to the theory of Epistemology', which still formed the crux of the matter (O'Donnell 1989: 144–5). Four years later, Ramsey presented the new theory of subjective probability, directly attacking Keynes's epistemology: 'there really do not seem to be any such things as the probability relations he [Keynes] describes. He supposes that, at any rate in certain cases, they can be perceived; but speaking for myself I feel confident that this is not true' (Ramsey 1926, 1978: 63). Yielding to Ramsey, Keynes abandoned the epistemology on which his theory rested. He also conceded that the probability calculus is part of formal logic and only ensures consistency among one's beliefs, as in Ramsey's theory, according to which a priori probabilities are exogenous and the principle of indifference can be wholly dispensed with (Ramsey 1926, 1978: 91), but he retreated from full-blown acceptance of the conclusion that degrees of belief are purely subjective and induction merely a useful mental habit. The foundations of Keynes's logic of probability were shaken, but he did not relinquish his hopes of proving that rational belief implies something other than internal consistency. Keynes does not indicate how this ambitious task can be fulfilled: he merely hints at the possible replacement of his early epistemology by Ramsey's 'human logic'. In a letter to Urban, of 1926, which anticipates his change of opinion, he seems to nurture hopes that delving into the subject of 'vague' knowledge could help to clarify the epistemology of probability,[3] but he also admits that further versions of the frequency theory could stand up to his former criticism. The conclusion to be drawn from this scanty evidence is that by the late 1920s Keynes, who had ceased thinking 'very deeply about the subject', was unsatisfied with his book, in particular with its epis-temology, but was still looking for an extended theory of rational belief.

While Ramsey's influence in inducing Keynes to move away from his early approach to probability and rationality is well documented, the role of Wittgenstein is unclear. Any early intense dialogue between the two is very unlikely. When they first met, in 1912, their contrast on the nature of logic and logical propositions could not have been deeper, and such it remained throughout the early 1920s. Wittgenstein's *Tractatus* is typically remembered for its logical atomism and the referential theory of meaning, but recent scholarship has modified this cliché, pointing out that these two tenets, rather than foundational, were functional to explaining how language works. Neither tenet is in open contrast with Keynes's early philosophy; more telling for comparison with the *Treatise* are the propositions of the *Tractatus* that play havoc with Russell's Platonic realm of logical relations and entities (5.4) and with the idea that logic is analogous to natural science. For Wittgenstein, logical propositions are tautologies which have no empirical content but show the formal properties of language and the world (6.1, 6.11, 6.12). This also holds for probability, which belongs to the logical-formal domain: 'there is no special object peculiar to prob-ability propositions' (5.1511), as there is none peculiar to any logical notion whatsoever. Being deduced from the propositional calculus, Wittgenstein's probabilities are numerical and definable in terms of other logical notions (5.15). Thus, although both authors cham-pioned the logical interpretation of probability, their views diverged on the nature of logic and probability. On induction the two authors were likewise poles apart. In the *Tractatus*, induction falls outside of the logics and 'has no logical justification, but a psychological one' (6.3631), being instead a useful mental habit based on con-siderations of economy and simplicity (6.363). Wittgenstein never abandoned this view, whereas Keynes reproached Ramsey for his acceptance of this conception. It is no surprise that upon sending him a complimentary copy, Keynes anticipated Wittgenstein's dislike of the *Treatise* (Wittgenstein 1974: 116).

More difficult to assess is their intellectual intercourse after Wittgenstein's return to Cambridge, in 1929, when, recanting logi-cal atomism and the referential theory of meaning, he switched to the philosophy later revealed by *Philosophical Investigations*. In 1939, Keynes, who was involved with Wittgenstein's appointment to the Chair of Moral Philosophy, requested the English translation of the manuscript. At the time, he did not share the Neopositivistic blend of rationalism and empiricism inspired by the prevailing interpretation of the *Tractatus* and might well have appreciated the spirit of Wittgenstein's new book. However, no trace that he read the book survives, and neither does any report of their long conversations during the 1930s. This makes room for a host of hypotheses and much story-telling (Coates 1996), though no convincing proof has yet emerged that Keynes paid attention to the deeper aspects of the later Wittgenstein's philosophy.[4] Given their common anti-positivist approach, reciprocal influence is plausible but difficult to assess.

ECONOMIC FALL-OUT

In 1903, Cambridge also saw the culmination of Marshall's efforts to establish the Economics Tripos, of which Keynes would soon become a temporary student (1905) and teacher (1909). Recent studies of the relevance of Keynes's philosophy to his economics have unduly dismissed the role of the Marshallian background. If Moore, Russell and later Ramsey were the main inspirers of Keynes's philosophy, it was Marshall's approach that underpinned his economic method. Their common views on the instrumentality of economics and the limitations to mathematical and statistical reasoning have already been mentioned. Other resemblances are easily detected in their positive evaluation of common sense and ordinary language, as well as in their dislike of overpreciseness and the extremely simplifying assumption of the economic man. They also shared the fundamental view that economics falls within the moral sciences and deals with subjective and variable motives, a fact which explains the economist's influence and calls for his responsibility. Both thought economics should be realistic; nonetheless, they recognized the need for an analytical part made up of short deductive chains, and rejected the crass empiricism of the historical school.[5] Keynes's letter to Roy Harrod highlights his views on economic method in a passage that Marshall could have subscribed to:

Economics is a branch of logic, a way of thinking . . . is a science of thinking in terms of models joined to the art of choosing models which are relevant to the contemporary world. It is compelled to be this, because, unlike the typical natural science, the material to which it is applied is, in too many respects, not homogeneous through time . . . Good economists are scarce because the gift for using 'vigilant observation' to choose good models . . . appears to be a very rare one . . . economics is essentially a moral science, not a natural science.

(JMK XIV: 296–7)

Are these views Marshallian, or simply Marshallian-like because they stem from the same British stock? Marshall's direct influence faded with the passing of time, but Keynes's growing experience of the economic world may have led him to appreciate the need 'to disentangle the interwoven effects of complex causes' (Marshall 1961: vol. II, 173), instilling the cautiousness and catholicity of his master's approach. Be this as it may, most of the methodological aspects of Keynes's economics are part of the British tradition of social science, descending from the Scottish Enlightenment and reinvigorated by the Victorians.

Onto this background, which erected fences against the spreading of general equilibrium theory into Britain, the Edwardians grafted their iconoclastic revolt against conventional morality and their loss of faith in secular progress. As time went by, these two innovative drifts met with radically different fates. The chaotic, dramatic events of the first half of the twentieth century – two world wars and the Great Depression in between – shook Keynes's early belief that 'the human race consists of reliable, rational, decent people, influenced by truth and objective standards, who can be safely released from the outward restraints of convention and traditional standards and inflexible rules of conduct': this belief was replaced by the awareness 'that civilisation [is] a thin and precarious crust erected by the personality and the will of a very few and only preserved by rules and conventions skilfully put across and guilefully preserved' (JMK X: 447). On the other hand, these events stressed the need to concentrate on present evils, forgetting about secular progress, be it entrusted to Providence, Evolution, Reason or the Spirit of the World. This brings us back to Moore's idea that the distant future is beyond the reach of human reason. The young Keynes, as will be recalled, did not challenge this view, but only the paralyzing consequences resulting from Moore's wrong theory of probability. Burke likewise stressed the uncertainty of the future, drawing the conclusion that politics must be concerned with present evil, as no revolutionary uprising, with its inevitable load of present discomfort, is justified by the uncertain prospect of a brilliant, far-away future. Keynes shared Burke's distrust of attempts to dispel this inherent myopia[6] and agreed that political action must be restricted to the present. It can be surmised that while studying economics with Marshall and Pigou he disregarded their belief in the continuity of time and doubted the power of their Victorian telescope to unveil the secret of the long period, thereby paving the way to his famous witticism that 'in the long run we are all dead'. The feeling of radical change and uncertainty that permeates chapter 12 of the *General Theory* finds some echo in the early papers; so does the feeling, wonderfully expressed in *The Economic Consequences of the Peace*, that stability and progress cannot be taken for granted.[7] These themes extend throughout all of his writings and permeate the last lines of his last article: 'We shall run more risks of jeopardising the future if we are influenced by indefinite fears based on trying to look ahead further than any one can see' (JMK XXVII: 446).

The purest presentation of these views and their economic implications is the 1937 retrospective essay on *The General Theory and After*, integrated with the almost contemporaneous Galton lecture. Far from being unconcerned with unpredictable change and radical uncertainty, economics is where they rule supreme. Deprived of the possibility of applying the Benthamite calculus, we discover the naked truth that 'the fact that our knowledge of the future is fluctuating, vague and uncertain, renders wealth a peculiarly unsuitable subject for the methods of the classical economic theory' (JMK XIV: 112). On issues of paramount importance for investment decisions, Keynes's verdict is beyond appeal: 'We do not know what the future holds. Nevertheless, as living and moving beings, we are forced to act' (JMK XIV: 124) and devise strategies to lull ourselves into the false belief that we do know: extrapolating present circumstances into the future, assuming that the present state of opinion embodies a correct prediction of the future and, above all, falling back on the judgement of the rest of the world and hoping they are better informed than ourselves. This game of reciprocal imitation gives rise to social conventions erected on flimsy foundations and therefore subject to sudden breakdown. Mass psychology and herd behaviour are transferred from politics and ordinary life to the Stock Exchange, the alleged Olympus of economic rationality. The vagaries of financial speculation had long been known, but Keynes emphasized that they were more than bubbles on the smooth surface of the market economy. Confidence was of paramount importance for Marshall's cycle theory, and indeed Keynes's rediscovery of its role, after his enthusiasm in the early 1930s for objective explanations which would make the crisis more easily tractable by economic policy, was 'a return to Marshall' (Bateman 1996: 99–100); but Keynes's boot-strap theory of economic equilibrium, dependent only on widespread conventional trust in its stability, was novel. So was Keynes's convention: heir to the Classical economists' custom, but, unlike the latter, not progressively forged through interaction with the objective world; it resulted from social interplay, like the later Wittgenstein's uses and rules, but lacked the solidity that social practice and tradition confer on these. Classical custom is the cumulative, tested result of natural selection, Keynes's convention is artificial and fragile; Wittgenstein's social rules look after themselves and are there to stay, Keynes's conventions are ephemeral, unless preserved by continuous and careful stewardship. And when they evaporate and the precarious equilibrium they supported breaks down, we retreat to another trench, finding refuge in the possession of money, a placebo that 'lulls our disquietude', nurturing the sham belief that, if we hold money, we are shielded from unpredictable shocks. The social intercourse thus generated is completely different from that originating from the early Keynes's ambitious plan of an extended logic, careful though it was to make room for 'caprice'. Rather, the new perspective reminds us of Freud's Unconscious, popular with Bloomsbury, but also of Hume's remedies against scepticism. Lacking any trace of direct influence, an explanation can be found in Keynes's permeability to the intellectual atmosphere of his times, which experienced the breakdown of the golden age of reason and progress. Literature and the arts abound with similar images, and Keynes's open-mindedness, his ability to wake up every morning 'as innocent as a new-babe' (Harrod 1951: 470), his proverbial quickness and the uniquely rich set of intellectual solicitations he was exposed to, may account for his new perspective. Where Keynes's philosophy of uncertainty proved original was in eroding the certainties of economics, the citadel of perfect rationality.

The outcome was a philosophy of action which, against traditional economic wisdom, praised bold enterprise over calculating parsimony. The healing virtue of detaining money is a poor substitute for the healthier situation in which investment is prompted by vigorous 'animal spirits'. For Keynes, however, economic action, deprived though it was of rationalistic foundations, was not altogether blind. Human reason should concentrate on framing contexts capable of channelling energies towards better aims than simply 'beating the gun' in the zero-sum game of financial speculation. The remedial measures that Keynes 'skilfully' devised, at least in the way they were applied during the Keynesian era, have been superseded, but his legacy, calling for responsible human action within a fragile horizon of radical uncertainty, is still unsurpassed.

NOTES

I am grateful to Alberto Baccini, Marco Dardi and Aldo Gargani for comments on an earlier draft.

1   Keynes's early interest in politics is confirmed by the paper 'Modern civilisation' (Moggridge 1992: 129) and his participation in the Union Society political debates (Cristiano 2004).

2   The epistemology that lies behind the logic is no matter of logic: 'in *all* knowledge there is some direct element; and logic can never be made purely mechanical' (JMK VIII: 15).

3   Whereas in the *Treatise* vagueness is either left aside (JMK VIII: 17–18) or declared to need amendment (JMK VIII: 57), later on it is accepted (JMK XXIX: 36).

4   Wittgenstein himself rules out this possibility in a letter to Moore (Wittgenstein 1974: 176).

5   Cf. Marshall (1961, vol. I: vii, 26–27, 77, 129, 460, 772) and JMK (XIV: 300; XXIX: 36, 294). On Marshall's impact on Keynes, see chapter 7 of Raffaelli (2003).

6   'Our powers of prediction are slight, our command over remote results infinitesimal' (KCKP, UA/20/3/82). 'Burke' – Keynes wrote in another early paper, "Panacea" – 'emphasized the slightness of our power over the future, the inutility of attempting means to ends remote' (KCKP, UA/37/2).

7   'It is rarely and with difficulty that we can envisage the incredible change which has come and is coming on the face of society . . . We take these things so much for granted . . . The real fabric of phenomenal society is being shaken' (KCKP, UA/22/1–2).

10 Keynes's political philosophy[1]

WHY DID KEYNES'S 'POLITICAL PHILOSOPHY' BECOME A BIG ISSUE?

One reason why Keynes's political philosophy has become a big issue is the realization that Keynes started out as a philosopher and regarded his *Treatise on Probability*, which was published in 1921, but mainly written before the First World War, as a work of philosophy rather than mathematics. This view was flattering to economists who liked to think of their subject as being an application of a broader political outlook, which in turn rested on some profound metaphysical view of the universe and man's place in it. But the evidence suggests to me that the evolution of Keynes's political and economic views was much more pragmatic and did not depend on such a philosophical edifice. The term 'political philosophy' has many different meanings; Keynes was a political philosopher only in the very broad sense of the term, synonymous with 'having a political outlook', much of it implicit.

A second reason for the interest in Keynes's political outlook was the revival of market liberalism in the 1980s. This took much of the academic world, Whitehall and the media by surprise, as it had previously been believed that this way of thinking was dead. The academic critics were, as so often, belatedly catching up with changes in the political world. Looking for an antidote to what they regarded as the neo-liberal blight, they hoped to resurrect a political philosophy associated with Keynes. This raised the question of who represented the alternative political outlook to which Keynes's was opposed and which lay behind the speeches of Ronald Reagan and Margaret Thatcher. The obvious choice was Milton Friedman.

However, the differences between Keynes and Friedman were too technical and depended on unfolding empirical evidence. The main alternative seemed to be Friedrich Hayek, who had enjoyed an earlier moment of fame, or notoriety, with *The Road to Serfdom* (1944), which was quoted by Winston Churchill in a 1945 election broadcast mentioning 'the Gestapo'. Hayek did indeed have a comprehensive political philosophy which could be contrasted with that implicit in the work of Keynes, but he became a symbol of the revived classical liberal outlook largely because Thatcher, who had read both *The Road to Serfdom* and *The Constitution of Liberty* (1960) at an early age, referred to these works whenever she could. Another Austrian-born economist, Ludwig von Mises, fulfilled this role with Reagan, but the references here were more casual and infrequent.

In my view, however, the real contrast was between Keynes and the Austro-American political economist Joseph Schumpeter. The latter is well known as the father of the economic theory of democracy, nowadays often called Public Choice. He conceived of democratic representatives as akin to other economic agents: they deal in votes as steel men deal in steel or oil men in oil. The democratic character of their behaviour results from the competition between different politicians and parties for votes. To gain or retain power, they must offer policies, or more characteristically promise results, that will attract votes away from their rivals. These basic insights have been incorporated by many economists, especially in North America, into the edifice of modern neo-classical theory, and their equations often model political influences on policy choices.

In their desire to build this mathematical edifice, modern political economists have tended to overlook the main conditions emphasized by Schumpeter for the insulation of liberal representative democracy from the internally generated forces that would tend to destroy it, such as a bias towards excessive public expenditure or the temptation to run inflationary risks which need not come home to roost until after the subsequent election. Above all, the discipline imposed in the commercial marketplace by the personal budget constraint is absent. Interest groups tend to press their demands as forcefully as possible without any real discipine on the sum total of their claims.

Schumpeter himself put forward three main constraints on such forces. They were the limitation of the area of effective political decision-making, the existence of a well-trained bureaucracy and the exercise of political self-restraint. Such constraints were taken for granted in the atmosphere in which Keynes grew up. Harrod refers to these as the 'preconceptions of Harvey Road', referring to the Cambridge street in which Keynes grew up. Skidelsky prefers to call them the preconceptions of Cambridge as such.

This outlook is what Bernard Williams once described as 'government house utilitarianism'. It reflected a battle that had taken place in the late nineteenth century between utilitarians, who judged policies in terms of their effect on the sum of human happiness, and intuitionists, who believed that there were objective moral rules, into which they had insight. A *de facto* compromise was reached on the basis that existing rules and institutions might after all have some utilitarian justification. Similarly, Alfred Marshall, the founder of Cambridge economics and one of Keynes's teachers, spoke of the need for democracy to be restrained in its own interests.

Although Keynes was, as a young man, avowedly contemptuous of Benthamite concerns with happiness and material welfare, he never abandoned the assumptions of government house utilitarianism when he came to turn his mind to politics and policies. He took for granted the existence of special agencies of a non-political nature such as the pre-1914 Bank of England. But however much he castigated the conduct of such institutions, he never lost hope that morality and the permeation of ideas could be relied upon to disseminate enlightened thinking after, at worst, a lag of a generation. Macroeconomic debate would then be largely confined to technical problems, with no danger of its becoming the tool of competing political teams. More generally, he took for granted a powerful, well-entrenched bureaucracy which would keep government in the hands of experts whose knowledge could be expected to improve. A government that could, for reasons of prestige or dogma, go back to the pre-1914 gold parity in 1925 at the expense of considerable unemployment, would surely be able to resist popular pressure when it was pursuing better ideas which really would promote the public interest.

In the background was the class composition and attitudes of politicians and civil servants who were to some extent enlightened

amateurs with sufficient means and independence to resist democratic pressures. They were not under financial pressure to continue
at their posts carrying out policies in which they no longer believed.
Much of economic policy could therefore be insulated from the
political process. Added to all this was the presence of tolerance
and democratic self-control. In the early twentieth century, electo-
rates were able to exercise this self-restraint partly because they
were slow to realize their power and partly because of events such
as the First World War, which produced an external threat and a
patriotic myth to override sectional conflicts and which weakened
the pressure that could be asserted, for instance by unions, on
government and business alike.

Neither Keynes nor Schumpeter, both of whom died soon after
the Second World War, lived long enough to appreciate the erosion
of these constraints. But Schumpeter clearly thought that the
amount of government intervention advocated by Keynes was only
tolerable and workable in the restricted arms-length democracy of
the early twentieth century.

KEYNES, MARKET LIBERALISM AND THE MIDDLE WAY

A third reason for the interest in Keynes's thinking arose from the
reaction of market liberals themselves to Keynes. In some American
Republican circles he was regarded as the fount of all political and
economic evil. But there were others, especially in Britain, who
tried to distinguish between Keynes, with a more liberal view of
the market, and social democratic versions of his teachings, which
they liked to regard as a distortion.

However, my own reading suggests that Keynes was far from a
classical liberal. It is true that he had little sympathy with what
came to be called 'Labour values'. Beatrice Webb qualified an appreciation of Keynes, written in 1926, by remarking 'he is contemptuous of common men, especially when gathered together in herds . . .
He . . . has no desire to enlist the herd instinct on his side. Hence his
antipathy to trade unions, to proletarian culture, to nationalism and
patriotism as distinguished from public spirit' (Skidelsky 1992: 257).
He was not very interested in equality, and his support for the
redistributive welfare state was perfunctory. All he would say on
wage push under full employment was, 'One is also, simply because

one knows no solution, inclined to turn a blind eye to the wages problem in a fully employed economy' (JMK XXVII: 385). As their name suggests, market liberals emphasized the benefits of market forces and the pitfalls of discretionary government intervention.

But just as important was the search for policy rules that might recreate Schumpeter's conditions for effective democracy. Heads of government were never so keen on having their hands tied by such rules as were their supposed academic inspirers. But these were nevertheless a central plank of the revived doctrines. The most famous of these was Milton Friedman's advocacy of a fixed growth of some specified version of the money supply. There were also rules for the allowable amount of the budget deficit related to the state of the economic cycle. Indeed, a British Conservative Chancellor, Nigel Lawson, summarized his medium-term financial strategy of the 1980s as 'rules rule'.

So, far from withering away, these rules had a new lease of life when the political pendulum swung to the left. The Euro was launched with both an independent European Central Bank committed to price stability and the ill-fated Growth and Stability Pact which aimed to limit budget deficits. In Britain there was no firmer advocate of government by rules than the Labour Chancellor Gordon Brown, who came to office in 1997, and who kept on republishing a fiscal strategy that aimed to lay down strict rules for government borrowing over the whole of a carefully defined business cycle. Another aspect was the operational independence of the Bank of England, which devised some rules of its own in implementing the inflation targets laid down by the government.

Market liberalism did not have to be nearly as hardhearted or as inflexible as its opponents claimed, or as it appeared to be in the literature emanating from some of the more doctrinaire think tanks. For instance, it was consistent with a considerable degree of income redistribution and also government intervention where there were glaring market failures, provided it was borne in mind that there could be government failures too. The distinguishing feature of classical liberal doctrines was that intervention should be bound by rules and not depend on discretionary deals between governments and interest groups.

Keynes is rightly identified with what was called in his time 'The Middle Way'. Indeed, he reacted favourably to a book of just that title by his friend and publisher, Harold Macmillan. But it must be remembered that the interwar Middle was in between *laissez-faire* capitalism and state socialism. When the *General Theory* was written, Marxism was still a live force in Western intellectual circles; Keynes himself believed, as he remarked in a letter to Bernard Shaw, that he had found a better antidote to the evils of capitalism than was to be found in the teachings of Marx, which he found arid and scholastic. By contrast, the later Third Way, as proclaimed for instance by Tony Blair's government in Britain, was meant to be in between the Thatcher–Reagan model of competitive free enterprise and 'Rhenish' corporate capitalism.

Obviously, Keynes lived too soon to pronounce on this Third Way. Nevertheless, to the extent to which the issues developed in his time, he was a corporatist. This comes out clearly from his excursions into current issues and in his support for the Liberal Industrial Inquiry of the 1920s. He was a strong advocate of both public corporations and large private concerns that were ready to do deals with the government and look beyond shareholder value. From the 1920s to the 1940s, he frequently referred approvingly to the two-thirds or three-quarters of fixed investment which he regarded as already effectively under public control or influence. This was pretty far removed from the privatization of later governments. He was, indeed, an early exponent of what have come to be called public–private partnerships; and their role in keeping public investment out of the budget arithmetic was seen by him as a positive advantage.

KEYNES AND INDIVIDUALISM: THE FOUNDATIONS OF KEYNES'S POLICY VIEWS

The reader will have noticed that this discussion has concerned Keynes's political economy rather than anything that might strictly be called his political philosophy. In fact, although Keynes read mathematics at Cambridge as an undergraduate, his main academic interests were in philosophy, and they continued to be so until the First World War. He had a few economics supervisions from Alfred Marshall, who urged him to take the Tripos in that subject. But he resisted and took the Civil Service exam and went into the India Office instead. It is even possible that if he had obtained a King's

Fellowship when he first applied in 1908, on the basis of a dissertation on probability, his interests might have turned permanently to philosophy. But the Fellowship was delayed until 1909, by which time he had already taken up the offer of a lectureship in economics. It is not entirely clear why he did so. Skidelsky (2003: 107–11) suggests that he discovered an aptitude for the subject having worked on Indian currency and finance, which became the subject of his first book. But in any case, he devoted almost all his spare time to his probability study – which was held up by the First World War and eventually published as the *Treatise on Probability* in 1921.

Although Keynes published very little on philosophy after 1921, he maintained his interest between the wars. He was a close friend of Frank Ramsey, the genius who died tragically in 1930 at the age of 27. He also saw quite a lot of Ludwig Wittgenstein. Indeed, some have seen a parallel between Keynes's abandonment of Classical economic theory, with its occasionally counter-intuitive conclusions, and the shift of Wittgenstein to ordinary language philosophy.

Nevertheless, Keynes was not a political philosopher in the sense that Hobbes, Plato or Michael Oakeshott in the twentieth century can be said to have been. The closest he came was in an unpublished, hundred-page paper on Edmund Burke as an undergraduate; but he never went on to formulate an explicit scheme of his own. His primary philosophical interests were in ethics, logic and probability.

By far the most important formative influence on Keynes was his membership of a highly selective Cambridge society known as the Apostles. It was founded in 1820, and Keynes joined in 1903 as Apostle number 243. Its objectives were summarized as 'the pursuit of truth in absolute devotion and unreservedly by a group of intimate friends'. The society later became notorious because four of the Soviet spies later unmasked in Britain were members, and many others became Marxists of one kind or another. These young men, oblivious of Keynes's own work, came to despair of Western capitalist nations either finding cures for unemployment and poverty or confronting the rising menace of Nazism. But that was all three decades ahead. In the twelve years from 1903, in which they had their greatest influence on the young Keynes, the Apostles were marked by a deliberate unworldiness. One feature that many members then had in common was a strong homosexual or bisexual element.

Those whom Keynes particularly recalled in 'My early beliefs' (JMK X) included Lytton Strachey, Leonard Woolf and the economist Ralph Hawtrey. But the dominating influence was the philosopher G. E. Moore, who was ten years older than Keynes and who attended as an 'Angel', the name given to members who had already graduated but returned for meetings. Keynes admitted that 'what we got from Moore was by no means entirely what he offered us' (JMK X: 436). The greater part of the latter's *Principia Ethica* consisted of an analytical examination of the meaning of 'good'. It became famous for its exposure of the naturalistic fallacy, by which Moore meant identifying goodness with some other quality such as happiness. In Keynes's words, goodness was 'a matter of direct inspection, of direct unanalysable intuition about which it was useless and impossible to argue' (JMK X: 437).

Apostles were, however, influenced mainly by Moore's final chapter, 'The ideal'. Here, he asserted that 'the most valuable things, which we know or can imagine, are certain states of consciousness, which may be roughly described as the pleasures of human intercourse and the enjoyment of beautiful objects' (Moore 1903: 188; quoted in JMK X: 440–1). One might wonder whether Moore did not himself commit the naturalistic fallacy in identifying goodness with these aspects. Moreover, he provided little argument for identifying the enumerated states of mind as the ideal, simply saying 'once the meaning of the question is clearly understood, the answer to it in its main outline, appears to be so obvious' (*ibid.*). Fortunately, however, my concern here is not with Moore but with what Keynes derived from him. He described it as a religion 'altogether unworldly – with wealth, power, popularity or success . . . thoroughly despised' (JMK X: 437). Even three decades later, Keynes believed that it remained 'nearer the truth than any other that I know . . . It was a purer, sweeter air by far than Freud cum Marx' (JMK X: 442). In the halcyon days before the First World War, the Apostles were mainly concerned with their own feelings, and treated politics and the outside world with contempt. But anyone with experience of such societies knows that however much they profess individualism, there is an enormous pressure to conform with the prevailing ethos. As Keynes confesses, 'In practice, of course, at least so far as I was concerned, the outside world was not forgotten or forsworn' (JMK X: 445).

How did he get from there to justifying his later activities as a political economist, inevitably concerned with promoting welfare in the Benthamite manner? In his memoir, he puts the emphasis on there being worthy categories of human emotion other than Moore's, including 'spontaneous, irrational outbursts of human nature' (JMK X: 448) of a kind that interested D. H. Lawrence, who hated the Apostles and Bloomsbury. This may not bring us any nearer to political economy. A more formal reconciliation, not mentioned in the memoir, was that certain attributes such as happiness, or even material wealth, could enhance the value of the more basic qualities, as explained in Moore's doctrine of the 'organic unities'. Keynes himself came to regard success in tackling the economic problem as a prerequisite to a better society in which most people – and not just a tiny elite – could concentrate on the matters of supreme value. This was one, but only one, element in his desire to accelerate investment, as discussed below.

There is a respect in which Keynes, as he matured, came closer to Moore. The latter had accepted the duty of the individual to obey society's rules as an indirect way to promote his form of 'Ideal Utilitarianism'. This was initially repudiated by Keynes and his friends, who utterly disregarded 'customary morals, conventions and traditional wisdom' (JMK X: 446). After his experiences in the political world, Keynes came to doubt that the human race consisted of 'reliable, rational, decent people' who could be 'safely released from the outward restraints of convention and traditional standards and inflexible rules of conduct, and left . . . to . . . reliable intuitions of the good' (JMK X: 447).

Looking back in 1938, he said, 'We were not aware that civilisation was a thin and precarious crust, erected by the personality and the will of a very few, and only maintained by rules and conventions skilfully put across and guilefully preserved' (JMK X: 447). This brought him closer to the respect for rules and conventions he had found in Burke, and which Hayek was to regard as a necessary constraint on the freedom he espoused. Keynes never quite resolved the issue, remarking, even in 1938, that he would always remain an immoralist and still insisting that 'Nothing mattered except states of mind' (JMK X: 436). Some would say that his immoralism consisted mainly of a continuing rejection of the somewhat hypocritical Victorian constraints on sexual and other personal behaviour which carried over for a surprisingly large proportion of the twentieth century. (The publishers of D. H. Lawrence's *Lady Chatterley's Lover* were prosecuted as late as 1960.) Moreover, his references to 'guile' would hardly have been echoed in the writings of Burke and Hayek.

There are indeed three themes to which Keynes stuck fairly consistently throughout all his changes of outlook and interest. These were:

1. A suspicion of fixed rules, although he sometimes, as his 1938 memoir shows, reluctantly accepted the case for them.

2. An intense dislike of what he called the money motive. This was not just a contempt for those who had an anal fixation on the accumulation of wealth for its own sake rather than what it could buy. It was a hostility to the whole idea of material gain as a motive. Indeed, what attracted him to his first great hero, the philosopher G. E. Moore, was that he believed that the latter had for the first time disposed of the Benthamite calculus of pleasure and pain as a guide to conduct.

   A contempt for business and money-making was fairly common among comfortably off Oxbridge intellectuals. What marks Keynes out was the combination of this contempt with a strong personal interest in the detailed processes of money-making in the City, going far beyond anything possessed by most mainstream utilitarian economists.

3. An interest in non-conclusive inference – that is, the logic of drawing tentative conclusions from facts or propositions that could not be known with certainty. It was this that formed the basis of his work on probability.

These interests were interrelated. He was quite content to accept Burke's suspicion of revolutionary change. But he could not accept Burke's insistence on fixed rules of conduct any more than his reverence for established property rights. And, in contrast to both conservative and revolutionary theorists, he was always suspicious of arguments for enduring present suffering for the sake of future benefits. He was not one of those who identified bourgeois civilization with postponed gratification.

KEYNES'S POLITICS

Was Keynes an individualist? At the personal level, he was so to an extreme degree. In my view, the most valuable part of the ethic of the Apostles and Bloomsbury consisted of a dictum of William Paley quoted in 'My early beliefs': 'Although we speak of communities as of sentient beings and ascribe to them happiness and misery, desires, interests and passions, nothing really exists or feels but individuals' (JMK X: 449). When Keynes in 1938 qualifies this by saying that 'we carried . . . individualism . . . too far', he probably had in mind his later strictures on economic individualism, as well perhaps as the need to identify with a wider group than particular coteries of close friends.

Although no formal political theorist, Keynes had a pronounced and surprisingly stable political outlook. He was himself politically engaged in the 1920s and 1930s. He took a prominent part in the deliberations of the Liberal Party and was instrumental in merging the *New Statesman* and the *Nation*. Indeed, he became the first chairman of the merged journal, and in this capacity he was a considerable thorn in the flesh of the more conventionally left-wing editor, Kingsley Martin, berating him for his opposition to rearmament in the 1930s.

A recherché argument has developed on whether Keynes was one of the New Liberals. This was a group of intellectuals who, in the period 1870–1914, exerted their influence towards weaning the Liberal Party away from free market economics towards more state intervention. Many of them were Oxford-based and included the philosopher T. H. Green, the sociologist Lionel Hobhouse and the radical economist J. A. Hobson, on whom Lenin drew for his work on imperialism. Keynes was not personally a member of this group. Nor would he have sympathized with the Hegelian view of some of them which exalted the collective above the individual. (In fact, Hobhouse himself vigorously repudiated that notion, if he had ever held it, in his magnificent First World War polemic entitled *The Metaphysical Idea of the State*, in which he blamed the war partly on the influence of such doctrines in Germany.) The short answer is that Keynes was not associated with this group either in terms of personalities or high theory but accepted many of its interventionist conclusions – although even there he put more emphasis on the inefficiencies of capitalism, as he knew it, and less on its inequities than they did.

Keynes considered that one of his main roles in the Liberal Party was to wean it away from the last vestiges of Gladstonian free market doctrine, emphasizing that 'the world is *not* so governed from above that private and social interest always coincide' (JMK IX: 287–8). Indeed, he was most struck by cases where they did not. Although he was best known at the time for his opposition to the return to gold in 1925 at the pre-war parity, he was also heavily involved in the Lloyd George plans for public works to reduce unemployment, and he took a personal part in schemes for a Lancashire cotton cartel.

Some have detected a shift back towards economic individualism after he had completed his *General Theory*. He himself wrote there that once government had assumed responsibility for managing effective demand, some of the other implications of his teachings were 'moderately conservative' – by which he meant liberal in the classical sense. Indeed, it is difficult to imagine that the hymn of praise to individualism, which seems to mix together personal individualism with the economic variety, at the end of the *General Theory* could have been written at any earlier time during his career as an economist. The swing had its limits. During the Second World War, he took a great interest in such ideas as commodity stabilization and buffer stocks; and even his proposed rules for an international monetary system, partially realized in Bretton Woods, left a strong element for discretion in defining such notions as 'fundamental disequilibrium'. He also envisaged controls over capital movements as a permanent feature of the international scene.

KEYNES AND INVESTMENT

Some aspects of Keynes's political beliefs require one to go a little further into his economics. His main heresy in the *General Theory* was the doctrine of oversaving. He explained how attempts to save more could in some circumstances lead not to increased investment and faster growth but to a slump, with lower output and employment. This collided with the conventional wisdom that savings were always virtuous. This tension was still present nearly seventy years later, when a Labour Chancellor of the Exchequer was on the one hand trying to stimulate private savings to help with the pensions problem, and then on the other hand boasting of his flexible fiscal rules that allowed a deficit – i.e. public dis-saving – in recessions or periods of slow growth. This fundamental heresy could be kept under the carpet by concentrating on policy implications. These were in terms of what was known in the jargon as 'aggregate demand'. If this rises too quickly, the result is likely to be inflation. On the other hand, a sudden or unexpected drop in total spending – or even its rate of increase – is likely to produce not merely lower price increases, but recession and unemployment. These two assertions taken together are compatible both with Keynesian policies and with the monetarist counter-revolution. The greater importance attached by the latter to monetary policy was an empirical matter of a kind on which Keynes was always prepared to adjust his views to changing evidence. What Keynes did insist upon as far back as his *Tract on Monetary Reform* was that aggregate demand would not manage itself. But this was not really so very far from the original Friedman policy of using control over the money supply to promote sustainable growth without inflation or deflation.[2]

Keynes himself had a more radical interpretation from the 1930s onwards. He did not then see economic management merely as a matter of smoothing out the business cycle. He believed it was quite easy – indeed historically likely – for an economy to get stuck in a state of underemployment which would take a long time to cure. The absence of a Great Depression since the Second World War has fortunately made this a difficult matter on which to adjudicate. The nearest approximation to a long-lasting Keynesian depression has been the decade and more of stagnation that Japan suffered in the 1990s and afterwards. But despite premature alarms about more widespread deflation, the possibility of longer-term stagnation is sufficiently real that governments should be prepared for it.

It is precisely because of Keynes's pessimism about maintaining adequate demand in the long run that he came to adopt a few policy guidelines in place of complete discretion. He never clarified exactly what he meant by 'the socialisation of investment' in the famous last chapter of the *General Theory*; and his late thoughts on employment policy were never put together systematically. After his recovery from his pre-war heart attack, he was almost entirely preoccupied with war finance, the postwar international monetary order and postwar negotiations with the Americans for financial support.[3] Thus his final views on domestic policy have to be pieced together from *obiter dicta* on official postwar planning documents, letters to correspondents and similar sources. From these hints, Bateman (1996) has put together a plausible picture of a policy framework that Keynes favoured in his last years. These may not have amounted to rules in the late twentieth-century sense, but they were a long way removed from the complete discretion that both Keynesians and anti-Keynesians later came to attribute to him.

The basic part of this framework was a commitment to cheap money pushed through to such an extent that business would believe that low long-term nominal interest rates were here to stay. These would be reinforced by such institutions as a national investment board to co-ordinate the activities of public corporations and a separate national capital budget to secure a continuing high level of investment. He advocated such policies and institutions not as temporary anti-recession expedients, but as a continuing framework to prevent national economies from lapsing for long periods below their potential levels of output and employment. It is easy enough to say how unsuitable these ideas proved to be for much of the second half of the twentieth century, when cheap money was the first casualty of both open and repressed inflation. Moreover, Keynes's reverence for the public corporation did not survive the privatization drives of governments of all political persuasions, motivated not only by high-minded public choice analysis, but also by a primitive desire to make their budgets seem nearer to balance.

Rather than speculate how Keynes might have adjusted his doctrines to changing needs, it is more interesting to ask what would be appropriate if a threat of long-term stagnation were again to emerge. This may or may not be likely, but it is more useful to look at what would be appropriate if this happened than to engage in a battle of rival prophecies, none of which have any scientific basis.

Keynes might not have quarrelled with present-day central bankers who regard low nominal interest rates as the first line of defence against stagnation and slump. But he was concerned with situations where interest rates, as low as practicable, would not be enough to shift the economy out of a rut. It was here that he saw a role for fiscal policy.

The question raised for political theory is why he attached such importance to public investment as a way of raising expenditure, both in relation to deep-seated stagnation and to more conventional business-cycle recessions. After all, if a recession or slump is due to attempted savings exceeding investment, why not then tackle the savings side by stimulating consumption, if necessary by means of a budget deficit? Why, then, did Keynes himself concentrate almost entirely on the investment route? This question was put to him several times in correspondence during the Second World War (cf. JMK XXVII). He offered various answers, even though the question seemed to irritate him. The empirical mainspring of his attitude was the view that past business cycles had been touched off by fluctuations in investment. Therefore, stimulating investment artificially to make up for shortfalls seemed a natural route and involved less structural dislocation.

He also believed that it was much easier to win over public opinion to investment promotion than to stimulate consumption through budget deficits. This came over very clearly in his interchanges with James Meade, who in the wartime economic service was more consistently 'Keynesian' than the master. Meade argued, for instance, in favour of varying national insurance contributions according to the state of the business cycle, even if this meant current budget deficits, which the public was very far from accepting.

Keynes was reinforced in his bias by the fact that Parliament had, in Victorian times, provided governments with the authority to borrow for certain projects which were then called 'below the line' and which would nowadays be called 'off budget', and which did not contribute to official estimates of the fiscal balance. More important, however, was his belief that three-quarters of fixed investment, not merely of the public corporations but also of the larger private businesses, was, or could be, influenced by the government – in his view, more predictably and effectively than consumption could be. He also made a great deal in his interwar calculations of the return flow to the exchequer that would arise from investment promotion schemes that led to higher economic activity. He usually fell short of saying that the expenditure would pay for itself, although he had some hopes from the use of public money to top up schemes in transport and construction, a greater part of which could be privately funded. He was thus in a sense a spiritual father of today's public–private partnerships.

Nevertheless, some of Keynes's wartime correspondents did probe him on what would happen when investment was pushed as far as was practicable. He connected this back to his earlier statements in 'The economic possibilities for our grandchildren' (JMK IX) and the *General Theory*. It was only last in his line of reasoning that he brought in his hope of saturating the economy with capital and bringing forward the situation in which the economic problem would be solved, and men and women could concentrate on nobler pursuits.

Even then, he did not espouse anything like permanent injections of purchasing power to maintain demand. Indeed, he once said in reply to a letter from T. S. Eliot (JMK XXVII: 383–4) that the remedy would then lie in shorter hours. He did not make it clear whether he was thinking of compulsion or a natural drift.

It seems to me that Keynes was skating very near to what I call the saturation fallacy. This was exemplified by all the people who used to ask, 'What will we spend our money on when every family has two cars, a refrigerator, television and other consumer durables?' Needless to say, I regard such a possibility as unlikely in the extreme and raised by people who could not envisage the expansive nature of human desires and requirements stimulated by modern technology.

It is, of course, possible that people will shift away from the desire for ever more products and move voluntarily towards shorter working hours, a more congenial working environment or more sabbaticals, or some mixture of all three. This will not mean that saturation has been reached, but that at above certain levels of income the demand may be for leisure and a better environment rather than for more take-home pay and more tangible goods.

If, in this situation, a long-term deficiency of demand were to develop, it could be tackled by a regular cheque in the post financed by money creation, thus helpfully blurring the division between monetary and fiscal policy. Friedman (1969: ch. 4) has used the metaphor of money being dropped from the sky by helicopter, and Keynes himself spoke at an earlier stage about burying pound notes in the ground and leaving it to the forces of self-interest to dig them up (JMK VII: 129). In such a world, the cash receipts would be used to finance more leisure or a more congenial style of work. The economic problem would not have been solved, but we would enjoy a less puritanical and work-obsessed culture. It would be nearer to a utopia than a nightmare.[4]

There could clearly be problems in adjusting to such a world, where business investment would presumably be much lower and the structure of business activity very different from the present. But adapting to a world with such problems of success would be a much more cheerful prospect than a world governed by the Wall Street imperative of 'grow, grow, grow' and cries of disaster whenever the GDP change in the most recent quarter is found by analysts to be disappointing.

CONCLUSIONS

Keynes had such a flexible outlook and was so responsive to newly emerging facts that it is easy to imagine him changing his mind on many of the issues on which his followers clashed with the market liberals and monetarists in the decades after his death. It would not have been at all surprising if he had, along with some of the American Keynesians, given a greater role to monetary policy; and he might even have become disillusioned with public investment. On any of these specifics he would have been pretty pragmatic. But trying to work out in detail what he might have said if he had lived longer but maintained the intellect of his prime is a futile exercise.

The fundamental reason for his remaining disagreement with Hayek after the publication of *The Road to Serfdom* (1994) did not have so much to do with technical economics as with his belief that a much higher degree of intervention and planning would be compatible with personal liberty if carried out by 'right-thinking' leaders. He carried over from his Apostles period a belief in the importance of disinterested elites. It would have been difficult for Keynes to have persisted in his idealized view if he had lived long enough to see the way in which democratic politics developed as an auction for votes and in which crude personal rivalries and political spinning have come to dominate.

But there is another respect in which it is difficult to see him moving very near recent thinking. This refers to the doubts that Keynes expressed about rigid rules for public policy throughout his career; and it is here that he might, had he lived, have had a profitable dialogue with Hayek. (Keynes's partial and unenthusiastic re-espousal of rules in 'My early beliefs' probably referred mainly to private conduct.) The issue is far from settled. The expression 'rules' can have many different applications. They may, for instance, mean rules of personal conduct, constitutional and political rules, or operational rules, for policy. Keynes's scepticism applied, to varying degrees, to all spheres. But the contrast drawn with Hayek is incomplete. Hayek, for instance, was always pretty sceptical about anything like a money supply rule, a scepticism that was expressed as early as his *magnum opus, The Constitution of Liberty* (1960). Nor was he optimistic about central bank independence, remarking that whatever the legal form, the central bank would have to be closely intertwined with the finance ministry of the day.

An innovation of the 1990s was the idea of constrained discretion under which the Bank of England and other central banks were given operational freedom to fix interest rates, but subject to overriding inflation targets laid down by the government. It would be stretching the analysis of 'might have been' too far to guess what Keynes would have made of this concept, although doubtless he would have been happier with the discretionary than with the constraint part of it.

Indeed, there may well have been too sharp a swing back to rules in reaction to the monetary failures of the 1970s. The fiscal and monetary framework, both in the Euro area and in the UK, may be hampering government ability to respond to asset-price bubbles, systemic failures or, should they arise, deflationary threats.

The problem in talking about trends and tendencies is that they are not the same in all directions. We may now be too rule-bound in certain limited areas of financial policy – so much so that they may discredit themselves – yet as far as ever from the old classical liberal idea of a government of laws rather than of men, in which there are limits on what a temporary majority can achieve, or on a concept of law that goes beyond the whims of individual ministers or their advisers and appointees.

NOTES

1   I have tried wherever practicable to use Keynes's original texts as sources. I have also relied on Skidelsky (1983, 1992, 2000 and 2003).

My earliest knowledge of Keynes came from Harrod (1951). Although it is now fashionable to denigrate this work because it downplayed Keynes's personal and political unorthodoxies, it is still a helpful starting-point. Other important secondary sources include O'Donnell (1989), Coates (1996) and Bateman (1996). I have also benefited from Harcourt and Turnell (2003). I would still stand by most of my own early assessment of Keynes (1977).

2   It is not well known that, late in his career, Friedman modified his views on money supply control by saying that once inflation was low and stable, the money supply would have to fluctuate to offset short-term changes in velocity. He thus accepted pragmatically the success of central banks in holding down inflation from the mid-1980s onwards (Friedman 2004).

3   I cannot entirely support the admiration that seems to be showered on him for his latter role. It seems to me that he powerfully reinforced, even if he did not himself inaugurate, the begging-bowl attitude 'Support me or I will fall down dead.' It is hardly surprising that other countries that did not solicit special favours from the United States, but at most joined in the general Marshall aid handout (and, in the case of Germany, not for long), made a more rapid postwar recovery. Indeed, the UK did not finally escape from this posture until the repayment of its last IMF loan at the end of the 1970s.

4   I have explored the matter of a change in tastes away from material goods in Brittan (1988 : ch. 3).

11 Keynes and probability

INTRODUCTION

Keynes is most famous as an economist, but he was involved with probability from the very beginning of his research career, and in fact his first piece of academic research was in the philosophy of probability. Keynes's interest in probability began as an undergraduate. He started his degree in 1902, and in 1903 he was initiated into Cambridge's secret society of elite intellectuals, known as the Apostles. A paper that he read to this society in January 1904 contains his first discussion of the philosophy of probability (Skidelsky 1983: 152). In those days, the PhD degree did not exist in Cambridge, and bright graduate students were expected to submit dissertations in the hope of obtaining college Fellowships. In 1907, Keynes submitted a dissertation on probability for the prize competition at King's College Cambridge, but surprisingly he was unsuccessful. The college awarded Fellowships instead to two gentlemen by the names of Dobbs and Page. In 1909, however, Keynes did win a Fellowship at King's with a revised version of his dissertation on probability. Incidentally, Alan Turing, the computer pioneer, won a Fellowship to King's with a dissertation on probability on his first attempt in 1935. Keynes was on the committee which awarded Fellowships that year.

Reverting to Keynes in his early days, however, he turned his Fellowship dissertation into a book in the years 1909–12, and it was even set up in proof in 1913 (Skidelsky 1992: 56). At this point, however, the First World War intervened, and the book was only published, with the title *A Treatise on Probability*, after the war in 1921. This book is a natural starting-point for the study of Keynes and probability, and in the next section I shall give a sketch of the theory of probability that Keynes developed in it. This theory is a version of what is known as the *logical theory of probability*.

KEYNES'S LOGICAL THEORY OF PROBABILITY

Keynes's basic idea is that probability constitutes a generalization of deductive logic. In the case of deductive logic, a conclusion is entailed by the premises, and is certain given those premises. Thus, if our premises are that all ravens are black, and George is a raven, it follows with certainty that George is black. But now let us consider an inductive, rather than deductive, case. Suppose our premises are the evidence (*e*) that several thousand ravens have been observed, and that they were all black. Suppose further that we are considering the hypothesis (*h*) that all ravens are black, or the prediction (*d*) that the next observed raven will be black. Hume argued, and this is in agreement with modern logic, that neither *h* nor *d* follow logically from *e*. Yet even though *e* does not entail either *h* or *d*, could we not say that *e partially entails* h and d, since *e* surely gives some support for these conclusions? This line of thought suggests that there might be a logical theory of partial entailment which generalizes the ordinary theory of full entailment found in deductive logic. This is the starting-point of Keynes's approach to probability. He writes (JMK VIII: 52): 'Inasmuch as it is always assumed that we can sometimes judge directly that a conclusion *follows from* a premiss, it is no great extension of this assumption to suppose that we can sometimes recognise that a conclusion *partially follows from*, or stands in a relation of probability to a premiss.' So, a probability is the degree of a partial entailment. Keynes further makes the assumption that if *e* partially entails *h* to degree p, then, given *e*, it is rational to believe *h* to degree p. For Keynes, probability is degree of *rational* belief, *not* simply degree of belief. As he says (JMK VIII: 4):

. . . in the sense important to logic, probability is not subjective. It is not, that is to say, subject to human caprice. A proposition is not probable because we think it so. When once the facts are given which determine our knowledge, what is probable or improbable in these circumstances has been fixed objectively, and is independent of our opinion. The Theory of

Probability is logical, therefore, because it is concerned with the degree of belief which it is *rational* to entertain in given conditions, and not merely with the actual beliefs of particular individuals, which may or may not be rational.

Here, Keynes speaks of probabilities as being fixed objectively, but he is not using objective to refer to things in the material world. He means objective in the Platonic sense, referring to something in a supposed Platonic world of abstract ideas.

The next question that might be asked regarding Keynes's approach is the following: 'How do we obtain knowledge about this logical relation of probability?' Keynes's answer is that we get to know at least some probability relations by direct acquaintance or immediate logical intuition. As Keynes says (JMK VIII: 13): 'We pass from a knowledge of the proposition *a* to a knowledge about the proposition *b* by perceiving a logical relation between them. With this logical relation we have direct acquaintance.'

A problem that arises on this account is how we can ever assign numerical values to probabilities. Keynes indeed thinks that this is possible only in some cases, and writes on this point (JMK VIII: 41): 'In order that numerical measurement may be possible, we must be given a number of *equally* probable alternatives.' So, in order to get numerical probabilities we have to be able to judge that a number of cases are equally probable, and to enable us to make this judgement we need an a priori principle. This a priori principle is called by Keynes the *principle of indifference*, and he gives the following statement of it (JMK VIII: 42): 'The Principle of Indifference asserts that if there is no *known* reason for predicating of our subject one rather than another of several alternatives, then relatively to such knowledge the assertions of each of these alternatives have an equal probability.' So, to take a simple example, if we have in front of us a standard die which appears to be fair, and we have no reason to suppose that there is a bias in favour of any of the possible results, then we assign the probability of 1/6 to each of these results.

Unfortunately, the principle of indifference leads to a number of paradoxes. An example of such a paradox is the so-called *wine/water paradox*. Suppose we have a mixture of wine and water and we know that at most there is three times as much of one as of the other, but nothing more about the mixture. We have

$$1/3 \leq \text{wine/water} \leq 3$$

and by the principle of indifference, the ratio wine/water has a uniform probability density in the interval [1/3, 3]. Therefore

$$P(\text{wine/water} \leq 2) = 5/8$$

But also

$$1/3 \leq \text{water/wine} \leq 3$$

and, by the principle of indifference, the ratio water/wine has a uniform probability density in the interval [1/3, 3]. Therefore

$$P(\text{water/wine} \leq 1/2) = 15/16$$

But the events 'wine/water $\leq$ 2' and 'water/wine $\geq$ 1/2' are the same, and the principle of indifference has given them different probabilities. Keynes gives a full account of the paradoxes of the principle of indifference in chapter 4 of his *Treatise on Probability* and makes an attempt to solve them. Yet it has to be said that his solution is far from satisfactory.[1]

PROBABILITY IN KEYNES'S ECONOMICS

After the publication of his *Treatise on Probability* in 1921, Keynes never again wrote extensively on the theory of probability. He devoted his research time largely to problems in economics and politics. It would seem therefore that this chapter on Keynes and probability should come to an abrupt stop at this point, but of course this is not so. Although Keynes never again wrote explicitly and at length on probability, he certainly used the concept implicitly in his later works on economics. From a study of his writings on economics, therefore, we can get an idea of how his ideas about probability developed after 1921.

The claim that probability appears implicitly in Keynes's economics might, however, appear to some rather surprising, since many of the standard textbook presentations of Keynesian economics do not involve probability at all. The reason for this, however, is that such textbooks are not based on Keynes's original writings, but usually on what is known as the IS-LM diagram. The IS-LM diagram was introduced, not by Keynes, but by John Hicks. It is not to be found in the classic writings in which Keynes developed his mature theory. These writings are, of course, Keynes's 1936 book *The General Theory of Employment, Interest and Money* and his 1937 article 'The general theory of employment', which Keynes wrote to summarize and defend his book. I shall next argue that in these works of Keynes, probability is certainly to be found.

In his 1936 and 1937 publications, Keynes argues that the *amount of investment* is the key factor in determining the performance of the economy as a whole. He regards the amount of investment as the *'causa causans'* (or principal cause) of 'the level of output and employment as a whole' (JMK XIV: 121). Let us start, therefore, with Keynes's analysis of investment. We shall consider two of the concepts that Keynes introduces in this connection, namely: *prospective yield* and *demand price of the investment*. Keynes defines these as follows (JMK VIII: 135, 137):

When a man buys an investment or capital-asset, he purchases the right to the series of prospective returns, which he expects to obtain from selling its output, after deducting the running expenses of obtaining that output, during the life of the asset. This series of annuities $Q_1, Q_2, \ldots Q_n$ it is convenient to call the *prospective yield* of the investment. . .
If Q_r is the prospective yield from an asset at time r, and d_r is the present value of £1 deferred r years *at the current rate of interest*, $\Sigma Q_r d_r$ is the demand price of the investment; and investment will be carried to the point where $\Sigma Q_r d_r$ becomes equal to the supply price of the investment . . . If, on the other hand, $\Sigma Q_r d_r$ falls short of the supply price, there will be no current investment in the asset in question.

So, any decision to invest depends crucially on the quantity $\Sigma Q_r d_r$ (the demand price of the investment), which is the sum of the prospective annual yields discounted at the current rate of interest. But now the crucial problem arises, because the prospective yield $Q_1, Q_2, \ldots Q_n$ of an investment is not known, and consequently $\Sigma Q_r d_r$ cannot be calculated. As Keynes puts it (JMK VII: 149–50):

The outstanding fact is the extreme precariousness of the basis of knowledge on which our estimates of prospective yield have to be made. Our knowledge of the factors which will govern the yield of an investment some years hence is usually very slight and often negligible. If we speak frankly, we have to admit that our basis of knowledge for estimating the yield ten years hence of a railway, a copper mine, a textile factory, the goodwill of a patent medicine, an Atlantic liner, a building in the City of London amounts to little and sometimes to nothing; or even five years hence.

Since the actual future yields are unknown, they must be replaced, in calculating $\Sigma Q_r d_r$ to make an investment decision, by expected yields. A decision to invest consequently depends on what Keynes calls *the state of long-term expectation* (the title of the famous chapter 12 of the *General Theory*). Now, the notions of expectation and of probability are interdefinable. If we take expectation as the starting-point, we can define probabilities in terms of expectations, and vice versa. If, then, Keynes is using the notion of expectation in its standard sense, he is implicitly operating with a concept of probability, and we can therefore ask what the interpretation of the probabilities involved should be.

Since Keynes published a book advocating the logical interpretation of probability in 1921, it would seem most natural to suppose that he used this interpretation of probability in his economic writings of 1936 and 1937. However, the issue turns out not to be a simple one. It is after all possible that Keynes changed his views on probability between 1921 and 1936. Keynes was not a man who stuck dogmatically to a view he had once advocated. The other problem is that Keynes does not explicitly state what interpretation of probability he is adopting in the *General Theory* of 1936. It is possible to infer something about the sense in which he means probability by examining the way in which he uses such concepts as expectation, but there is certainly room for disagreement about what inferences can be drawn here.

These questions have been the subject of a fascinating debate which took place in the 1980s and 1990s among scholars studying Keynes's ideas. One point of view is the *continuity thesis*, that Keynes held much the same view of probability throughout his life. This thesis is advocated by (among others) Lawson (1985), Carabelli (1988) and O'Donnell (1989). Opposed to this is the *discontinuity thesis*, that Keynes changed his views on the interpretation of probability significantly between 1921 and 1936. This thesis is advocated by Bateman (1987, 1996) and Davis (1994).

If the discontinuity thesis is to be at all plausible, there must be some reason why Keynes changed his mind on probability between

1921 and 1936. In fact, as far as the interpretation of probability is concerned, a most important intellectual event did indeed take place in those years. In 1926, Frank Ramsey, the brilliant young prodigy of Cambridge philosophy, read a paper entitled 'Truth and probability' to the Moral Sciences Club in Cambridge. In this paper, Ramsey subjected Keynes's logical interpretation of probability to a profound criticism and introduced a new view of probability. In my opinion, there is strong evidence that Keynes, who had the greatest respect for Ramsey, took this criticism very seriously, and, in effect, altered his views on probability in the light of Ramsey's objections. This is why I support the discontinuity thesis. Before considering the arguments for this, however, we must first take a brief look at Ramsey's contributions to the philosophy of probability, which I shall do in the next section.

RAMSEY'S CRITICISMS OF KEYNES, AND RAMSEY'S SUBJECTIVE THEORY OF PROBABILITY

Ramsey begins his paper of 1926 by criticizing Keynes's views on probability. According to Keynes, there are logical relations of probability between pairs of propositions, and these can be in some sense perceived. Ramsey criticizes this as follows (1926: 161):

But let us now return to a more fundamental criticism of Mr. Keynes' views, which is the obvious one that there really do not seem to be any such things as the probability relations he describes. He supposes that, at any rate in certain cases, they can be perceived; but speaking for myself I feel confident that this is not true. I do not perceive them, and if I am to be persuaded that they exist it must be by argument; moreover I shrewdly suspect that others do not perceive them either, because they are able to come to so very little agreement as to which of them relates any two given propositions.

This is an interesting case of an argument which gains in strength from the nature of the person who proposes it. Had a less distinguished logician than Ramsey objected that he was unable to perceive any logical relations of probability, Keynes might have replied that this was merely a sign of logical incompetence, or logical blindness. Indeed, Keynes does say (JMK VIII: 18): 'Some men – indeed it is obviously the case – may have a greater power of logical intuition than others.' Ramsey, however, was such a brilliant mathematical logician that Keynes could not have claimed with plausibility that Ramsey was lacking in the capacity for logical intuition or perception – and Keynes did not in fact do so.

Ramsey did not confine himself to criticizing Keynes, but went on in his paper to develop a new interpretation of probability, known as the *subjective interpretation of probability*. This interpretation was developed independently at the same time by a distinguished Italian mathematician–philosopher: Bruno de Finetti. In the logical interpretation, the probability of h given e, P(h / e), is identified with the rational degree of belief that someone, who had evidence e, would accord to h. This rational degree of belief is considered to be the same for all rational individuals. The subjective interpretation of probability abandons the assumption of rationality leading to consensus. According to the subjective theory, different individuals (Ms A, Mr B and Master C say), although all perfectly reasonable and having the same evidence e, may yet have different degrees of belief in h. Probability is thus defined as the degree of belief of a particular individual, so that we should really not speak of *the* probability, but rather of Ms A's probability, Mr B's probability or Master C's probability.

Now, the mathematical theory of probability takes probabilities to be numbers in the interval [o, 1]. So, if the subjective theory is to be an adequate interpretation of the mathematical calculus, a way must be found of measuring the degree of belief of an individual that some event (E, say) will occur. Thus we want to be able to measure, for example, Mr B's degree of belief that it will rain tomorrow in London, that a particular political party will win the next election, and so on. How can this be done? Ramsey argues (1926: 172): 'The old-established way of measuring a person's belief is to propose a bet, and see what are the lowest odds which he will accept. This method I regard as fundamentally sound.' Ramsey defends this betting approach as follows (1926: 183):

... this section ... is based fundamentally on betting, but this will not seem unreasonable when it is seen that all our lives we are in a sense betting. Whenever we go to the station we are betting that a train will really run, and if we had not a sufficient degree of belief in this we should decline the bet and stay at home.

The betting approach to probability can be made precise as follows. Let us imagine that Ms A (a psychologist) wants to measure the degree of belief of Mr B in some event E. To do so, she gets Mr B to agree to bet with her on E, under the following conditions. Mr B has to choose a number q (called his *betting quotient* on E), and then Ms A chooses the stake S. Mr B pays Ms A qS in exchange for S if E occurs. S can be positive or negative, but must be small in relation to Mr B's wealth. Under these circumstances, q is taken to be a measure of Mr B's degree of belief in E.

If Mr B has to bet on a number of events $E_1, \ldots, E_n$, his betting quotients are said to be *coherent* if, and only if, Ms A cannot choose stakes $S_1, \ldots, S_n$ such that she wins whatever happens. If Ms A can choose stakes so that she wins whatever happens, she is said to have made a *Dutch Book* against Mr B.

It is taken as obvious that Mr B will want his bets to be coherent, that is to say he will want to avoid the possibility of his losing whatever happens. Surprisingly, this condition is both necessary and sufficient for betting quotients to satisfy the axioms of probability. This is the content of the following theorem.

The Ramsey–De Finetti theorem

A set of betting quotients is coherent if, and only if, they satisfy the axioms of probability.

This theorem gives a rigorous foundation to the subjective theory of probability. The chain of reasoning is close-knit and ingenious. The first general idea is to measure degrees of belief by betting. This is made precise by introducing betting quotients. What is known as the Dutch Book argument then shows that for betting quotients to be coherent, they must satisfy the axioms of probability and so can be regarded as probabilities. In this way Ramsey established his new interpretation of probability.[2] In the next section we shall examine how Keynes reacted to all this.

KEYNES'S REACTION TO RAMSEY

Frank Ramsey died in 1930 at the age of only 26, having already made major contributions not only to probability theory, but also to the philosophy of mathematics, mathematical logic and mathematical economics. Ramsey died of a liver disease for which he had an operation. He pulled through the operation itself but died of a postoperative infection, a common eventuality in the days before antibiotics. Ironically, Alexander Fleming published the paper in which he announced the discovery of penicillin in 1929, the year before Ramsey's death, but penicillin was not developed into an antibiotic which could be used for human patients until the 1940s.

Keynes paid a tribute in chapter 29 of his 1933 *Essays in Biography* to this remarkable Cambridge philosopher, mathematician and economist. This is what Keynes says about Ramsey's treatment of probability (JMK X: 338–9):

Ramsey argues, as against the view which I had put forward, that probability is concerned not with objective relations between propositions but (in some sense) with degrees of belief, and he succeeds in showing that the calculus of probabilities simply amounts to a set of rules for ensuring that the system of degrees of belief which we hold shall be a *consistent* system. Thus the calculus of probabilities belongs to formal logic. But the basis of our degrees of belief – or the *a priori* probabilities, as they used to be called – is part of our human outfit, perhaps given us merely by natural selection, analogous to our perceptions and our memories rather than to formal logic. So far I yield to Ramsey – I think he is right. But in attempting to distinguish 'rational' degrees of belief from belief in general he was not yet, I think, quite successful.

In this passage, Keynes does appear to concede that Ramsey was correct in his criticisms of Keynes's logical theory. Keynes in fact says: 'So far I yield to Ramsey – I think he is right.' This surely suggests that Keynes did change his views on probability in the light of Ramsey's criticisms, and indeed that he had done so by 1933. Of course, those who advocate the continuity thesis would say that, as Ramsey had just recently died at a tragically young age, Keynes was prepared to praise Ramsey's views more than he would have done in other circumstances. However, I do not find the claim that Keynes might be being insincere in the interest of politeness very convincing. Ramsey's criticisms of Keynes were very powerful, and I am sure that Keynes would have accepted this and would consequently have changed his views on probability to some extent. Thus I accept what he says in the passage just quoted as being entirely sincere.

This point of view is also adopted by Bateman, a leading advocate of the discontinuity thesis. In his interesting 1987 article on 'Keynes's Changing Conception of Probability', Bateman argues that Keynes did adopt the subjective interpretation of probability. After quoting the above passage from Keynes, he writes (1987: 107): 'While [Keynes] had originally advocated an *objective epistemic* theory of probability in *A Treatise on Probability* he was now willing to accept a *subjective epistemic* theory.'

While I agree with Bateman that Keynes did change his views on probability in the light of Ramsey's criticisms, I find less convincing his claim that Keynes adopted the subjective theory. While Keynes makes clear that he yields to Ramsey on some points, he also adds that there were some other points on which 'he was not yet I think quite successful'. This suggests that Keynes may have moved towards a position somewhat intermediate between his original logical interpretation of probability and Ramsey's subjective theory of probability. There is, moreover, a general consideration in favour of such a suggestion. It is very characteristic of Keynes as a thinker that he always emphasizes groups rather than individuals, and this makes it unlikely that he would have wholeheartedly adopted Ramsey's view of probability as degree of individual belief. But if Keynes moved to a position on probability somewhat intermediate between the logical and subjective theories, what might that view have been? Before trying to answer this question, I shall present a further piece of evidence that Keynes did abandon the logical interpretation of probability in the 1930s.

This further piece of evidence comes from Keynes's *General Theory* of 1936. As we saw earlier, Keynes's version of the logical interpretation of probability makes use of what he called the *principle of indifference*. Admittedly, Keynes does give a full discussion of the paradoxes to which this principle leads, and he is not very successful in resolving these paradoxes. Yet in his 1921 *Treatise on Probability*, he still regards the principle of indifference as essential for probability theory, as the following remarks about it show (JMK VIII: 87):

On the grounds both of its own intuitive plausibility and of that of some of the conclusions for which it is necessary, we are inevitably led towards this principle as a necessary basis for judgments of probability. In *some* sense, judgments of probability do seem to be based on equally balanced degrees of ignorance.

By contrast, in the *General Theory* Keynes wrote (JMK VII: 152):

Nor can we rationalise our behaviour by arguing that to a man in a state of ignorance errors in either direction are equally probable, so that there remains a mean actuarial expectation based on equi-probabilities. For it can easily be shown that the assumption of arithmetically equal probabilities based on a state of ignorance leads to absurdities.

This amounts to a complete repudiation of the principle of indifference, and it is interesting to note that Keynes may here be echoing Ramsey who wrote (1926: 189): 'To be able to turn the Principle of Indifference out of formal logic is a great advantage; for it is fairly clearly impossible to lay down purely logical conditions for its validity, as is attempted by Mr Keynes.'

So far I have tried to analyze what Keynes might have been thinking about probability in the 1930s in reaction to Ramsey's criticisms of his earlier logical theory, but now a note of caution must be introduced. In this period, and indeed until the end of his life, Keynes was taken up with social, political and economic problems. He never returned full-time to the philosophy of probability and never attempted to make an explicit revision of his earlier views on this subject. My opinion is that Keynes did realize, in the light of Ramsey's criticisms, that his earlier views on probability needed to be changed, and he may well have had some rough ideas about how this should be done, but he never settled down to work out a new interpretation of probability in detail. What we have to do therefore is not so much try to reconstruct, on the basis of rather fragmentary evidence, Keynes's exact views on probability in the 1930s. I don't believe that Keynes had very exact views on probability at that time. I suggest therefore that we should switch to trying to develop an interpretation of probability that fits the economic theory that Keynes presented in 1936 and 1937, but without necessarily claiming that this theory was precisely what Keynes himself had in mind. In the next section I shall expound such a theory – which I call the intersubjective theory of probability.[3] Then, in the final section of this chapter, I shall argue that this interpretation of probability agrees very well with the theory of long-term expectation that Keynes presented in 1936 and 1937.

The subjective theory is concerned with degrees of belief of particular individuals. However, this abstracts from the fact that many, if not most, of our beliefs are social in character. They are held in common by nearly all members of a social group, and a particular individual usually acquires them through social interactions with this group. If we accept Kuhn's analysis (1962), then this applies to many of the beliefs of scientists. According to Kuhn, the scientific experts working in a particular area nearly all accept a paradigm, which contains a set of theories and factual propositions. These theories and propositions are thus believed by nearly all the members of this group of scientific experts. A new recruit to the group is trained to know and accept the paradigm as a condition for entry to the group. Much the same considerations apply to other social groups such as religious sects, political parties and so on. These groups have common beliefs which an individual usually acquires through joining the group. It is actually quite difficult for individuals to resist accepting the dominant beliefs of a group of which they form part, though of course dissidents and heretics do occur. One striking instance of this is that individuals kidnapped by a terrorist organisation do sometimes, like Patty Hearst, adopt the terrorists' beliefs. All this seems to indicate that as well as the specific beliefs of a particular individual, there are the consensus beliefs of social groups. Indeed, the latter may be more fundamental than the former. What will be shown next is that these consensus beliefs can be treated as probabilities through an extension of the Dutch Book argument.

Earlier we imagined that Ms A (a psychologist) wanted to measure the degree of belief of Mr B in some event E. To do so, she gets Mr B to agree to bet with her on E, under the following conditions. Mr B has to choose a number q (called his betting quotient on E), and then Ms A chooses the stake S. Mr B pays Ms A qS in exchange for S if E occurs. S can be positive or negative, but S must be small in relation to Mr B's wealth. Under these circumstances, q is taken to be a measure of Mr B's degree of belief in E. In order to extend this to social groups, we can retain our psychologist Ms A, but we should replace Mr B by a set $B = \{B_1, B_2, \ldots, B_n\}$ of individuals. We then have the following theorem.

Theorem. Suppose Ms A is betting against $B = \{B_1, B_2, \ldots, B_n\}$ on event E. Suppose B_i chooses betting quotient q_i. Ms A will be able to choose stakes so that she gains money from B whatever happens *unless* $q_1 = q_2 = \ldots = q_n$.

Proof.[4] Let us begin by taking $n = 2$, and let us assume without loss of generality that $q_1 > q_2$. Suppose Ms A chooses $S > 0$ on her bet with B_1, and $-S$ on her bet with B_2. Then if E occurs, Ms A's gain G_1 is given by:

$$G_1 = q_1 S - S - q_2 S + S = (q_1 - q_2)S$$

If E does not occur, Ms A's gain G_2 is given by:

$$G_2 = q_1 S - q_2 S = (q_1 - q_2)S$$

It is clear that $G_1 > 0$ and $G_2 > 0$, unless $q_1 = q_2$.

The generalization from 2 to n is perfectly straightforward. Suppose we have $q_1, q_2, \ldots, q_n$, which are not all equal. Then there must exist q_j and q_k such that $q_j > q_k$. Suppose Ms A chooses $S > 0$ on her bet with B_j, $-S$ on her bet with B_k, and $S = 0$ on her bet with B_i where $i \neq j$ and $i \neq k$. Then, arguing as in the first part of the proof, we conclude that Ms A gains money from B whatever happens. Thus Ms A can gain money from B whatever happens, unless $q_1 = q_2 = \ldots = q_n$.

Informally what this theorem shows is the following. Let B be some social group. Then it is in the interest of B as a whole if its members agree, perhaps as a result of rational discussion, on a common betting quotient rather than each member of the group choosing his or her own betting quotient. If a group does in fact agree on a common betting quotient, this will be called the *intersubjective* or *consensus* probability of the social group. This type of probability can then be contrasted with the *subjective* or *personal* probability of a particular individual.

The Dutch Book argument used to introduce intersubjective probability shows that if the group agrees on a common betting quotient, this protects them against a cunning opponent betting against them. This, then, is a particular mathematical case of an old piece of folk wisdom, the claim, namely, that solidarity within a group protects it against an outside enemy. This point of view is expressed in many traditional maxims and stories. A recent example occurs in Kurosawa's film *Seven Samurai*. In one particular scene, Kambei, the leader of the samurai, is urging the villagers to act together to repel the coming attack by bandits. 'This is a rule of war,' he says. 'Collective defence protects the individual. Individual defence destroys the individual.'

One helpful way of regarding the intersubjective interpretation of probability is to see it as intermediate between the logical interpretation of the early Keynes and the subjective interpretation of his critic, Ramsey. According to the early Keynes, there exists a single rational degree of belief in some conclusion c given evidence e. If this were really so, we would expect nearly all human beings to have this single rational degree of belief in c given e, since, after all, most human beings are rational. Yet in very many cases different individuals come to quite different conclusions, even though they have the same background knowledge and expertise in the relevant area, and even though they are all quite rational. A single rational degree of belief on which all rational human beings should agree seems to be a myth.

So much for the logical interpretation of probability, but the subjective view of probability does not seem to be entirely satisfactory either. Degree of belief is not an entirely personal or individual matter. We very often find an individual human being belonging to a group that shares a common outlook, has some degree of common interest and is able to reach a consensus as regards its beliefs. Obvious examples of such groups would be religious sects, political parties or schools of thought regarding various scientific questions. For such groups the concept of intersubjective probability seems to be the appropriate one. These groups may be small or large, but usually they fall short of embracing the whole of humanity. The intersubjective probability of such a group is thus intermediate between a degree of rational belief (the early Keynes) and a degree of subjective belief (Ramsey).

I shall now try to show in the final section of this chapter that the intersubjective interpretation fits perfectly with Keynes's theory of long-term expectation developed in his 1936 and 1937 publications (see p. 203 above).

KEYNES'S THEORY OF LONG-TERM EXPECTATION

In his 1937 article, Keynes argues that our knowledge of the future yields of investments is 'uncertain' in a sense that he distinguishes from 'probable'. This is what he says (JMK XIV: 113–14):

By 'uncertain' knowledge, let me explain, I do not mean merely to distinguish what is known for certain from what is only probable. The game of roulette is not subject, in this sense, to uncertainty; nor is the prospect of a Victory bond being drawn. Or, again, the expectation of life is only slightly uncertain. Even the weather is only moderately uncertain. The sense in which I am using the term is that in which the prospect of a European war is uncertain, or the price of copper and the rate of interest twenty years hence, or the obsolescence of a new invention, or the position of private wealth owners in the social system in 1970. About these matters there is no scientific basis on which to form any calculable probability whatever. We simply do not know. Nevertheless, the necessity for action and for decision compels us as practical men to do our best to overlook this awkward fact and to behave exactly as we should if we had behind us a good Benthamite calculation of a series of prospective advantages and disadvantages, each multiplied by its appropriate probability, waiting to be summed.

Keynes here uses 'uncertain' in much the same sense as Knight, who in 1921 had distinguished between risk and uncertainty.

Keynes next asks, regarding situations of uncertainty in the above sense (JMK XIV: 114): 'How do we manage in such circumstances to behave in a manner which saves our faces as rational, economic men?' He answers this question by saying that we resort to 'a variety of techniques', of which the most important is the following (JMK XIV: 114):

Knowing that our own individual judgment is worthless, we endeavour to fall back on the judgment of the rest of the world which is perhaps better informed. That is, we endeavour to conform with the behaviour of the majority or the average. The psychology of a society of individuals each of whom is endeavouring to copy the others leads to what we may strictly term a *conventional* judgment.

Keynes's point is that because of lack of information and because of the general uncertainty of the future, entrepreneurs cannot form a rational expectation which then determines their investment decisions. As a result, their expectation is largely conventional, and because of this, it is subject to waves of optimism or pessimism, the general state, that is of the famous 'animal spirits', which Keynes describes as follows (JMK VIII: 161–2):

. . . there is the instability due to the characteristic of human nature that a large proportion of our positive activities depend on spontaneous optimism rather than on a mathematical expectation, whether moral or hedonistic or economic. Most, probably, of our decisions to do something positive, the full consequences of which will be drawn out over many days to come, can only be taken as a result of animal spirits – of a spontaneous urge to action rather than inaction, and not as the outcome of a weighted average of quantitative benefits multiplied by quantitative probabilities . . . Thus if the animal spirits are dimmed and the spontaneous optimism falters, leaving us to depend on nothing but a mathematical expectation, enterprise will fade and die; – though fears of loss may have a basis no more reasonable than hopes of profit had before.

Keynes does not postulate, as a strict follower of Ramsey might have done, that each entrepreneur forms his or her own individual expectation which differs from that of every other entrepreneur. On the contrary, the entrepreneurs imitate each other, so that the group comes to have more or less the same expectation. However, this expectation is not based on a rational assessment, but depends on factors like the state of the 'animal spirits'. What we are dealing with is the intersubjective degree of belief of a group of entrepreneurs which, through a process of social interaction, reaches a consensus. Keynes's long-term expectation is the intersubjective expectation of a group of entrepreneurs and implicitly involves the notion of intersubjective probability. This view is reinforced by the way Keynes sees the role of expert professionals who deal in stock market investments (JMK VII: 154):

. . . most of these persons are, in fact, largely concerned, not with making superior long-term forecasts of the probable yield of an investment over its whole life, but with foreseeing changes in the conventional basis of valuation a short time ahead of the general public. They are concerned, not with what an investment is really worth to a man who buys it 'for keeps', but with what the market will value it at, under the influence of mass psychology, three months or a year hence.

So, my general conclusion is that in his economic writings of 1936 and 1937, Keynes had abandoned his earlier logical interpretation of probability and had in mind a notion of probability that he had not clearly formulated, but that can be explicated by the intersubjective interpretation of probability.

NOTES

1   A more detailed account of Keynes's logical theory, including further examples of paradoxes of the principle of indifference and a discussion of Keynes's attempt to solve them, is to be found in Gillies (2000: ch. 3, 25–49).

2   A more detailed account of Ramsey's views on probability, including a full proof of the Ramsey–De Finetti theorem, is to be found in Gillies (2000: ch. 4, 50–65, and ch. 8, 180–4).

3   What follows is an informal sketch of the intersubjective interpretation of probability. A more detailed account is contained in Gillies and Ietto-Gillies (1991). This is a joint paper written with my wife, who was then Professor of Applied Economics at the University of the South Bank, London. The theory of intersubjective probability as applied to economics was worked out by the two of us together. An account of the theory is also to be found in Gillies (2000: ch. 8, 169–80).

4   I have here included the proof, as it is quite simple, but those lacking in mathematical inclination can omit the proof without losing the general thread of the argument.

12 The art of an ethical life: Keynes and Bloomsbury

Keynes is the only major economist who spent a substantial part of his life embedded (in all the meanings of that term) in a community of artists and creative writers. The most important of these for Keynes were members of the so-called Bloomsbury Group: the artists Duncan Grant, Vanessa Bell, Roger Fry and Dora Carrington; the novelists E. M. Forster, Virginia Woolf and David Garnett; the critics Lytton Strachey, Clive Bell and Desmond McCarthy; and others. To disentangle the impact of Bloomsbury on Keynes from other influences is difficult. Many have worked on the question, notably the biographers of Keynes, Harrod (1951), Moggridge (1992) and Skidelsky (1983, 1992 and 2000), who have examined the complex personal interactions. Others, such as Williams (1980), Annan (2002) and Mini (1991), have pictured Bloomsbury as an intellectual community with deep roots in British cultural history. They have documented, for example, how Keynes's close involvement with the artists Grant and Bell, and his great respect for Roger Fry, help to explain his extraordinary commitment to such institutions as the London Artists Association, the Contemporary Art Society, the Cambridge Arts Theatre and the Arts Council. But was Keynes's professional life as well as his personal life affected by Bloomsbury?

In this chapter, in order to address this question, we examine two closely related topics that intrigued Keynes and the other Bloomsburys. First, how should humans live their lives? And second, how in fact do humans behave in the societies in which they live? The first was an ethical question, the other a behavioural one. This examination leads to a consideration of two related questions about the Bloomsburys, including Keynes. How did they select the subjects of their works of art and literature? And second, why did they employ the distinctive style common as much to Keynes as to the others?

At various points in his writings, Keynes made it clear that he believed that economic activity, and therefore the discipline of economics, should be concerned with far more than simply the production of goods and services to satisfy human wants. There was more to life than increasing consumption under consumer sovereignty. He was not comfortable with the notion of utility as a proxy for human welfare, and his discomfort was especially intense when he looked to the future. In his 1930 essay 'Economic possibilities for our grandchildren' (JMK IX), Keynes argued that 'the economic problem', meaning satisfaction of the biological needs of human beings, was rather close to being solved. As a result of technological progress and capital accumulation, all reasonable human demands for consumption might soon be met, and what was thought of by economists as the eternal 'economic problem' of scarcity would no longer be 'the permanent problem of the human race'. He wrote: 'Thus for the first time since the creation man will be faced with his real, his permanent problem – how to use his freedom from pressing economic cares, how to occupy the leisure, which science and compound interest will have won for him, to live wisely and agreeably and well' (JMK IX: 328). He was not speculating about life in the stationary state, as John Stuart Mill had done. For Keynes, even in the very long run increase in the production of goods and services would not cease; it would simply be directed to other than biological ends. Keynes's question was about how to lead a virtuous life when faced with abundance rather than scarcity.

So where did this heretical suggestion originate, that the economists' stock in trade, the perpetual problem of allocating scarce resources to unlimited consumer wants, would soon disappear? By Keynes's own testimony the disillusionment began in Cambridge during his undergraduate days while under the influence of the philosopher G. E. Moore, and while a member of the exclusive student society the Apostles. Through Moore, Keynes claimed, he and his friends were 'amongst the first to escape Benthamism' (JMK

X: 447). Unlike Bentham, who saw 'the good' as a set of activities that led to the greatest social utility (Bentham 1962), Moore, in his *Principia Ethica*, saw 'the good' as consisting of things that ought to exist for their own sake, things that were 'indefinable' (Moore 1903, 1993: 3). To equate 'the good' with something else, like pleasure or utility, Moore claimed, was a 'naturalistic fallacy'. Moreover, Moore was confident that he knew the things that were most likely to lead to a person experiencing a 'good' state of mind. 'By far the most valuable things, which we know or can imagine,' he said, 'are certain states of consciousness, which may be roughly described as the pleasures of human intercourse and the enjoyment of beautiful objects' (1993: 237).

Moore's ethical doctrine was exhilarating and intensely liberating for the young Cambridge undergraduates, and especially for those who were philosophically inclined, like Keynes and his young friends Leonard Woolf and Lytton Strachey. Moore told them what they wanted to hear, that means should be distinguished from ends, and that aesthetic objectives were the most exalted of ends. But was Moore the inspiration for the comments about economic norms expressed in Keynes's 1930 essay, and did he remain the guiding force among the Bloomsburys who assembled in London after the young men left Cambridge in the early years of the new century? The evidence suggests that the answer may be no, for two reasons at least. First, after drawing a philosophical roadmap, Moore did not prescribe the best path to follow for these young people who were planning their lives, except perhaps that they might practise certain kinds of self-indulgence with a clear conscience. Second, Moore's writings were not easy to read or to interpret, especially for those not trained in philosophy. Take, for example, the experience of Virginia Stephen (later Woolf), who was introduced to the young Cambridge students and to Moore by her brother Thoby. She began to read *Principia Ethica* in August 1910, and she wrote to Clive Bell: 'I am climbing Moore like some industrious insect, who is determined to build a nest on the top of a Cathedral spire. One sentence, a string of "desires" makes my head spin with the infinite meaning of words unadorned. . .' (V. Woolf 1983: 340). Ten days later she was still mired down, and she wrote to Saxon Sydney-Turner: 'I have been reading a good deal, and make some way with Moore, though I have to crawl over the same page a number of times, till

I almost see my own tracks. I shall ask you to enlighten me, but I doubt that I can even ask an intelligent question' (V. Woolf 1983: 352–3). Finally, after three weeks, it was done, and she wrote to her sister Vanessa: 'I finished Moore last night; he has a fine flare of arrogance at the end – and no wonder. I am not so dumb foundered [sic] as I was; but the more I understand, the more I admire' (V. Woolf 1983: 364).

Principia Ethica became a sacred text in Bloomsbury, but paucity of references to it after the Cambridge years suggest it was not of great continuing direct influence. Another body of thought on social values and norms that did, however, come to influence Bloomsbury and Keynes profoundly originated with Group member Roger Fry. A Cambridge undergraduate and Apostle a decade before most of the young men who made up the core of Old Bloomsbury, Fry approached life partly as a painter and art historian, partly as a trained scientist and partly as a journalist. He was rigorous but also comprehensible to a wide audience. Like Moore, among the Bloomsburys Fry was a subject almost of worship – but worship of a different kind. He continued to interact with them closely and guided them in their daily lives. Virginia Woolf expressed the consensus of the Group in a letter to her sister in 1928: 'Roger is the only civilised man I have ever met, and I continue to think him the plume in our cap; the vindication, asservation – and all the rest of it – If Bloomsbury had produced only Roger, it would be on a par with Athens at its prime' (V. Woolf 1977: 566).

Fry's reflections on the nature of human accomplishment began in the 1890s as he explored the history of art, and in particular the role of artistic entrepreneurs such as Joshua Reynolds. His first synthetic statement came in a talk in 1909 that ultimately became 'An Essay in Aesthetics' and a chapter in his book *Vision and Design* (1920b). The essay was concerned principally with the nature of aesthetic experience that Fry, following Tolstoy, saw as the communication of aesthetic emotion from artist to audience. This communication was facilitated by the presence in works of art of 'purposeful order and variety' (Fry 1909 in Goodwin 1998: 80), what Clive Bell would later call 'significant form' (C. Bell 1914). Fry pictured human life as divided into two separate compartments, the 'actual life' and the 'imaginative life'. The former included eating, drinking, procreating and making a living, and could be understood using Darwinian biological metaphors such as competition for scarce resources. Here the Benthamite calculus was useful to portray forces on both sides of market interactions. Fry was trained in evolutionary biology at Cambridge, and he did not doubt the need for humans to attend carefully to their actual life. But he believed that the imaginative life, meaning the life of the mind, distinguished humans from other biological organisms and was of a higher order of significance than the actual life. Here were the arts, literature and disinterested inquiry, which included pure (in contrast to applied) science. He wrote: 'most people would, I think, say that the pleasures derived from art were of an altogether different character and more fundamental than merely sensual pleasures, that they did exercise some faculties which are felt to belong to whatever part of us there may be which is not entirely ephemeral and material' (Fry 1909: 76). Progress in human affairs for Fry included enrichment of both the imaginative and actual lives, but because there was declining marginal utility from goods consumed in the actual life but not in the imaginative life, human progress should witness a steadily increasing proportion of resources devoted to the imaginative life. Although, Fry conceded, it should not be claimed that the imaginative life was necessarily more moral than the actual life, as Ruskin had done (G. C. Moore 2005), the imaginative life could establish moral standards to be used in the actual life. He observed that 'the imaginative life comes in the course of time to represent more or less what mankind feels to be the completest expression of its own nature, the freest use of its innate capacities, the actual life may be explained and justified by its approximation here and there, however partially and inadequately, to that freer and fuller life' (Fry 1909: 76). A danger in making the best allocation of resources between the actual and imaginative lives, Fry noted, were 'feelings of rivalry and emulation' that receive 'encouragement' they 'scarcely deserve' (Fry 1909: 79). In later works (especially *Art and Commerce* (1926)), Fry, following Veblen (1899), made emulation virtually a third sphere of life that humans must make efforts to constrain.

The graphic arts for Fry, the artist, not surprisingly had a critical role in the imaginative life. 'Art, then, is, if I am right, the chief organ of the imaginative life; it is by art that it is stimulated and controlled within us, and, as we have seen, the imaginative life is distinguished by the greater clearness of perception, and the greater purity and freedom of its emotion' (Fry 1909: 77).

In the Fry framework, the ethical objectives of a society must be to meet the biological needs of humanity generously, limit the emulative instincts vigorously, and devote residual resources to the arts and sciences. Adherence to these principles came to be called by the Bloomsburys 'civilization'. Precisely how resources should be used in a civilized life was for them a legitimate matter for dispute, but as a rule the Bloomsburys hoped that as much as possible could be accomplished in the private sector rather than through the public sphere. In his 1928 book *Civilization*, Clive Bell attempted to reconcile Fry and Moore. He saw Fry's prescription for civilization as the way to achieve Moore's states of mind. It was necessary fundamentally, Bell said, to instil in society 'a sense of values and reason enthroned'. The sense of values had, in turn, to be expressed as effective demands for the products of 'art and thought and knowledge'. This conclusion presented a problem for conventional economic analysis because these items had to be purchased 'for their own sake and not for their possible utility' (C. Bell 1928 [1973]: 72).

If we examine Keynes's propositions in his 'Economic Possibilities' essay against the Fry doctrine of civilization, they are easily understood. Keynes is looking ahead through Fry's eyeglasses to a time only barely anticipated by Fry, when no additional resources would be needed for the actual life and society could concentrate most of its attention on the imaginative life. Keynes observed shrewdly that when this time came, attitudes and institutions would have to change dramatically – if not, the 'relative needs' of the emulative side of life would eat up any amount of surplus product. The following statement by Keynes could easily have come from Fry:

Now it is true that the needs of human beings may seem to be insatiable. But they fall into two classes – those needs which are absolute in the sense that we feel them whatever the situation of our fellow human beings may be, and those which are relative in the sense that we feel them only if their satisfaction lifts us above, makes us feel superior to, our fellows. Needs of the second class, those which satisfy the desire for superiority, may indeed be insatiable; for the higher the general level, the higher still are they. But this is not so true of the absolute needs – a point may soon be reached, much sooner perhaps than we all of us are aware of, when these needs are satisfied in the sense that we prefer to devote our further energies to non-economic purposes.

(JMK IX: 326)

Addressing an urgent concern of the Bloomsburys, Keynes added that warfare might also put off the day when ample resources would be available for 'the real values of life'. He added that another danger lay with unconstrained population growth. 'I draw the conclusion that, assuming no important wars and no important increase in population, the *economic problem* may be solved, or be at least in sight of solution, within a hundred years. This means that the economic problem is not – if we look into the future – *the permanent problem of the human race*' (JMK IX: 326).

Each of the Bloomsburys had a distinctive conception of what should take place in the imaginative life, what constituted 'civilization'. For example, in 1905 Virginia Woolf declared: 'To be civilised is to have taken the measure of our own capabilities and to hold them in a perfect state of discipline. . .' (V. Woolf 1986: 29). Clive Bell declared that a true civilization was characterized by 'reasonableness and a sense of values' (1928: 54). They all agreed that human welfare involved much more than the consumption of goods and services in the actual life – and that the most important events occurred in the imaginative life. Keynes chose his words carefully when he concluded his speech at a dinner honouring his retirement from the editorship of the *Economic Journal*. He offered a toast 'to economists, who are the trustees, not of civilisation, but of the possibility of civilisation' (Skidelsky 2000: 168). The true trustees of civilization, he might have added, were the artists and writers with whom he spent much of his life.

HOW HUMANS BEHAVE

At the core of Keynes's *General Theory of Employment, Interest and Money* is the conviction that because all economic actors face uncertainty about the future, their decisions about what to do down the road, no matter how 'rational', are likely to be inconsistent one with another. Savers may decide to save more than investors invest, employers may plan to hire more labour than workers supply. But these variables must somehow be reconciled in the event, and sometimes this reconciliation has unfortunate consequences, such as unemployment and stagnation. Keynes knew that the economy had built into it mechanisms designed to resolve inconsistencies, notably competitive markets that caused prices, wages and interest rates to fluctuate and thereby to achieve market-clearing equilibria. Most economists in Keynes's time, and since, have been confident in the power of these adjustment mechanisms to do their jobs. They acknowledge that there may be delays in adjustment, as well as impediments introduced by market concentration, but these are merely transitory. So why was Keynes so concerned about these inconsistencies? One answer may simply be that he reflected the generally gloomy Bloomsbury view about the capacity for human accommodation. Much of the Bloomsbury literature and works of art, and indeed their style of life, was predicated on the presumption that personal, social, political, cultural, international and economic institutions inherited from the Victorian age were no longer able, if they ever had been, to resolve the destructive tensions resulting from inconsistent expectations. The First World War was the most catastrophic example of the results of inconsistent expectations in their experience. Instead of starting from the presumption that existing adjustment mechanisms would work, the Bloomsburys usually presumed just the opposite, and they looked immediately for alternatives. But to find satisfactory alternative mechanisms the biggest challenge, they discovered, was to change the basic psychological attitudes of actors as well as the institutions through which they interacted. To emerge from the Great Depression, Keynes suggested, one of the major challenges was to achieve 'the readjustment of the habits and instincts of the ordinary man, bred into him for countless generations, which he may be asked to discard within a few decades' (JMK IX: 327). The Bloomsburys made similar claims about countless other habits and instincts throughout society. A few examples will illustrate this point.

One of the serious sources of tension in contemporary life, the Bloomsburys believed, arose from inconsistent expectations within Victorian marriage. A familiar plot line in their fiction portrays a dysfunctional family torn apart by divergent hopes, aspirations and expectations of the members. Failure to achieve reconciliation of crucial differences results in tragedy. In E. M. Forster's short fable *Other Kingdom*, an English country gentleman sets out to train an untamed Irish bride to become lady of the house. But she has a different set of values and expectations for the marriage, and these cannot be shaken; indeed, her obstinacy is made worse by an education he mistakenly provides in classical literature. Eventually, when no accommodation can be found, she simply disappears into the wood, apparently to become a tree (Forster 1928). A similar story can be found in David Garnett's novel *Lady into Fox* (1923). Again, an insensitive husband forces his young bride to accept his values and his expectations for her behaviour, including participation in a fox hunt. They argue, after which she herself inexplicably turns into a fox. The husband then attempts to explore alternative forms for their relationship, but it is too late, and ultimately the vixen is killed by hounds. Both of these stories centre on tensions in marriage that grow from a supposedly greater sensitivity to nature in women than in men. Because of their subservient position, the wives are forced to acquiesce in behaviour destructive of nature, and they rebel. There is no mechanism for successful reconciliation of these differences, and the marriages collapse.

In the novels of Virginia Woolf, the dysfunctional families are of a less fabulous kind than in Forster and Garnett. In *Mrs. Dalloway* (1925) most of the principal characters are trapped in failed marriages of easily recognizable kinds, and all are constrained by inconsistent expectations, with no way to achieve reconciliation. Clarissa Dalloway and her friends Sally Seton and Peter Walsh all dreamed in their youth of 'civilization', and of abundant time spent in 'the imaginative life'. Instead, they find themselves at middle age in empty relationships with spouses who do not share their aspirations and committed to suffocating actual and emulative lives in politics, business and the colonial service. By contrast, the Italian war bride Rezia has come to England with dreams of a family and peace of mind. Instead, she finds herself bound to a suicidal victim of post-traumatic stress and with no obvious way out. In her novel *To the Lighthouse* (1927), Virginia Woolf explores relationships within her own family, with her tyrannical father the centrepiece and her self-sacrificing mother the heroine. In this story, the children as much as the parents are victims of a Victorian marriage founded on inconsistent expectations from which there seems no escape.

All of these fictional Bloomsbury marriages revolve around the problem of male–female relationships in a modern society. Although for the most part women are portrayed as the victims of an oppressive and obsolete institution, there is little assignment of blame to the men, and in a sense everyone is portrayed as a victim. Moreover, there is no leap to a public-policy conclusion and recommendation except that, by implication, there is unanimous agreement on the importance of greater equality and economic independence for women in marriage. In their own personal lives, the Bloomsburys certainly experimented with a number of creative solutions to the marital problems described in their fiction, including psychoanalysis and relationships 'à trois'.

At a higher level of generality, Bloomsbury fiction focused regularly on problems that arose out of inconsistent hopes and expectations among classes, cultures and nations. The novels of E. M. Forster demonstrate this concern very clearly. The main tension in *Howards End* (1910), for example, arises from the interaction of three social classes. The lower-middle-class Leonard Bast yearns to rise above his station; the upper-middle-class Schlegel sisters would like to help but don't know how and make things worse. The Wilcoxes, a family of *nouveaux-riches* tycoons, misunderstand both the Basts and the Schlegels, and tragedy occurs for all three families on a grand scale. The moral of the story seems to be that class division leads to costly misunderstandings and inconsistent behaviour among humans living together in one society. If the elimination of social classes is too utopian a dream, then tolerance and improvement in communication might reconcile some of the differences.

Two novels by Forster illustrate how tragedy can result from inconsistent expectations at still other levels of society. In one of his early novels, *Where Angels Fear to Tread* (1905), an Englishwoman flees the stifling constraints of Victorian Britain for a holiday in a free-spirited Italian mountain village. To the horror of her British family, she marries a local man and then dies in childbirth. The British and Italian families battle over custody of the baby, and in the process the child dies in an accident. The root cause of the final conflict between the families is differing expectations over how a child should be raised, and the tragedy cannot be averted because the dominant cultural practices and institutions will not permit a reconciliation. In *A Passage to India* (1927), Forster deals with the insurmountable difficulties present in empires because the governors simply cannot understand the governed, and vice versa. Whenever the British and Indians plan something together, even something as simple as a visit to a cave, it fails because of their incapacity to look ahead and plan co-operatively. The powerful message of this novel, as it was in Leonard Woolf's *Village in the Jungle* (1913) and David Garnett's *Sailor's Return* (1925), is that empires are doomed to failure. The inconsistencies are simply too great to be solved by any improvements in communication, education or institutional reform.

The closest parallel in Bloomsbury to the inconsistent expectations that play such a large part in Keynes's *General Theory* can be found in Leonard Woolf's three-volume political history of the West, initially entitled *After the Deluge* but with the last volume bearing a title of its own, *Principia Politica*, suggested by Keynes with a side-glance undoubtedly to Newton and to Moore, two of his idols. In this trilogy, Woolf sees Western history dominated by the ebbs and flows of 'communal psychology' that reflect bodies of thought. At the beginning of volume I, he stresses the importance of ideas, even inchoate ones, which determine man's fate: 'Whether in individuals or in communities, nothing is so unusual or so dangerous as thought. Thought leads to action and action to change, and once things begin to change with thought as the impulse, a movement is started the end of which can neither be controlled nor foreseen' (L. Woolf 1931: 23). He continued: 'The ideas which form the content of communal psychology, and which are causes of world catastrophes and landmarks in history, are not simple. They have puzzled the wisest and subtlest minds, and few if any of those who are prepared to die or to make others die for them could express them in intelligible language' (L. Woolf 1931: 31).

Woolf's comments about the influence of deceased thinkers on current affairs, published five years before the *General Theory*, may be compared to Keynes's words on the same subject. Woolf wrote:

At every particular moment it is the dead rather than the living who are making history, for politically individuals think dead men's thoughts and pursue dead men's ideals . . . These dead ideas which are inconsistent and unmeaning in their new environment necessarily come in conflict with the new ideas which new circumstances have brought to life. But the old is

nearly always stronger than the new, and the dead than the living . . .
Practically every political principle and idea, every social principle or aim,
if it is widely accepted, will be found to be controlled to a considerable
extent by the dead mind.

(L. Woolf 1931: 33, 34, 36)

It is hard to believe that Keynes did not have these words of his
close friend and frequent collaborator in mind when he commented
at the beginning and end of the *General Theory*. In the preface he
says: 'The difficulty lies, not in the new ideas, but in escaping from
the old ones, which ramify, for those brought up as most of us have
been, into every corner of our minds' (JMK VII: viii). He ends the last
chapter with one of his most oft-cited passages:

The ideas of economists and political philosophers, both when they are
right and when they are wrong, are more powerful than is commonly understood. Indeed, the world is ruled by little else. Practical men, who believe
themselves to be quite exempt from any intellectual influences, are usually
the slaves of some defunct economist. Madmen in authority, who hear
voices in the air, are distilling their frenzy from some academic scribbler
of a few years back. I am sure that the power of vested interests is vastly
exaggerated compared with the gradual encroachment of ideas. Not, indeed,
immediately, but after a certain interval; for in the fields of economic and
political philosophy there are not many who are influenced by new theories
after they are twenty-five or thirty years of age, so that the ideas which civil
servants and politicians and even agitators apply to current events are not
likely to be the newest. But soon or late, it is ideas, not vested interests,
which are dangerous for good or evil.

(JMK VII: 383–4)

The ideas from the past that concerned Keynes were not the same
as those that concerned Woolf. Whereas Keynes was concerned with
Say's Law, the Treasury view and whether *laissez-faire* was an
appropriate posture for the state, Woolf was concerned with notions
of freedom, nationality, democracy and empire. The inconsistencies in economic and political expectations that Woolf outlined
could not, even in theory, be resolved by competitive markets.
Early in the eighteenth century, he observed, there was still widespread acceptance of the economic and political status quo. The
existing distribution of both political power and economic goods
and services, whatever it was, was thought to be 'natural' and in-
equality inevitable. Inherited social and political status and wealth

were widely accepted as immutable, and this view was sustained
by cultural and religious doctrine. Towards the end of the eighteenth century, however, the situation changed dramatically. Political thinkers such as Thomas Jefferson, Thomas Paine, William
Godwin, William Cobbett and Jeremy Bentham proposed variants
of a new democratic theory that promised liberty, equality and
fraternity for all citizens. The power of these ideas was reflected
in the French and American revolutions. At the same time, however, the 'hand of economics' was emerging in a body of new
economic theory that had very different messages. It promised
efficiency and consumer sovereignty through free market capitalism, and required instead of the promised conditions of the new
democracy adherence to the rules of competitive markets, respect
for property rights and rewards determined by contribution to production rather than a commitment to equality. Woolf suggested
that it would be hard to imagine a better recipe than this for
inconsistent expectations. Political theory promised one set of outcomes, economic theory another, and disappointment was inevitable. The inconsistency had quickly become obvious. However, the
Western democracies were reluctant to acknowledge the contra-
dictions and continued to live by the myths. They refused to
explore new policies and institutions that might resolve the tensions and prescribe a new way ahead. The result was mounting
political conflict, labour strife, monopolistic exploitation and ideological cynicism during the nineteenth century. By the 1930s, a
crisis had been reached.

   The whole of this economic organization is inconsistent with
the fundamental tenets of democracy. The common happiness,
which is the object of social organization, according to the demo-
crat, can only be attained by the co-operation of free and equal
individuals. For the working of our industrial organization, we rely
upon a complicated system of privilege, monopoly and class war.
Here there is no co-operation of free and equal individuals for
any common object; there is a struggle between the employer for
profits and the employed for wages. The quantity of material things
or wealth that each side can snatch for itself from the operation
of the economic system is determined ultimately by a kind of
economic war, by the force that it can bring to bear upon some
section of the community (L. Woolf 1931: 316).

Matthew Arnold appreciated the seriousness of this mounting problem of inconsistent promises and expectations by the middle of the nineteenth century, but he could not come up with a solution. The Jacobins, Marx, Nietzsche and even H. L. Mencken too had essentially thrown up their hands and called for violent change. The characteristic Bloomsbury response that Woolf gave was that there could be a moderate and constructive alternative that would involve change in ideas, attitudes (communal psychology) and social institutions. The challenge was to put the alternative in place.

TOPICS FOR ATTENTION

The subjects to which Keynes devoted much of his scholarly career and the style with which he addressed them follow directly from the Bloomsbury concern with the two questions of how to live the virtuous life and how humans actually do live their lives. The Bloomsburys were far from being starry-eyed utopians on the question of how to achieve the ethical life. They concluded that humans faced formidable obstacles, within themselves and within society, in approaching perfection. But they seldom counselled inaction or resignation. They were confident that it was possible to discover the obstacles and to defeat them. The first task, however, was to understand what the obstacles were and how they might be addressed. For this, the novelists had a key role. Let us examine only one example: the first widely successful novel to come out of Bloomsbury, *Howards End* (1910), by Keynes's friend and fellow Kingsman E. M. Forster (briefly discussed on p. 226 above). A brief review of the plot suggests the parallel to Keynes's later research in economics. A principal character is Leonard Bast, a lower-middle-class clerical worker who tries desperately to experience an imaginative life that he senses is out there but that he cannot fully grasp. With little formal education he reaches clumsily for guidance and attends a large public concert and lecture with a charismatic speaker who sounds very much like Roger Fry. Bast is taken under the wings of two well-meaning, upper-middle-class, intellectual young women (based on Vanessa and Virginia Stephen?) who are sympathetic towards but also puzzled by his pretensions. Ultimately, despite taking advice from a rich friend, the sisters do little for Bast except get him permanently unemployed; their fumbling efforts at private charity lead ultimately to his premature death. Central themes of *Howards End* are thus the yearning of the working classes to rise above their biological lives and the feckless response, or total disregard, they experience from both the leaders of the market economy and concerned intellectuals. Although Forster, like the other novelists, does not take the next step of proposing policy solutions to the problems he has identified, the reader is led to appreciate the need for, first, more systematic public education in the art of how to live as much as how to work, and, second, for a governmental programme to relieve the human costs of unemployment. It is surely not coincidence that these two needs became lifelong concerns of Keynes's.

The Bloomsburys were certain that human progress would not occur automatically through some sort of Benthamite accumulation of ever larger amounts of utility. As Clive Bell insisted, civilization was not 'natural'; it required education of the citizens and creative leadership (Bell 1928: 119). The siren song of emulative competition could always be heard in the background, and humans had to be led by the hand along the paths of ethical spending. The Bloomsburys did not have much faith in the capacity of government to operate a Pigovian programme of encouraging activities with positive externalities and discouraging those with negative ones. Experience during the First World War convinced them of the callous and inefficient character of many senior civil servants, personified by Hugh Whitbread in Virginia Woolf's *Mrs. Dalloway* (1925).

Leadership in the achievement of human progress had to be accepted as a responsibility by those who had the capacity to provide it. An intellectual elite, whom Morgan Forster called 'an aristocracy of the sensitive, the considerate and the plucky' (Forster 1951: 70), must discover and demonstrate ways of living and forms of social organization that would achieve desired objectives while preserving fundamental values of personal freedom. Some of the Bloomsburys spent their energies attacking practices and institutions that they found to be inimical to civilization, such as empire, militarism, racial prejudice and the oppression of women. Keynes set out to discover public policies that would achieve economic progress, upon which civilization depended, while at the same time protecting human liberty. His proposals for institutional reform were mainly for the creation of advisory bodies at the national level and international organizations that would introduce the heavy hand of bureaucracy as little as possible.

Public education was also an essential reform for Keynes – less to relieve the pain of industrialization, as desired by Adam Smith, than to equip the citizen for self-government, as demanded by John Stuart Mill. Education for Keynes also had two other purposes: to guide humans to get the most out of their brief stay on earth through participation in the imaginative life, and to reduce instability in the economy and society by providing wide and open access to proven fact. This position was similar to that of Roger Fry who, on the last point, applauded the stability that well-trained critics brought to art markets (Goodwin 1998: 33–4).

Because they recognized that understanding human behaviour was the key to comprehending human institutions and practices, and to making them better, the Bloomsburys turned very early to the young discipline of psychology. They canvassed thoroughly the authorities of the time for answers to questions about the arts and creativity, the family, sources of conflict and the seemingly mercurial fecklessness of humans: they examined Freud, Jung, James, Trotter, Ross and others, and several in the Group became practising psychoanalysts (Meisel and Kendrick 1985, and Fry 1924). But for the most part, they came away disappointed; their questions remained unanswered. And so they set themselves up as amateur psychologists, as biographers. They were determined to learn through close case studies. The high proportion of the Bloomsbury literature and works of art that is concerned with biography – including fictional characters and painted portraits by the artists – is striking (Shone 1976). And this was true across the Group, even to the social scientists. Has any great economist, other than Keynes, produced a volume of *Essays in Biography*? Keynes's fascination with biography was definitely not merely a personal eccentricity or an exercise in hagiography; it had deep heuristic roots.

A conviction shared in Bloomsbury by the end of the First World War was that progress in the achievement of civilization was incompatible with warfare or internal conflict, not simply because of the resources that were destroyed and wasted but especially because of the psychological impact on the participants. In particular, they were horrified at what otherwise right-minded people would do when gripped by fear, first during the war and then during the depressed two decades that followed. They watched in anguish as outrageous propaganda was tolerated, civil liberties were eroded and opportunities in the imaginative life were foreclosed. They responded both by trying to explain the mass psychology of fear (e.g. L. Woolf 1925, 1935) and by combatting it through the arts, notably the decoration of Berwick Church, and the activities of the Council for the Encouragement of Music and the Arts by Keynes during the Second World War (Skidelsky 2000: 286–99). Fear was a major consideration in Bloomsbury political analysis; they concluded that it contributed to the rise of totalitarian regimes in the 1930s, and they favoured gradual political change over revolution partly because of the difficulty of controlling violence once fear had taken hold. Fear also held an important place in Keynes's economics, as a spur to saving during the early years of industrialization, and as a block to consumption and investment-spending during recession. The distinguished art historian and disciple of Roger Fry, Kenneth Clark, was horrified in the 1960s when his celebrated book and television series *Civilisation*, in which he identified social tranquility and absence of fear as conditions for creative progress, were applauded by political conservatives as simply a defence of their own values (Secrest 1986: 232).

Religion was another topic on which everyone in Bloomsbury typically had strong views. They were in most cases neither typical atheists nor even agnostics. They accepted mystical elements in human life, and in varying degrees they appreciated some ceremonial aspects of formal religion. Duncan Grant and Vanessa Bell were buried side by side in Firle churchyard, and Keynes asked that his ashes be placed in King's College Chapel, a request that was forgotten (Skidelsky 2000: 473). Yet they found religion to be a prime source of both fear and unreason – two enemies of civilization. The concept of original sin as perpetrated in the Garden of Eden they found to be especially noxious, and in their writings and their works of art they returned often to the Book of Genesis to revisit and discredit this and other stories that they decided had been told as much for political as for literary reasons or for reasons of faith (Goodwin 2000). Keynes joined in their repeated references to Adam and Eve, Noah, Jonah and other Old Testament figures who personified values and judgements of which they disapproved.

RHETORICAL STYLE

By the time Keynes sat down to write his first major work, the Bloomsbury rhetorical style was well established, and he adopted it with alacrity for at least two reasons – first, because it was dramatically successful in reaching a wide audience and stimulating discussion, and, second, because it was good fun. The style had its roots in the year 1910, when Bloomsbury shocked the respectable British public by bringing to London an exhibition of Post-Impressionist paintings that enraged both the viewers and the artistic establishment (Stansky 1996). In so doing, they declared themselves committed iconoclasts, and in their own commentary on the exhibition they confronted and attacked a wide range of old verities and respected leaders of polite opinion. In particular, they learned to use well-known individuals as personifications of revered institutions and points of view. For example, Roger Fry repeatedly attacked the Victorian artist Sir Lawrence Alma-Tadema as representing all conventional Victorian artistic values, and also the Royal Academy of which he was president. In some respects, this rhetorical device was unfair, but it proved very effective. It was widely perceived as 'bad form' and incurred the wrath of respectable people, wrath that rains down upon Bloomsbury still. This iconoclastic style was extended and perfected by Clive Bell in his highly popular little book *Art* (1914), by Lytton Strachey in *Eminent Victorians* (1918), by Virginia Woolf in *Mr. Bennett and Mrs. Brown* (1924) and by others in the Group. In Keynes's writings, the Bloomsbury style appears first in *Economic Consequences of the Peace* (1919), where the Treaty of Versailles is attacked through the character of the negotiating heads of state. But it remained a characteristic feature of his later writings as well; repeatedly he emphasized the revolutionary nature of his own contributions, and he personified classical economics through Ricardo and what we now call neoclassical economics through Pigou. And just as Roger Fry and Lytton Strachey, as a result of their exhilarating style, found themselves at the head of bands of young rebels, so too did Keynes – and it was sweet.

Other distinctive features of Keynes's style that may be explained by his immersion in Bloomsbury include his apparently insatiable thirst for publicity, as befits a public intellectual who seeks to reach an audience of doers as much as scholars. Like Fry, he often irritated his followers by seeming never to declare a subject closed. Fry explained his own attitude towards this approach thus: 'I have always looked on my system with a certain suspicion. I have recognised that if it ever formed too solid a crust it might stop the inlets of fresh experience' (Fry 1920a: 87). Keynes famously allowed his great works almost to merge together. He had barely finished the *Treatise* before he declared it obsolete and announced work on the *General Theory*. A related Bloomsbury trait was a reluctance to engage in extensive controversy outside the Group. To persuade sceptics or disarm critics was simply not high among their priorities. After Roger Fry was attacked viciously by Wyndham Lewis over an incident at the Omega Workshops, he astonished his friends and irritated his enemies by refusing to reply (Collins 1984: 54–9). Similarly, it remained a puzzle why, after the abundant comment on the *General Theory*, both positive and negative, Keynes did not straighten out the commentators.

A distinctive feature of much Bloomsbury art and literature is the repeated reference to stories from classical and biblical writings. Some of these references can be explained simply by the authors' classical education and upbringing in the Protestant religion. They referred to what they knew. But there was more! It seems that they were struck by the continuing value of these texts to an understanding of contemporary issues. For example, ancient Athenians were as concerned as were modern Britons with how to achieve lasting peace, how to reform empire and above all how to enjoy the good life. Sometimes the Bloomsburys found in the early texts wisdom of a general kind – for example, to pursue moderation in all things. Sometimes the advice was more precise. They claimed the approach of Euripides to lessen fear rooted in religious superstition was useful still (L. Woolf 1953: 68). They too set out to retell and reinterpret the old myths so as to remove their sting. They found other devices, like the personification of nature in the god Pan, to be a clever way of drawing attention to the destruction of wild flora and fauna that occurred during industrialization (Forster 1928: 3–38). In Keynes's writings we see frequent references to Adam, Midas, Jonah and other characters as shorthand for behavioural qualities that deserved special attention. He and the other Bloomsburys were intrigued by how these early societies made the case for saving over consumption even though they had subsistence economies. The need for savings they took to be the sub-text of the Book of Genesis as well as of other parts of the bible. The Bloomsbury painters selected as the subject for one of the large murals in Berwick Church the biblical parable of the Wise and Foolish Virgins. Here the economic moral is clear. The profligate, foolish virgins use up all the oil for their lamps, so that when God arrives he cannot see them; the wise and economical virgins, by contrast, save their oil and have ample illumination for the critical moment. The Bloomsburys concluded that as the time arrived when adequate aggregate spending, rather than saving, needed to be sustained, myths of this kind had to be re-examined and, through re-telling, have their message changed. A biblical parable that especially intrigued Keynes was that of the widow's cruse, a vessel that remained full no matter how much was taken from it (JMK V: 125). He used this to demonstrate how 'profits as a source of capital increment' would return to entrepreneurs no matter whether they were spent on consumption or investment and would remain 'undepleted however much of them may be devoted to riotous living'.

CONCLUSIONS

Keynes perceived that the art of the ethical life was far more complex than that understood by the typical neo-classical economist of his time. Just as the economics discipline was agreeing to the Benthamite doctrine that virtue consisted in taking advantage of all opportunities to maximize utility subject to constraints, he accepted the Bloomsbury–Moore–Fry doctrine that virtue lay in attending well to the biological needs, resisting emulation and then moving as quickly as possible into the imaginative life, with assistance offered to others to follow suit. Keynes himself seems to have lived by this doctrine. But the thesis of this chapter goes beyond this, to suggest that Bloomsbury principles affected his professional as well as his personal life and may have made him both a more ethical human being and a more ethical economist as well.

13 Keynes and ethics

MOORE

In his famous essay 'My early beliefs', written in September 1938, Keynes bears witness to the impact of Moore's *Principia Ethica* (1993), first printed in 1903, on his early beliefs: 'I went up to Cambridge at Michaelmas 1902, and Moore's *Principia Ethica* came out at the end of my first year. I have never heard of the present generation having read it. But, of course, its effect on *us*, and the talk which preceded and followed it, dominated, and perhaps still dominate, everything else' (JMK X: 435). He continues: 'It seems to me looking back, that this religion of ours was a very good one to grow up under. It remains nearer the truth than any other that I know, with less irrelevant extraneous matter and nothing to be ashamed of . . . It is still my religion under the surface' (JMK X: 442).

Several aspects of Moore's work were important. Moore's claim that there has been a fallacy, the 'naturalistic fallacy', in almost all previous ethical theories released Keynes and his friends from the weight of tradition and, they thought, set them free to approach ethics afresh. Looking back at it in 1938, the publication of Moore's book was 'the opening of a new heaven on a new earth' (JMK X: 435), and this is indeed just how Keynes expressed himself at the time: in 1906 when he was studying ethics for his Civil Service entry examinations, Keynes expressed his enthusiasm for Moore in a letter (21 February 1906) to Lytton Strachey:

It is *impossible* to exaggerate the wonder and originality of Moore. People are already beginning to talk as if he were only a logic-chopping eclectic. Oh why can't they see!

How amazing to think that we and only we know the rudiments of a true
theory of ethics, for nothing can be more certain than that the broad outline
is true. What is the world doing? It does damned well bring it home to read
books written before *PE*. I even begin to agree with Moore about Sidgwick –
that he was a wicked edifactious person.

(KCKP, PP/45/316/2/122)

As these remarks indicate, for Keynes Moore's book not only
legitimated a contemptuous dismissal of the past, it also offered a
new method of ethical inquiry, the method of 'reflective isolation',
which gave confidence to Keynes and his friends that they themselves could arrive at ethical knowledge. For Moore taught that if
one clears one's mind of inherited assumptions and unambigu-
ously identifies the ethical questions that one needs to answer, the
answers to these questions are not difficult to find. In 'My early
beliefs', Keynes quotes Moore's notorious presentation in this way
of his 'Ideal':

Indeed, once the meaning of the question is clearly understood, the answer
to it, in its main outlines, appears to be so obvious, that it runs the risk of
seeming to be a platitude. By far the most valuable things, which we can
know or can imagine, are certain states of consciousness, which may be
roughly described as the pleasures of human intercourse and the enjoyment
of beautiful objects.

(Moore 1993: 237)

But it was not just Moore's unfettered method of ethical inquiry
that appealed to the young Keynes; Moore's own ideal, his affirmation of the supreme value of love and beauty, also attracted him. For
it offered the thought that a life organized round these values would
be the best of lives, since, as Moore put it, 'it is only for the sake of
these things – in order that as much of them as possible may at some
time exist – that any one can be justified in performing any public
or private duty' (Moore 1993: 238).

A century later, we cannot sensibly share Keynes's youthful enthusiasm for Moore's *Principia Ethica*, even though the book remains an essential point of reference for subsequent ethical debate.
Moore's thesis that there is a fundamental mistake, the 'naturalistic
fallacy' or some similar error, in the work of his predecessors is
itself mistaken. Most of them simply do not propose the kind of
reductive theory of ethical value, naturalistic or metaphysical,

whose incoherence Moore seeks to expose. Although they maintain that there are connections between ethical values and possibilities for human fulfilment, these connections are usually taken
to express the fact that we are intrinsically ethical beings, not that
ethical value can be defined in terms of a neutral conception of
human nature. Moore's own ideal is a good case to think about.
Love and beauty are indeed of great value; but Moore's view that
one cannot give reasons for this judgement and that we should
therefore accept it as if it were as self-evident as an elementary
truth of arithmetic is unpalatable. By contrast, if one adopts the
traditional view that ethical values connect with possibilities for
human fulfilment, the question of the value of love and beauty
should be, in principle, susceptible of explication and sensible discussion. For what is needed is a sensitive account of the role of love and
beauty in our lives, and while this is far from straightforward, the
complex lives, writings and other achievements of Keynes's friends
in the Bloomsbury Group, such as Virginia Woolf, are in fact a
profound resource for this project, since it is only through engaging
with such complexities as these that it is possible to arrive at a just
estimation of the value of love and beauty and set them alongside
other values such as truth, loyalty and compassion.

   It is notable that among the works that Keynes studied and wrote
about, both as a student and later, there is scarcely any reference to
those by John Stuart Mill. There are occasional references to Mill's
Political Economy throughout Keynes's writings, but there is no
discussion of Mill's attempt at a synthesis of Benthamite utilitarianism and Coleridgean romanticism, as in his famous essay *On
Liberty*. This omission is probably to be explained by the influence
of Moore's notorious critique in *Principia Ethica* of Mill's alleged
'proof' of utilitarianism, in which he accuses Mill of 'as naive and
artless a use of the naturalistic fallacy as anybody could desire'
(Moore 1993: 118) in proposing that the only evidence that something is desirable is that people actually desire it. It is in fact clear
from the context of Mill's essay on 'Utilitarianism' in which the
offending discussion occurs that Mill is not guilty of the fallacy of
which Moore seeks to convict him, since Mill's 'evidence' is only
intended to be, in Mill's phrase, a 'consideration capable of determining the understanding', and not a strict proof of a kind that
Mill, like Moore, takes to be unavailable concerning fundamental

ethical judgements. But Moore's discussion seems to have persuaded a generation of readers that as far as ethics is concerned Mill had little to add to Bentham. In truth, however, Mill's writings, especially his *Autobiography* and *On Liberty*, are among the most profound explorations of the difficulties inherent in balancing a concern for public welfare with the practice of creative individual achievement. Since Keynes himself recognized this tension both in such early writings as his 1905 Apostles essay 'Modern civilisation' and in such later political essays as 'Am I a Liberal?' and 'Liberalism and labour' (JMK IX), it is, I think, to be regretted that Keynes never engaged seriously with Mill's ethical and political writings.[1] They might well have helped him to develop his own liberal ideas and to respond creatively to his critics; they might even have led him to moderate his enthusiasm for his Moorean 'religion' by recognizing that Moore's ethics omits much of what is important by refusing to discuss the ways in which ethical values connect with the possibilities for human life.

In 'My early beliefs', this omission is in effect acknowledged, in the acknowledgement there that there was some justice in D. H. Lawrence's denunciation of the brittle superficiality of the irreverent chatter of Keynes and his Cambridge friends. I shall return at the end to this point, which connects with Keynes's enlarged understanding of human psychology and social institutions. But first I want to discuss a remarkable but unappreciated episode in Keynes's thought, in which he first developed, and then abandoned, an ethical theory that is in some respects a significant improvement on Moore's theory.

'MISCELLANEA ETHICA'

In June 1905, Keynes successfully completed the Mathematics Tripos at Cambridge. He immediately commenced detailed study of *Principia Ethica*, and, noting Moore's last-minute commendation in his preface of Franz Brentano's *The Origin of Our Knowledge of Right and Wrong* (1969), whose English translation had just been published in 1902, he turned to Brentano's book. As Moore's commendation would lead one to expect, Keynes found here a position similar in many respects to that of Moore, but with one crucial difference: where Moore takes goodness to be the fundamental and indefinable ethical value, for Brentano goodness is defined as that which is 'correctly' loved. Keynes was at this time increasingly dissatisfied with Moore's method of ethical inquiry (this dissatisfaction is clearly expressed in his correspondence with Lytton Strachey[2]); hence, feeling that Brentano's position offered advantages over that of Moore, he quickly wrote up his own reformulation of Brentano's position as an extended sketch of an ethical treatise, 'Miscellanea Ethica' (composed July–September 1905) (KCKP, UA/21).

Although it is unclear whether this sketch had any long-term significance for Keynes, it is well worth some attention for its own sake. But in order to understand the significance of Keynes's position it is necessary to return briefly to Moore. As we saw earlier in connection with Moore's claims about the value of love and beauty, Moore takes it that no reasons can be given for fundamental judgements concerning the goodness of different kinds of thing. For Moore, because these judgements do not just concern putative natural matters of fact, they are not amenable to inductive justification by empirical investigation; equally, because they are not putative truths of reason, they cannot be established by conceptual analysis and proof. Hence, he holds, all we can do when discussing fundamental questions of value is to clarify the judgements in question and hope that our unargued judgements carry conviction. The resulting position is scarcely satisfactory: it offers ethical inquiry no prospect of a way of resolving serious disagreements apart from the search for as yet undiscovered ambiguities or unclarities concerning the points at issue. Moore's theory implies that a great variety of situations are valuable, and that their value depends on their properties; but he denies that there is any systematic account of this dependence to be had. So all that ethical theory can do is point us to the existence of this unsystematic variety of fundamental truths and then invite us to make up our mind about them without offering us any substantive guidance as to how to go about this. While this invitation can seem liberating at first, as indeed the young Keynes found it to be, its shortcomings are rapidly exposed when one confronts someone such as D. H. Lawrence, whose experience of life leads them to quite different judgements.

In most respects, Brentano's ethical theory is similar to Moore's: he holds that ethical truths are distinctive and in particular not reducible to the truths of any positive science. Equally, he holds that these truths concern the goodness of different kinds of thing, and that right action is that whereby one makes the world as good as possible. But the crucial difference between Moore and Brentano is that Brentano defines goodness: to be good, he says, is to be something which it would be correct to love. The emphasis on correctness here serves to differentiate Brentano's position from that of a simple subjectivist who holds that being good is simply a matter of being loved (or being preferred), and Brentano compares the concept of correctness employed here with that which occurs in connection with truth: 'We call a thing *true* when the affirmation relating to it is correct. We call a thing *good* when the love relating to it is correct. In the broadest sense of the term, the good is that which is worthy of love, that which can be loved with a love which is correct' (Brentano 1969: 18).

Thus for Brentano the good and the true are to be precipitated out of the conception of a 'correct' attitude, love in the one case, affirmation or judgement in the other. Given Brentano's comparison, an important initial question is how he can sustain a conception of the correctness of a judgement that is distinct from that of its truth. The answer is that in this case he draws on the potential 'evidence' of a judgement,[3] which he interprets as experience of its certainty; for he claims that this experience of the certainty of a judgement is constitutive of its truth: 'it is only inasfar as we discern certain judgments that the word "true" takes on significance' (Brentano 1973: 131). This, now, is his model for thinking about the relationship between goodness and the correctness of love: he holds that antecedent to any judgement about the goodness of what is loved, we experience some loves as correct in a way that then authorizes us to infer the goodness of that which is loved. He sets out his position clearly in the following passage:

I have said that the temptation into which Aristotle fell seems quite understandable. It may be traced to the fact that whenever we have a positive emotion that is experienced as being correct, we also acquire knowledge that the object of the emotion is something that is good. It is easy to confuse the relation between the emotion and the knowledge. One may then assume, mistakenly, that the love of the good thing is a consequence of the knowledge that it is good, and that the love is seen to be good because it is seen to be appropriate to the knowledge.

(Brentano 1969: 89)

It is not easy to be satisfied with any of this. There are many truths, such as truths about the past and the future, concerning which certainty is not possible. More deeply, our own experience and the history of philosophy teach us to distinguish subjective from objective certainty, and to recognize that the former does not suffice for the latter and thus for truth. So Brentano's account of truth is untenable. A similar dissatisfaction attaches to his account of goodness. Brentano's appeal to a fundamental experience of the intrinsic correctness of love is unpersuasive. The point is most clearly grasped by considering cases of 'incorrect' love: we have plenty of experience of inappropriate or illusory loves, but in each case what makes the loves inappropriate or illusory is dependent upon a mistaken judgement about that which is loved, and not vice versa. Brentano is rightly famous for insisting upon the 'intentionality' of psychological phenomena, their inherent 'object-directedness'. His accounts of truth and goodness, however, fail to recognize a crucial development of this point, which is that the evaluation of psychological states is in this respect dependent upon the evaluation of their objects, and not vice versa.

In the end, therefore, Brentano's position does not offer any great advance on Moore's. Where Moore relies on unsupportable intuitive judgements of the goodness of things, Brentano invokes unverifiable experiences of the correctness of love for the same things. And yet there is a passing phrase in the passage quoted above in which Brentano omits his talk of correctness, when he simply says that 'the good is that which is worthy of love'. I suspect that this was just a slip, but it is this idiom that Keynes exploits in his account of goodness. Laying out Keynes's position is a bit tricky, because he shifts the terminology around, but his basic thought is that judgements about the goodness of things are best conceived as judgements to the effect that these things are 'fit' to be loved, except that Keynes generally writes, not simply of love, but of 'good feelings'. Thus for Keynes there is one fundamental kind of evaluation, which is that of feelings; and then there is a dependent evaluation of the objects of feelings, in so far as they are fit to be objects of good feelings. This second evaluation is just a rephrasing of that encountered in Brentano, concerning whether something is 'worthy' to be loved; but instead of Brentano's problematic conception of a 'correct' love, Keynes simply has that of a 'good' feeling.

Keynes says very little about what feelings are good or what makes them good, and it may be that at this point he himself would have been content to rely on Moorean intuitions about the intrinsic goodness of different states of consciousness. But this is by no means necessary: one could easily develop his approach into one whereby feelings are evaluated in the light of a broader conception of human life which identifies some feelings as, say, 'life-affirming' and others as 'life-denying'.

Such a development would be, of course, entirely speculative. Keynes himself is content in his programmatic sketch to look forward to an 'ethics of ends', which would have the 'two functions of analysing and enumerating the different kinds and degrees of good feelings and fit objects'. An important part of this would be a 'natural history of fit objects', what we might now call a phenomenology, which would explore 'the nature of beauty and tragedy and love and the attitude a man should have towards truth' so that 'there would be very little in the field of experience or of passion which writers could not introduce if they had a mind for it' (KCKP, UA/21/7–8).

Despite its only sketchy outlines, Keynes's programme for an ethics is a remarkable achievement. Composed in only a couple of months straight after doing the Mathematics Tripos, Keynes, probably without realizing it, provides a conceptual schema that enables one to avoid both the unhelpful abstractness of Moore's conception of goodness and the wishful thinking of Brentano's conception of the experience of correct love. A good way to think about the position is to start from Keynes's notion of the 'fitness' of things. As I have indicated, Keynesian fitness is derived from Brentano's goodness and, therefore, provides a way of thinking about Moorean goodness, the intrinsic value of a kind of state of affairs. For Keynes, the key point is that fitness is inherently relational – it is fitness to be loved (admired etc.). So, goodness conceived as fitness is not an abstract property dependent in some ineffable way on the natural properties of the things involved; instead, it is a way of affirming that things with these natural properties are, ipso facto, fit or worthy to be loved. Another way of capturing this relationship is to describe it in terms of rationality: that which is good, or fit, is so because its natural properties imply that there is reason to love it. This final step, the transformation of Keynesian fitness into rationality, suddenly gives the position a contemporary sound: for what we have here is precisely Tim Scanlon's recent 'buck-passing' account of goodness, that 'to be good or valuable is to have other properties that constitute such reasons' – namely, reasons 'to respond to a thing in certain ways' (Scanlon 1998: 97).

Where Scanlon differs from the young Keynes is in not providing a role for Keynesian goodness, the evaluation of feelings, or 'responses' in Scanlon's idiom. Scanlon (1998: 99–100) remarks that different responses are appropriate to different kinds of thing, for example to different kinds of music (think of folk song vs dance vs chamber music). Scanlon is clearly right about this point, which implies that Keynes's category of 'good feelings' needs to be disaggregated. But, equally, it seems to me that Keynes is right to hold that an account of which type of response is appropriate is bound to be evaluative in a different way from a judgement about the fitness, or rationality, of that which calls for some response. Keynes does not himself say anything significant about this kind of evaluation, but as I indicated earlier, it seems to me that some broader conception of human life and the possibilities for fulfilment will need to be involved. If this is right, it points to a significant lacuna in Scanlon's general theory; but I shall not pursue the issue here. Instead, I should just acknowledge that even if this lacuna is filled, these judgements about the ways in which the properties of things provide us with reasons for responses to them have an irreducible status, belonging neither to a positive, value-free psychology nor to an abstract a priori rational ethics. So, it may be objected, does not my objection to Moore's position recur here? I think not: for, once we have a substantive theory of Keynesian goodness and a relational conception of the fitness of things, there is plenty of material for constructive ethical debate.

I have tried to show here how Keynes's sketch for an ethics in 'Miscellanea Ethica' is a remarkable achievement. By separating the 'fitness' of things from the 'goodness' of feelings, Keynes opens up the possibility of an approach that avoids the objectionable features of the positions advanced by Moore and Brentano; and it is really only in Scanlon's recent work that, one might say, academic moral philosophy has caught up with the young Keynes. For Keynes himself never published this line of thought or developed it any further. He wrote 'Miscellanea Ethica' in the summer of 1905; later in the same year he wrote a long 'Theory of Beauty', into which he copied parts of the earlier piece. But, early in 1906, Keynes declares himself to have reconverted to his Moorean faith: 'I was a little shaken in my newfound Moorism', he writes to Lytton Strachey on 20 January, and soon after this he writes in the extravagant idioms I cited at the start of this chapter. At this time, Keynes was studying Moore's new paper 'The Nature and Reality of the Objects of Perception' (reprinted in Moore 1922), and it has been suggested that his appreciation of this paper brought him back to his earlier faith (Bateman 1996: 13). But this latter paper deals with the reality of colours and other 'sense-contents', as Moore calls them, so it has no implications for ethics and cannot account for Keynes's reconversion. Keynes was, however, also preparing himself for his Civil Service examinations by re-reading Moore's *Principia Ethica* at this time, and I think he just found himself overwhelmed by Moore's rhetoric.

There is, however, one significant and enduring legacy of Keynes's brief period of heresy. One feature of Keynes's position had been that the only genuinely good things are feelings; things of other types are (improperly) judged to be good only in so far as they are fit objects of a good feeling. Even when Keynes has reconverted, he retains the claim that it is only feelings, or (more generally) 'states of consciousness', that are *intrinsically* good; in so far as things of other kinds are good, this is only because they are instrumentally good or good in virtue of their relationship to 'organic wholes' whereby the evaluation of a state of consciousness includes an essential reference to its object. The claim that it is only states of consciousness that are intrinsically good is one that Moore had explicitly rejected in *Principia Ethica*;[4] but Keynes's espousal of the opposite doctrine appears to have been decisive. His position became orthodoxy among the members of the Bloomsbury Group (JMK X: 436), and it gave extra significance to the explorations of consciousness undertaken by Virginia Woolf in her novels. What is perhaps most striking is that Moore himself changed his mind on this point and endorsed Keynes's position in his later (1912) book *Ethics* (1966: 129–30).

'ETHICS IN RELATION TO CONDUCT'

'Miscellanea Ethica' was not Keynes's first critical discussion of Moore's ethics. Instead, chapter 5 of *Principia Ethica* had already been the target of Keynes's critical attention in an Apostles paper of 1904 whose title was the title of Moore's chapter – 'Ethics in relation to conduct' (KCKP, UA/19/2). In 'My early beliefs', Keynes remarks concerning this chapter that 'There was one chapter in the *Principia* of which we took not the slightest notice.' As I have just indicated, this is misleading – for in fact it was precisely this chapter that first attracted Keynes's notice! It was only the conclusions of this chapter that Keynes and his friends took no notice of.

Moore argues in this chapter that because of our ignorance of the future we have no way of accurately calculating the relative benefits of all the possible courses of action open to us in some situation and thereby no way of working out which is the right action for us in that situation; so 'we never have any reason to suppose that an action is our duty' (Moore 1993: 199). But he mitigates this moral scepticism by proceeding to argue that where there are established general principles of conduct whose utility in general is well established, we ought *always* to be guided by these principles – which, for Moore, turn out to be 'most of the rules most universally recognised by Common Sense' (Moore 1993: 205). So Moore ends up prescribing a strict adherence to common sense morality, and it was this morality that Keynes and his friends rejected. In his paper, Keynes aims to undermine Moore's argument for this position by attacking his scepticism about the possibility of even rational probabilistic beliefs about the future.

A central part of Keynes's argument is the claim that Moore's sceptical argument relies on a frequency conception of probability, and, Keynes suggests, once we replace this conception with a conception of probability that simply expresses the 'bearing of the evidence at my disposal' (KCKP, UA/19/2/5), Moore's argument is undermined. This second conception of probability is of course that which Keynes was to develop as a 'logical' conception of probability and to present at length in *A Treatise on Probability* (1921), where he makes essentially the same criticism of Moore that he had made in his 1904 paper (see JMK VIII: 341–3). Although it is not part of my present purpose to assess Keynes's logical conception of probability (see instead chapter 11, 'Keynes and probability', in this volume by Donald Gillies), it is worth pointing out that Keynes's argument on this point is misconceived, since some

commentators have assumed otherwise (e.g. Skidelsky 1983: 153–4).
The point turns on the following passage in *Principia Ethica*:

The first difficulty in the way of establishing a probability that one course
of action will give a better total result than another, lies in the fact that we
have to take account of the effects of both throughout an infinite future. . .
We can certainly only pretend to calculate the effects of actions within what
may be called an 'immediate' future. . . Yet, if a choice guided by such
considerations is to be rational, we must certainly have some reason to
believe that no consequences of our action in a further future will generally
be such as to reverse the balance of good that is probable in the future we
can foresee. This large postulate must be made, if we are ever to assert that
the results of one action will be even probably better than those of another.
Our utter ignorance of the far future gives us no justification for saying that
it is even probably right to choose the greater good within the region over
which a probable forecast may extend.

(Moore 1993: 202)

Moore is concerned here with the possibility of establishing that
one course of action X is better overall than another Y. He accepts
that our evidence concerning 'the future we can foresee' may well
support a judgement that it is probable that over that period of time
X is better than Y. He asks, however, what reason we have to
extrapolate that difference 'throughout an infinite future', when
we have no evidence about the likely effects of X and Y over that
vast future which we cannot foresee; and his claim is just that,
without any such reason, we cannot establish the kind of conclusion we seek. It is obvious that Moore is not here even tacitly
invoking a frequency conception of probability: his sceptical argument does not in any way draw on our ignorance of the ratio of the
relative benefits of actions similar to X and Y assessed over an
indefinitely long series of trials. Instead, his argument simply
assumes our ignorance of the distant future, and thus our lack of
evidence about the relative benefits of X and Y over a long period of
time which includes the distant future.

In his response to Moore, Keynes prescribes 'a legitimate application of the principle of indifference' (JMK VIII: 342) to make the
extrapolation for which Moore seeks a reason. The suggestion seems
to be that if, concerning the distant future, we are ignorant of any
reason for thinking that X will then have greater benefits than Y

or vice versa, we are entitled to assume that their benefits then are the same, and thus that the overall comparison of X and Y can be based simply on evidence concerning the future we can foresee. The principle of indifference is, however, notoriously problematic (see pp. 201–2), and this application of it by Keynes certainly appears to be no more than a case of preferring theft over honest toil. The fact that we now have no reason to differentiate between the benefits of X and Y in the distant future is not by itself a reason for holding now that there will be no difference in their benefits. The correct response to Moore's argument is surely that at which he himself hints, namely that we have good inductive reasons for holding that in general 'the effects of any particular event become neutralised by lapse of time' (Moore 1993: 203), and thus that the only significant differences between X and Y are likely to be their short-term effects.

Moore's sceptical argument, therefore, does not rest on the mistake about probability of which Keynes seeks to convict him. Instead, it depends on an unwarranted scepticism concerning the future which it is surprising to find Moore, that inveterate critic of scepticism, employing. Nonetheless, Moore's discussion of morality connects in two other ways with important aspects of Keynes's thought.

One issue concerns the objective–subjective distinction. In his review of *Principia Ethica*, Russell (1904) had observed that there is a contradiction in Moore's position, since he holds that we ought always to act in accordance with generally useful moral rules despite the fact that he also holds that there are situations in which such actions are not maximally beneficial, and thus, by Moore's own ideal utilitarian principle, not actions that we ought to perform.[5] The context in which this inconsistency arises is that Moore thinks that we cannot identify these exceptional situations, despite the fact that we know that they exist, but the difficulty here is not dependent on Moore's excessively sceptical attitude to our capacity to identify some such exceptions, for our inescapable fallibility is by itself sufficient to create the problem, which has come to be known as that of adjudicating between 'subjective' and 'objective' conceptions of obligation. For the objectivist, it is the objective facts that constitute a situation which determine what ought to be done in that situation, even where an agent with an entirely reasonable but mistaken understanding of these facts acts in the light of this understanding. For the subjectivist, by contrast, by acting in accordance with his own understanding of what is required such an agent acts as he ought to act, even if his action is not in fact appropriate.

I shall not attempt here to adjudicate between these two positions (I myself regard the issue as one that still lacks a decisive resolution). Keynes himself was introduced to it by Moore in his 1903 lectures on 'Modern Ethics' that Keynes attended (I take it that Moore had by then been made conscious of the issue by Russell), though so far as I can judge, it is not a question that much exercised him, either then or later. But what is nonetheless striking is the parallel with the similar issue concerning objective *vs* subjective conceptions of probability. Like Moore, Keynes started out as an objectivist: his logical conception of probability is the conception of an objective relation between evidence and hypothesis. But he too, though in a different way, found himself confronted by a subjectivist challenge, in the account of probability propounded by Ramsey, according to which a probability judgement is fundamentally an expression of a degree of belief. Keynes was largely persuaded by Ramsey to change his position: 'I think he is right', Keynes famously wrote in his review of Ramsey's papers.[6] The considerations are not quite the same in the two cases, for a recognition of human fallibility is not, I think, the main consideration in favour of subjectivism about probability. Nonetheless, if one thinks of the objective–subjective issue as one that afflicts both theoretical and practical reason, it is not surprising to find significant similarities between the two cases.

The second topic to be considered here is Keynes's discussion of expectations in chapter 12 of the *General Theory*. Keynes is here discussing the rationality or not of decisions concerning investment, and he starts from a sceptical position which is strikingly reminiscent of Moore's discussion of decisions as to what one ought to do. Keynes writes: 'The outstanding fact is the extreme precariousness of the basis of knowledge on which our estimates of prospective yield have to be made. Our knowledge of the factors which will govern the yield of an investment some years hence is usually very slight and often negligible' (JMK VII: 149). What then are we to do? Keynes's answer is that: 'In practice we have tacitly agreed, as a rule, to fall back on what is, in truth, a *convention*. The essence of this convention – though it does not, of course, work out quite so simply – lies in assuming that the existing state of affairs will continue indefinitely, except in so far as we have specific reasons to expect a change' (JMK VII: 152).

Keynes does not suggest that this convention is warranted; on the contrary, it is 'in an absolute view of things so arbitrary' (JMK VII: 153). Nonetheless, it is important to us since it underpins the confidence in investment that is crucial to the development of the economy. Hence the authorities need to bear this convention in mind when developing new policies, and this, Keynes argues, will be a reason for a conservative attitude to the basic institutions of property:

It is safe to say that enterprise which depends on hopes stretching into the future benefits the community as a whole. But individual initiative will only be adequate when reasonable calculation is supplemented and supported by animal spirits, so that the thought of ultimate loss which often overtakes pioneers, as experience undoubtedly tells us and them, is put aside as a healthy man puts aside the expectation of death.

This means, unfortunately, not only that slumps and depressions are exaggerated in degree, but that economic prosperity is excessively dependent on a political and social atmosphere which is congenial to the average business man.

(JMK VII: 162)

This position is similar to Moore's, though the argument is different: where Moore defends common sense morality, including respect for property, as generally beneficial and not to be tampered with because of our ignorance of the long-term effects of such changes, Keynes argues from our ignorance of the future against radical changes in economic institutions on the grounds that such changes are likely to undermine business confidence and thus investment. So, despite his disdain for chapter 5 of *Principia Ethica*, at least with respect to those aspects of the 'political and social atmosphere' that matter to the average businessman's investment decisions, our ignorance of the future leads Keynes in his *General Theory* to take up a position remarkably similar to that which Moore had advanced quite generally for morality.

LATER BELIEFS

This development should be set alongside Keynes's later discussion in 'My early beliefs', in which he is critical of some aspects of his youthful irreverence. Before assessing in what respects Keynes really changed his mind, however, it is worth looking briefly at a characteristic expression of this youthful irreverence, in which he sets out a sharp critique of contemporary morality: his 1905 Apostles paper 'Modern civilisation' (KCKP, UA/22).

Having briefly acknowledged his Moorean ideal utilitarian starting-point, Keynes here introduces a conception of 'duties' which is recognizably that of the common sense morality Moore had affirmed: 'Duties, in fact, I am defining as those actions not good in themselves but so generally recognised to be useful as to claim our performance on all occasions irrespective of particular circumstances' (KCKP, UA/22/3). Keynes, however, so far from endorsing such duties, continues: 'What I wish to suggest is this – that there is and is coming a Revolution in duty. We may have reached a critical point in some matters where the general bank and capital of nations of ages is no longer useful to us' (KCKP, UA/22/3).

Although Keynes's reference here to 'bank' and 'capital' is primarily metaphorical, he goes on to say that one cause of the coming 'Revolution in duty' is primarily economic. He gives the example of contemporary affairs in the United States, where industrialists such as Rockefeller and Carnegie behave in a manner that, by the standards of traditional duty, would lead them to be condemned as 'scoundrels', but that, in present circumstances, cannot be so condemned. Their conduct shows that 'altogether new duties between buyers and sellers, whether of labour or commodity, must obtain in the future' (KCKP, UA/22/5). Similarly, he suggests, life in modern London cannot be conducted in accordance with 'the social and family duties of a village or a country town'. The old boundaries have gone, and 'the field that is relevant for any individual has grown, but the individual has not grown in proportion'; instead, we live in a world 'where men really bugger one another and go to prison for it' (KCKP, UA/22/7).

What then is Keynes's recipe for the future? He declares that he has none – 'heaven knows what the new moralities are to be'. But, he continues: 'I cannot believe that family relations, or business relations, or political relations will subsist much longer with any sincerity or useful purpose, unless we remember that all duties are with respect to time and place, and that sometimes old duties must go to be replaced by new' (KCKP, UA/22/8). In particular, Christian morality has now run its course: 'In the kingdom of moralities and duties the Galilean will himself be conquered, not by words or argument or proof, but equally with his predecessors by the irresistible trend of human affairs and the need for an adequate and relevant morality' (KCKP, UA/22/10). The only point of substance he ventures is that there will be, for his fellow Apostles and their generation, 'a greater contrast between our public and our private life', and thus the possibility of 'a far deeper intimacy' than was contemplated in the past.

This is a remarkable piece. In his refusal to be swayed by tradition and his openness to real social changes, Keynes expresses the attitudes of enlightenment liberalism. His main theme here is strongly reminiscent of Mill's writings, even though, as I remarked earlier, he never seems to have engaged with them. The question that arises here, however, is how far he came to qualify this position in the course of his life, and the context in which this question can be posed is that from which I started, his retrospective talk of 1938, 'My early beliefs'. The initial challenge he addresses in this talk is Lawrence's critical rejection of him and his friends on account of their brittle superficiality; but the way in which he responds to this charge can also be read as a critical comment on the early essay I have been discussing. For he begins with a self-description that exactly fits that essay:

We were among the last of the Utopians, or meliorists as they are sometimes called, who believe in a continuing moral progress by virtue of which the human race already consists of reliable, rational, decent people, influenced by truth and objective standards, who can be safely released from the outward restraints of convention and traditional standards and inflexible rules of conduct, and left, from now onwards, to their own sensible devices, pure motives and reliable intuitions of the good.

(JMK X: 447)

But, he now continues, this position which he and his friends then maintained does not provide an adequate understanding of human life:

In short, we repudiated all versions of the doctrine of original sin, of there being insane and irrational springs of wickedness in most men. We were not aware that civilisation was a thin and precarious crust erected by the personality and the will of a very few, and only maintained by rules and conventions skilfully put across and guilefully preserved. We had no respect for traditional wisdom or the restraints of custom. We lacked reverence, as Lawrence observed and as Ludwig with justice also used to say – for everything and everyone.

(JMK X: 447–8)

No doubt the experiences of the 1930s provided good reasons for Keynes both to temper his enlightenment 'meliorism' in the light of the manifold manifestations of human wickedness during this decade, and to acknowledge the value of traditional institutions in helping to withstand this wickedness. But it does not follow that this acknowledgement represented a profound change of heart on the part of Keynes from liberal reformer to conservative traditionalist. Instead, as his 1938 essay indicates, the change is primarily one of acknowledging that reform is more difficult and more risky than he had previously supposed. Keynes does not elaborate his position here, and there are no writings from this time in which he sets out his moral and political ideals. But his essays on politics from the 1920s provide a clear guide to his views then, and I see little reason to think that he subsequently changed his views in significant respects.

A remark from his 1926 essay on 'Liberalism and Labour' provides a good way into his position: 'The political problem of mankind is to combine three things: economic efficiency, social justice, and individual liberty' (JMK IX: 311). He already acknowledges that the pursuit of economic efficiency requires ways of promoting confidence in the future. For, he writes in his 1925 essay 'The end of laissez-faire', 'Many of the greatest economic evils of our time are the fruits of risk, uncertainty, and ignorance' (JMK IX: 291). Hence, he argues here, the cure for these evils lies in securing greater confidence about the future through state interventions which will diminish the risks for private investors; and, as we saw above, in the *General Theory* he takes the view that this requires the state to act in a way that will project 'a political and social atmosphere which is congenial to the average business man'. Thus, although reform is not ruled out, economic efficiency requires respect for the institutions of property and the rule of law. But his commitment at the same time to change in the area of individual liberty is unqualified, as in the call in his 1925 essay 'Am I a Liberal?' for reform of the laws concerning sexual behaviour and the position of women:

Birth control and the use of contraceptives, marriage laws, the treatment of sexual offences and abnormalities, the economic position of women, the economic position of the family – in all these matters the existing state of the law and of orthodoxy is still medieval – altogether out of touch with civilised practice and with what individuals, educated and uneducated alike, say to one another in private. . . Let no one suppose that it is the working women who are going to be shocked by ideas of birth control or divorce reform. For them these things suggest new liberty, emancipation from the most intolerable of tyrannies.

(JMK IX: 302)

What, finally, of the issue of 'social justice'? One might think that Keynes's attachment to the writings of Burke would have led him to develop a nostalgic love of traditional hierarchies. But this is not so. He was a consistent critic of Conservative politics and, despite his enduring attachment to the Liberal Party, was prepared to allow that the issue of social justice 'is the best possession of the great party of the proletariat' (i.e. the Labour Party) (JMK IX: 311). Perhaps the most striking expression of this attitude comes in his essay 'A short view of Russia' written in 1925 after a visit to Soviet Russia; for despite all his criticisms of the Soviet regime on both economic and liberal grounds, he ends by declaring that 'how much rather, even after allowing for everything, if I were a Russian, would I contribute my quota of activity to Soviet Russia than to Tsarist Russia! . . . I should feel that . . . out of the cruelty and stupidity of Old Russia nothing could ever emerge, but that beneath the cruelty and stupidity of New Russia some speck of the ideal may lie hid' (JMK IX: 271).

So, although his later beliefs include a new emphasis on the importance of retaining confidence in social and economic institutions, Keynes remained true to his youthful ideals, to his conviction that 'sometimes old duties must go to be replaced by new'. Despite acknowledging the threats and difficulties inherent in unpleasant human motivations and the reassurance provided by traditional loyalties, Keynes's position remains that we have no excuse for not seeking to remove old prejudices that are dressed up as morality, especially in the area of sexual morality. And since the public world of social, economic and political practice changes anyway, it is much better to understand these changes and adapt one's morality accordingly than to seek to preserve rules and conventions that have become irrelevant or worse – as Keynes himself put it in 1925:

Half the copybook wisdom of our statesmen is based on assumptions which were at one time true, or partly true, but are now less and less true day by day. We have to invent new wisdom for a new age. And in the meantime we must, if we are to do any good, appear unorthodox, troublesome, dangerous, disobedient to them that begat us.

(JMK IX: 305–6)

NOTES

1   This omission is made all the more remarkable by the similarities between the lives of the two men; it is as if Keynes unconsciously shied away from too close an engagement with someone whose very similarity to him might have inhibited him.
2   For discussion of this, see Bateman (1996: ch. 2).
3   The use of 'Evidenz' in German is not quite the same as that of 'evidence' in English. The 'evidence' of a judgement is not to be understood as the existence of evidence *for* the judgement; instead, it is the fact that the judgement itself is 'evident', i.e. compelling.
4   See his famous comparison between a beautiful world and 'the ugliest world you can conceive' (Moore 1993: 135–6).
5   See Moore (1993: 212), where the inconsistency is almost explicit.
6   JMK X: 339; but see Gillies (chapter 11 in this volume) for further discussion of this issue.

14 Keynes between modernism and post-modernism

INTRODUCTION

As an astute commentator on the economics of the early decades of the twentieth century has put it, the First World War acted as a watershed between an 'age of tranquility' and an 'age of turmoil' (Shackle 1967: 289). It marked a significant discontinuity in the intellectual, sociocultural and economic development of the Western hemisphere and beyond. The interwar period that followed witnessed severe financial crises and economic depression. In the wake of the Russian Revolution the world embarked on the competition of economic and political systems that dominated the twentieth century. At the same time, radio and television opened up the era of mass communication, which industrially was accompanied by the advent of mass production, brought to the consumer by ever more sophisticated uses of the new media for advertising. A solar eclipse in 1919 allowed adherents of Einstein's general theory of relativity to claim empirical confirmation of what newspapers around the world hailed as the overthrow of Newtonian physics, while Rutherford, building on his atomic model, eventually managed to split atoms. All these events and developments characterize the context of the culmination of modernism as a sociocultural style. In the world of fine arts Dadaism, expressionism and surrealism supplanted realist modes of representation. Similar shifts were experienced in architecture, literature, music and design.[1]

Keynes's economically most productive phase, from the *Economic Consequences of the Peace* (JMK II) of 1919 to the *General Theory* (JMK VII) of 1936, coincides with the early twentieth-century apex of modernism. While the extent to which his work departed from the British orthodoxy associated with Alfred Marshall and interwar business-cycle theory more generally has always been controversial, Keynes presented his work as a rejection of this orthodoxy. It is thus not surprising that some critics of 'modern' economics, sensitive to the ways in which the modern era and its categories have been questioned in the post-modernist literature, have sought to read Keynes's work as an alternative to and a critique of an economic 'modernism' epitomized by the neo-classical paradigm in economics.

Post-modernist discourse in itself has remained at the forefront of controversy and acrimonious division in the social sciences. Some regard it as tantamount to a return to the Dark Ages (e.g. Sokal and Bricmont 1999). Others see post-modernism as 'an adult's way to be a scientist' (McCloskey 2001: 122). In economics, self-declared post-modernist dissenters have remained few and far between. Nevertheless, comparable frictions arise from the dominance of an Anglo-American orthodoxy *vis à vis* a range of heterodox traditions, with Keynes studies having proved a fertile battleground for the resulting skirmishes.

Whether or not neo-classical economics is appropriately interpreted as modernist, there are good grounds for firmly placing Keynes's work in the context of its particular early twentieth-century modernist origins. Keynes was a modernist in that his work displays the central hallmarks of literary and artistic modernism. What is more, he found himself at the core of the most prominent British modernist movement of the time, alongside Virginia Woolf and other members of the Bloomsbury Group. The following section revisits how economic modernism has hitherto been interpreted in economic methodology. Postmodernist readings of Keynes are then explored. Finally, Keynes's economic modernism is reasserted.

ECONOMIC MODERNISM

Economists commonly look at the history of their discipline in epochal terms (e.g. Dasgupta 1985). The classical era, for example, is broadly understood to reach from the late eighteenth century to what has become known as the 'marginal revolution' of the 1870s, encompassing the canonical work of Adam Smith, David Ricardo and John Stuart Mill. The marginal revolution, in turn, marked the advent of neo-classical economics, carried chiefly by the Lausanne school of Léon Walras and Vilfredo Pareto, the Marshallian tradition and the Austrian school around Carl Menger. For a long time, it was common to see an underlying continuity in microeconomics throughout most of the twentieth century, but to see a new, Keynesian epoch in macroeconomics originating in the 1930s.[2] More recently, historians of economics have argued for regarding the neo-classical era as historic, having been superseded, at a date usually placed between the 1930s and the 1950s, by what is often, for want of a better term, referred to as 'modern' economics (e.g. Backhouse 1985, Colander 2000; see also Blaug 1999, Mirowski 2002).

In the light of these developments, some methodologists turned to describing the methodological traits of modern economics in terms of an economic 'modernism'. From the middle of the twentieth century onwards, economists have, by and large, seen themselves as adhering to the broad outlines of a critical rationalist methodology (Popper 1934, 1963). This 'official' methodology of economics[3] has been characterized as modernist in the sense that it is committed to a scientistic belief in the progress and accumulation of knowledge acquired as a result of the formulation of hypotheses and their subsequent testing against empirical evidence, all within a mathematical formalist framework of analysis (McCloskey 1983, 1994; Dow 1991; Klamer 1993, 1995). Economic modernism, a term favoured by some critics of economic orthodoxy for summarizing its problematic features, refers to a kind of economics that 'has kept in place the fetishism of the unified rational subject, the bottom line of "prediction", the reliance on mathematical "rigor", and much else that has given economics its specifically "modern" character' (Ruccio and Amariglio 2003: 4).

Consider Paul Samuelson's (1939a) multiplier-accelerator model (Klamer 1995), central to the development of business-cycle theory in Keynesian economics (Heertje and Heemeijer 2002). Samuelson's article is barely four pages long, much of it devoted to mathematical notation, tables and graphs.[4] According to Klamer, it represents the modernist spirit *par excellence*. While intended to advance Keynesian business-cycle theory, the paper stands in stark contrast to Keynes's analysis of business cycles in chapter 22 of the *General Theory*.

Klamer argues that Keynes doubts the possibility of understanding the economy on the basis of time-invariant structures, emphasizing instead its fundamentally uncertain nature, which resists formal representation. An alternative method of analysis emerges, drawing heavily from narrative elements, and highlighting the historical dimension of economic events and the psychological dimension of economic actors.

Compared to the rich textures of economic life in which Keynes revels, Samuelson's model is austerity itself. It formalizes a hypothetical feature of the economy that, without any supporting argument, is simply posited as invariant. Moreover, the main thrust of the article is less concerned with analyzing the economy than with economics itself, since Samuelson develops the model as a vehicle to display the virtues of reductionist formalism. As it turns out thus, the format of the article mirrors the substance of its argument in a self-referential fashion.

Economic modernism has more generally been defined through its reflexive and inward-looking concern with representation, a strive towards uncovering invariant structures of reality, and an attempt to break with history by favouring abstract, ahistorical accounts over detailed studies of institutional processes (Klamer 1993, 2001: 81–2). In these more general interpretations, economic modernism displays many of the hallmarks of modernism as they are identified in other literatures outside economics. Strikingly, however, 'Keynes's text fails to live up to key characteristics of modernism' (Klamer 1995: 329).

POST-MODERNIST KEYNES STUDIES

If one interprets the emerging neo-classical orthodoxy of the 1930s as modernist, and as different in nature from Keynes's work, much of Keynes's writing must strike one not just as 'not modernist' but as outright anti-modernist. It is thus not surprising that, of the authors who point to a modernist kind of economics, some proceed by exploring links between Keynes and post-modernist critiques of modernism. Both Klamer (1995: 328, 332) and McCloskey (2001: 120–4) are open to such a reading, but reluctantly stop short of providing a post-modernist interpretation of Keynes's economics. Ruccio and Amariglio (2003) are more ambitious in this regard.[5] Pursuing an overall project of uncovering what they regard as the post-modern moments of modern economics, their analysis of Keynes explicitly deals with potential overlaps between his work and post-modernist thought.

While Amariglio and Ruccio also consider other aspects of Keynes, their main argument turns on Keynes's treatment of uncertainty. They hold that his outlook on economic uncertainty, in particular as expressed in the *General Theory*, differs significantly from the rational choice framework conventionally taken as characterizing the neo-classical tradition in economics. There is, of course, broad agreement that what came to be known as the IS-LM model of the emerging post-Second World War 'Keynesian' macroeconomic orthodoxy reflected the *General Theory* only in part.[6] Keynes (JMK XIV: 109–23) himself was quick to realize that it was in particular the emphasis in the *General Theory* on the condition of fundamental uncertainty and the handicap it posed to economic decision-making that failed to leave its mark on this orthodoxy. It is Amariglio and Ruccio's contention that Keynes in fact anticipated important elements of a post-modernist understanding of uncertainty, itself at odds with much of modern economics.

The interpretation of Keynes's concept of uncertainty is a contested matter (Rosser 2001; Weatherson 2002; and chapter 11 here, by Gillies). It is therefore not surprising that, in exegetical terms, Amariglio and Ruccio's interpretation remains open to debate. For example, one can argue that Keynes's thinking on uncertainty constituted less a radical departure from interwar thought than a continuation of the Cambridge tradition of monetary analysis and trade-cycle theory. A close reading of the *General Theory* reveals a concern less with uncertainty *per se* than with the response of economic actors and markets to it, which explains the central role played in the *General Theory* by business confidence and the stabilizing role of conventions (Bateman 1996: 101–40).

The main thrust of Amariglio and Ruccio's analysis is, however, of a methodological nature, informed by Lyotard's (1985, 1987) modal interpretation of post-modernism (see Brügger 2001). Modally conceived, the post-modern is a mode already present in the modern, pursued by the avant-garde in their efforts to push beyond the envelope of modernist strictures. Amariglio and Ruccio take up this modal interpretation by speaking of 'postmodern moments' that they identify in the work of Keynes.

Lyotard (1979, 1984) described post-modernity in terms of fragmented personal identities and a pervasive heterogeneity and indeterminacy of knowledge. Individual agents, while not assumed irrational *per se*, are regarded as lacking any rational basis of adjudicating between competing identities and knowledge claims, being thus exposed to a fundamental epistemological uncertainty.[7] Amariglio and Ruccio see this condition reflected in Keynes's distinction between uncertainty that can be analyzed in probabilistic terms and 'true' uncertainty for which, to quote from a well-known passage, 'there is no scientific basis on which to form any calculable probability whatever. We simply do not know' (JMK XIV: 114). According to this reading, Keynes sought to understand the behaviour of economic actors primarily in terms of the much-quoted 'animal spirits' and with reference to the role of social conventions in the formation of long-term expectations. Under conditions of true uncertainty, 'individual initiative will only be adequate when reasonable calculation is supplemented and supported by animal spirits, so that the thought of ultimate loss . . . is put aside as a healthy man puts aside the expectation of death' (JMK VII: 162).

This irrational element, while responsible for sudden fluctuations, does not reduce the economy to constant upheavals, however, but is kept in check by the stabilizing role that Keynes accords to the conventions that guide investment behaviour (JMK VII: 152). The attempt to extend rational decision-making to uncertainty has therefore led Keynes not only to spell out the limits of this approach, but to move beyond it in conceptual terms. One of the key building-blocks of modern economics, rational economic man, has given way to an exploration of his psychological make-up and of the nature of social conventions.

Amariglio and Ruccio argue further that placing Keynes's concept of uncertainty in the context of his *Treatise on Probability* (JMK VIII) reveals that this is a move not just in any direction but towards discursive conceptions of uncertainty found in the post-modernist literature, stressing the fragmentary, indeterminate and relative nature of knowledge claims. Again, in exegetical terms, this claim is controversial, but there are good grounds for accepting the underlying proposition: that economic actors mediate uncertainty by stabilizing co-ordinating economic conventions through discursive practices (see chapter 11 in this volume). No fully worked-out account of uncertainty along these lines can be extracted from Keynes's work, though. The link from Keynes to a post-modernist kind of economics remains thus projective.

KEYNES THE MODERNIST

Historically speaking, the case for regarding Keynes as a modernist seems clear cut. As is well documented, Keynes did not only write in the high modernist period, he formed a central part of the British modernist movement through his involvement in the Bloomsbury Group (see chapter 12 in this volume). Keynes became involved with Bloomsbury through his relationship with the painter Duncan Grant, whom he first met in 1905. By 1911, he was, together with Grant, one of the lodgers in the house of the writer Virginia Stephen and her brother Adrian, to be joined by Leonard Woolf, whom Virginia married the following year. Keynes also entertained close friendships with Virginia's sister, Vanessa (another painter), and with Lytton Strachey. After the First World War, Keynes took over the lease of 46 Gordon Square, the London house that had originally served as the focal meeting-place of the emergent Bloomsbury Group, and shared it with Vanessa and her husband and art critic, Clive Bell, until his own marriage in 1925. The years before the First World War, during which the Bloomsbury Group prospered, marked the apex of Keynes's bohemian lifestyle. While the inter-war years saw the gradual dissolution of the closely knit circle of friends, most of whom were now entering middle age, this was the time of their greatest recognition and influence.[8]

The significance of Bloomsbury in Keynes's life is now well established (Skidelsky 1992; Moggridge 1992). Keynes was not simply 'influenced' by Bloomsbury, as intellectual historians would have it. Keynes *was* Bloomsbury, in the same sense that his avant-gardist Bloomsbury companions were Bloomsbury. Together, they stood for and understood themselves as a modernist reaction to the latest expressions of modernity in the early decades of the twentieth century, a reaction which, despite its bohemian origins, assumed a prominent position in British society. Keynes, for example, played a leading role in reshaping British cultural policy, acting as a key figure in the setting-up of the British Arts Council, which marked the beginning of large-scale state patronage of the arts in Britain, thereby putting key Bloomsbury ideas into practice (Upchurch 2004).

But Keynes's Bloomsbury legacy cannot be relegated to policy involvement of this kind alone, or to 'extracurricular' activities outside his professional life, such as his founding of the Cambridge Arts Theatre, including sponsorship of its premises, architecturally reminiscent of mainstream modernist features. It is manifest from Keynes's approach to writing that he saw himself as an avant-garde writer, prolific not just academically but also an accomplished columnist, critic, biographer and polemicist. The unmistakably polemical dimension of Keynes's writing style made him notorious and somewhat the object of suspicion among economists. Take the following passage from the *General Theory*, in which he seeks to illustrate the implications of his theory in terms of the multiplier effects of increased consumption and investment, together with the real effects of monetary expansion, on the level of employment:

If the Treasury were to fill old bottles with bank notes, bury them at suitable depths in disused coalmines [sic] which are then filled up to the surface with town rubbish, and leave it to private enterprise to dig the notes up again . . . there need be no more unemployment . . . It would, indeed, be more sensible to build houses and the like.

(JMK VII: 129)

Keynes's accomplishment as a writer is widely accepted. Commonly, however, it is taken for granted as an expression of his exceptional talent and intelligence, as if it simply sprang from his unique personality. This undervalues Keynes's ambitions as a writer and neglects his writing as coming from a key member of the Bloomsbury Group. Of the few commentators who have taken Keynes's literary ambitions seriously, Elizabeth Johnson (1978: 30) has found the best epitaph to this artistic dimension of his economics: 'I doubt that there are many other economists whose work can be read as literature in their own right.'

Johnson compares Keynes's talents to Virginia Woolf's ability to crystallize complex impressions in aptly chosen metaphors. Recent literary studies have pursued the parallels between Keynes and Bloomsbury's most famous literary writer in more detail. Marzola (1994), for example, points to the close relationship between Keynes's rhetoric and his innovative theory-building as the most notable

Bloomsbury hallmark in his work, in particular in the *Economic Consequences of the Peace* and the *General Theory*. His use of language in the latter becomes a powerful tool of emancipation from the terminology of the Marshallian orthodoxy. Consciously employing an innovative economic writing style, Keynes resists systematic introduction and discussion of his theory. Instead, his arguments are developed by alternating linear and circular forms of exposition which, argues Marzola (1994: 212), amount to a 'non-positivist' methodological stance. It is in this regard that she finds the most clearly developed parallels to Woolf's (1925) break with the literary realist tradition.

Further parallels can be observed (Esty 2004). While Woolf's (1915) first novel, *The Voyage Out*, depicts a colonial journey, her last novel, *Between the Acts* (1941), deals with an English country ritual. Similarly, Keynes's first book, on Indian currency, was a result of his time as a civil servant at the India Office from 1906 to 1908 (JMK I), while Esty reads the *General Theory* as turning from the neo-classical perspective of abstract markets to the economic system as a geopolitical entity. This, according to Esty, reflects a contracting concern with the British economy, in place of the inter-related economies that made up the British Empire. While, in *Between the Acts*, Woolf revises her 'stream of consciousness' narrative style to take wider account of historical and cultural context, Keynes's *General Theory* accords a central role to social conventions in the stabilization of investor expectations. Therefore, Esty reads the mature work of both writers as thus marking the end-stage of the London-based modernism of the Bloomsbury Group.

Woolf's introspective radicalism, along with Keynes's psychologistic accounts of the formation of investors' expectations in chapter 12 of the *General Theory*, are arguably different facets of the same underlying Bloomsbury obsession with psychology and the fragmented nature of individual identity and experience (Bonadei 1994). Like Woolf's protagonists, Keynes's investors are portrayed from a perspective of psychological realism. Both Woolf's and Keynes's styles of writing have been described as attempts to find a new access to modern market forms in their dynamism and unpredictability (Wicke 1996: 110), to the extent that Esty (2004: 170) rightly regards Keynes as a mediating figure in modernism, not simply theorizing these markets but casting them in artful language.

The point here is not to argue from traces of literary modernism in Keynes's economics to Woolf's influence on Keynes, or indeed from Woolf's depiction of urban markets to Keynes's economic influence on Woolf. Similarities in style and ambition are best accounted for by their mutual background in that modernist circle of friends that became known as the Bloomsbury Group. The argument for Keynes's modernism is therefore both stylistic and sociological.[9] The work of other economists may well exhibit similar modernist elements. If ever there was, however, a case for placing an economist and his work at the heart of a sociocultural style that was so aware of its own emergence, alongside novelists, painters and art critiques, it must be Keynes's.

CONCLUSIONS

Robert Skidelsky (1992: 407) rightly cautions that 'Keynes's relationship to the twin movements of modernism and collectivism is both extraordinarily important in understanding his work as a whole and extremely difficult to say anything sensible about.' Intellectual historians, usually faced with the difficult enough task of tracing influences between texts and individuals, face significant historiographical obstacles when trying to assess the influence of a cultural sensibility such as modernism in the work of a single author, short of resorting to invocations of Hegelian *Geist* or the broad brush of an Arthur Lovejoy (1936). Sociologically, the answer seems reasonably clear though. To the extent that it makes sense to speak of a London-centred high-modernist movement around the Bloomsbury Group, Keynes was one of its key figures. To the extent that Keynes may be usefully characterized as a writer, his ambitions, even and most visibly in his mature economic work, were modernist. To the extent that one can define a modernist approach in economics in well-established sociocultural terms, Keynes's economics as culminating in his *General Theory* is best regarded as modernist.

Proponents of modernism questioned individual identity, displayed profound scepticism towards realist accounts of the world, and embraced dissonance and uncertainty as defining aspects of life. Regarding themselves as the cultural avant-garde, they developed ever more sophisticated forms of representation and display of formal technique (Childs 2000: 18–25). However, modernist preoccupation with form and technique constituted less a celebration of formalism and abstraction as an end in itself than a questioning of modes of representation. In literature, this led authors like Virginia Woolf to seek narrative methods distinct from the literary realist novel, with a particular focus on psychologistic perspectives such as her quasi-formalist variation on the modernist 'stream of conscious-ness' technique on display in *The Waves* (Woolf 1931). In painting, the move towards abstraction, as given expression in Kandinsky's (1911) manifesto *Über das Geistige in der Kunst*, liberated the artist from the constraints of figurative representation towards an explo-ration of the symbolic primitives of the visual field, and their pre-representational syntax and emotive content. In architecture, the functionalist legacy epitomized by the Bauhaus school went hand in hand with a fascination for reflexive renderings of space of which Mies van der Rohe's Landhaus Lemke (Berlin 1933) provides an illustration par excellence.[10]

Architectural modernism, reacting against the prevalent Gothic, classical or Renaissance mimicry of the Victorian era, rejected its refusal to accept the realities of the machine age and its attending functionalism (Schmiechen 1988) in quite the same way as literary modernists celebrated new communication and travel technologies (Whitworth 2000: 146). Similarly, modernist painters' fascination with the grid and the interpretive silence that it casts across the canvas (Krauss 1981: 158–61) resembles the psychological turning inward of literary modernist prose as a way of silencing the outer world and its transitory, materialist 'trivia' (Woolf 1925: 148). The latter as well as the former resorted to abstract technique in their attempts to radically break with extant traditions. Even the oft-quoted statement of Charles-Edouard Jeanneret ('Le Corbusier') that a house is 'a machine for living' needs to be read alongside his insistence that architectural style must also address the meditative side of the human psyche (Weston 1996: 100–5).

While there is thus some point in referring to both the formalist and the psychologistic dimensions of modernism (Klamer 1993), ultimately it remains difficult to keep them apart as two mutually exclusive kinds of modernism. To accept the work of Samuelson as modernist does not commit oneself to locating Keynes's work in a different way. As soon as one subjects Keynes to the same rhetorical exercise that Klamer applied to Samuelson, one will find equally persuasive grounds for regarding Keynes as a modernist. In fact, the modal reading of Amariglio and Ruccio's 'postmodern moments' provides the best argument for maintaining that Keynes's economics should be regarded as modernist.

It may of course be difficult for authors who see economic modernism, in its neo-classical orthodox manifestation, chiefly in a negative light to accept a dissenting voice such as Keynes's, that is continuous with a range of concepts and theories pushed to the margin by that orthodoxy, as arising in the same modernist context. It is not clear, however, why a post-modernist outlook on economics should imply a departure from the neo-classical tradition,[11] nor is a critic of this tradition bound to be committed to anti-modernism.

Whether or not Keynes should be regarded as a modernist does not thus come down to arguing a moot point but has implications for one's overall assessment of twentieth-century economics. Modernism has always been understood not as a phenomenon restricted to the arts but equally as something that pervades philosophy, science and politics (Gluck 1986: 846). To maintain Keynes's cultural modernism as a feature of his private life while pointing to anti-modernist elements in his professional economics merely perpetuates the separation between rationally reconstructed economics of the past on the one hand, and its historical, sociocultural institutionalization on the other (see Klaes 2001).

All this should not distract from exploring how parts of Keynes's work may enrich and be expanded in poststructuralist economic approaches. Discursive dimensions of economic responses to uncertainty, in particular in the context of Keynes's monetary theory, are worth further exploration. While economists have only sparingly and, with caution, referred to money as a language (e.g. Carabelli 1988: 167–72; Mirowksi 1994), there is a long tradition outside economics of arguing precisely that, and increasingly with reference to the work of Keynes (e.g. McLuhan 1964; Shell 1982; Goux 1990; Gray 1999; Gernalzick 2001). The time seems ripe for exploring opportunities for trade with these literatures on the basis of an economically and philosophically informed understanding of Keynesian themes.

NOTES

I am indebted to the editors for their insightful feedback. Thanks also, without implicating them in any way, to John Davis, Sheila Dow, Michael Hutter, Rolland Munro and my former colleagues at the Stirling Centre for Economic Methodology for useful comments.

1 See Gluck (1986) for a critical discussion of the debates surrounding the dating and very substance of modernism. The secondary literature on modernism is vast and exhibits numerous alternative interpretations and datings of modernism and modernity. For present purposes, suffice it to point to Childs (2000) and Weston (1996) as two useful introductory texts.

2 Today, the term 'neo-classical' is also often used in a more general sense to refer to the perceived mainstream in economics. Marx (1847: 118) was probably the first to refer to Smith and Ricardo as the 'Classics'. The coining of 'neo-classical' in the context of economics is commonly attributed to Veblen's (1900: 261) reference to a 'neo-classical' or 'modernized classical' school.

3 It is well established that actual practice of economic research proceeds along somewhat different lines (e.g. Blaug 1980).

4 One should note that a 'discursive' version of the model was published in parallel, which kept notation and graphs to a minimum (Samuelson 1939b).

5 See also Amariglio (1988), Ruccio (1991), Ruccio and Amariglio (2003) and Cullenberg, Amariglio and Ruccio (2001). Amariglio (1990) and Amariglio and Ruccio (1995) present earlier versions of the analysis of Keynes in chapter 2 of their 2003 book.

6 Keynes's orthodox reception constituted less an attempt to canonize the essential insights of the *General Theory* than a consolidation of various strands of interwar economic theorizing, of which Keynes's work was but one aspect (see Laidler 1999).

7 For a useful genealogy of post-modernism that manages to draw out some of the underlying disciplinary and geographical heterogeneity that characterizes the various discourses that champion the term, see Huyssen (1984).

8 For the Bloomsbury circle, see Skidelsky (1992: 10–18), Moggridge (1992: 213–23) and more generally Johnstone (1954), Gadd (1975).

9 See Williams (1980) for a critical but overall affirmative discussion of the sociological dimension of Bloomsbury.

10 The L-shape of the building gives rise in certain rooms to a visual reflexivity that, combined with the mirroring effects of the large window

fronts, undermines the distinction between inside and outside (Knüvener 2005).

11   Jameson (1991: 267–71, for example, regards the work of Gary Becker as representative of a post-modernist turn in economics, as Ruccio and Amariglio (2003: 7) themselves acknowledge. The post-modern theme of the fragmentation of identity and multiple selves has received in-depth coverage in modern economics (Davis 2003).

15   Keynes and Keynesianism

One of the most significant changes in the economic and political life of the twentieth century was the introduction of demand management in the industrialized democracies. From Japan to the United States, and from Sweden to Italy, national governments took on responsibility for a kind of economic function that had not previously been seen as a regular part of their brief: they began to use fiscal and monetary policy to try to stabilize the business cycle by stabilizing the total demand for goods and services.

Fiscal policy consists of the government's expenditures on goods and services (from pens and paper to fighter bombers), and monetary policy consists of controlling the creation of money and the level of interest rates. Both of these functions existed and were discussed in the previous two centuries, but they took on a new life in the twentieth century as a part of electoral politics and understood as a means to stabilize the swings in output that constitute the business cycle. Banking policy and government debt had been issues well before the twentieth century, but they had not been conceived of in a *systematic* way as the means to achieve economic stability. Inevitably, this revolution in economic management (indeed, in economic self-understanding) bears the name of John Maynard Keynes.

Most economists certainly have a very clear idea of the trajectory of Keynes's influence in the twentieth century. The stylized history runs as follows. First, they believe that he scored a theoretical breakthrough with his *General Theory of Employment, Interest and Money* (1936), the book that, by mid-century, established him as the world's leading economist. Before him, no one had ever produced a satisfactory theory of the demand for all goods and

271

services in the economy; no one had provided a way to talk clearly about the aggregate demand for an economy's output. Keynes's theoretical breakthrough thus amounted to the invention of macroeconomics, the theory of how the economy as a whole works. Once Keynes's theoretical prominence was established, his ideas spread quickly among economists, and many countries began to adopt his policy recommendation of 'continuing and increasing budget deficits' and 'a rapidly growing governmental sector' to keep the level of aggregate demand at a high level and so ensure full employment (Buchanan and Wagner 1977: 4). Eventually, amidst the inflation and unemployment of the 1970s, it became clear that trying to use monetary and fiscal policy to maintain aggregate demand could have perverse and unintended consequences, and economists began to see Keynes's theory as resting on several naïve assumptions. His theoretical framework and his policy recommendations were supplanted by the more conservative theoretical frameworks of Milton Friedman and the Chicago School. In this stylized history, Keynes and Keynesianism are one and the same.

For better or worse, work by scholars in several disciplines during the last two decades has brought virtually every piece of this stylized history into question. The economist David Laidler, for instance (1999), has questioned the idea that Keynes's work marked the birth of macroeconomics. While Keynes did successfully create a new way of thinking about economics, and while he did successfully formulate a theory of effective demand in a form that no one else had achieved, his ideas built directly on the work of others who had already done substantial work in developing macroeconomic thought over the preceding decades. Though they had not thought of it as macroeconomics, writing instead about money and the business cycle, economists had been working on recognizably macroeconomic problems for over a century.[1]

Likewise, scholarship by economic historians in the 1980s has shown that the stylized history does little or no justice to Keynes's influence on British economic policy-making. Economic historians such as George Peden have used newly available documents from the Public Record Office to show that Keynes had little success in directly influencing policy in the 1930s and that his influence in the 1940s, when he served as a special consultant in the Treasury during the Second World War, was of a very different nature than had traditionally been supposed. The Treasury *had* learned much from Keynes, but what they learned was not necessarily what the stylized history claimed.[2] The Treasury never did take it from Keynes that the running of 'ever larger deficits' was necessary to keep the nation at full employment. Indeed, the historian Peter Clarke (1997) has shown that following Keynes's death in 1946 there were only two years between 1947 and 1972 when there was a deficit in the British budget, when the deficit is calculated on a traditional, Gladstonian basis in which capital expenditure is not accounted in the ordinary budget.

Finally, a flurry of literature in the 1990s questioned whether it had even been Keynes's intention to argue for the regular use of budget deficits in managing the economy (Clarke 1997; Bateman 1996, 2005). With the newly published correspondence in the last volumes of Keynes's *Collected Works*, it has become clear that Keynes had been serious when he argued during the Second World War that 'the ordinary Budget should be balanced at all times' (JMK XVII: 225)

So much, then, for the naïve profligate from Cambridge. Likewise, so much for the father of macroeconomics and the corrupter of the modern state. Proceeding by half-truths, the stylized history gets almost everything wrong.

The purpose of this essay is to build upon this work that debunks the stylized history of Keynes's influence in order to build an alternative story of how Keynes has shaped the economic landscape that we live in at the beginning of the twenty-first century. If we understand what Keynes himself said about macroeconomic policy and how this might differ from Keynesian economic policy, then we can see twentieth-century economic history in a somewhat different light.

But to begin, we need to add another reinterpretation of Keynes's legacy that has been made possible by recent work in history, sociology, political science, economics and the history of economics. This reinterpretation initially became possible through the work in the excellent volume, *The Political Power of Economic Ideas: Keynesianism across Nations*, edited by Peter Hall (1989). Hall and his contributors set out to answer the previously unanswered question of exactly how Keynes's ideas had permeated the industrial democracies. How, they wondered, had Keynes's ideas penetrated into the policy-making apparatus in so many countries? The volume thus contains the first set of detailed country studies ever to examine the adoption of demand management policies in different industrialized democracies.

But, somewhat awkwardly, Hall discovered that the process he had intended to study, 'Keynesianism across nations', was not exactly what he had thought it was. 'One of the most striking findings of this study is the degree to which Keynes's ideas about demand management were resisted or ignored in many nations' (Hall 1989: 367). Likewise, '[t]he role of the state in the economy increased for many reasons that had little to do with Keynes: the legacy of the war economy, the demands of reconstruction, and the expansion of universal social benefits' (Hall 1989: 365). Put most simply, Hall discovered that it was *not* the fact that Keynes had invented a rationale for state intervention in the economy that had first swept economists off their feet and then been embraced by the economic policy-makers across the industrial democracies. 'Keynesianism across nations' is a more complex phenomenon than the simple triumph of Keynes's ideas over economists and policy-makers.

KEYNES'S OWN POLICY ADVICE

For most of the seventy years since the publication of the *General Theory*, the phrase 'Keynesian economic policy' has been a synonym for fiscal policy. If a country was said to be using Keynesian economic policy, it meant they were using the federal budget (expenditures or taxes) to stimulate or dampen the economy. During the decades immediately after the Second World War, it was almost always the case that the use of the term 'Keynesianism' meant not only the use of fiscal policy, but its use to *stimulate* the economy. Thus, Buchanan and Wagner could say in their well-known book *Democracy in Deficit: The Political Legacy of Lord Keynes* (1976) that Keynes had wrought a world of ever-increasing government budget deficits, and it raised nary an eyebrow; of course, people assumed, that was what Keynes had called for.

As George Peden suggests in chapter 6 of this volume, this idea of Keynes was not only erroneous, but somewhat ironic. The first important application of Keynes's ideas about the use of fiscal policy in his native Britain came in 1941, in response to the needs to *dampen* demand at the beginning of the Second World War to avoid inflation, and it resulted in fiscal *tightening*. Keynes had published his pamphlet 'How to pay for the war' in 1940 with the express hope of influencing such an outcome. Thus, Keynes himself was most certainly not interested in the one-way use of his ideas to stimulate the economy; nor did Keynes ever run a campaign suggesting the continued and increasing use of budget deficits.

Keynes's own ideas about economic policy were famously fluid. This is one reason why among his many biographies there are very few that are short. He was often willing to consider different policy recommendations simultaneously and to weigh their relative merits; he was rarely dogmatic about any one solution to an economic problem. Perhaps the single great consistency in his thinking on economic policy was his belief that, in most cases, there was *something* that could be done that would improve the current situation. In this sense, it is perfectly appropriate that he is so widely associated with his famous dictum, 'in the long run, we are all dead'; he did believe in most cases that there were ways to improve the short-run performance of the economy.

Actually, as regards the policy most associated with Keynes's name, deficit spending by the central government, his views were relatively consistent over time: the fact is that he rarely explicitly supported such a policy. What Keynes supported during the last two decades of his life was the use of public works projects to stimulate aggregate demand. He believed that building new housing, constructing new roads or developing a new port facility were effective ways to put people back to work. Furthermore, he believed that if capitalists came to believe that such projects would be initiated at the appropriate time in the business cycle, it would bolster confidence in the economy and help sustain a more regular stream of private investment.[3]

Because Keynes often termed these public works projects 'loan-financed expenditure', many people came to believe that he supported using government deficits to stimulate the economy. Keynes notes in a footnote to the *General Theory* that loan-financed expenditure *could* be financed by government borrowing, but that it does not need to be. In his own time and his own context, Keynes did not see government budget deficits as necessary to carry out public works projects.[4]

In accounting, it is standard practice to distinguish between ordinary expenditure on current consumption and capital expenditure on projects that generate income. Consumption expenditure is gone once it is made; capital expenditure, however, creates a stream of income that arises from the capital asset that is created. Capital expenditure requires an investment that might entail borrowing, but the borrowed money can be paid back from the stream of new income that has been created. It is standard accounting practice to distinguish between these two types of expenditure through the use of two different budgets, an ordinary budget and a capital budget. For instance, when General Motors borrows money for investment in new plant and equipment that they will use over a twenty-year horizon, the borrowing takes place on the capital budget, not the ordinary budget. There would be no need to take the full expense of the plant's construction (or the funds raised for its construction) into the current year's budget. Likewise, for Keynes, there should have been no need to put the ordinary budget in deficit simply by making capital expenditures.

Often, however, Keynes did not even see the need to borrow new money to undertake the public works projects that he supported during hard times. Instead, he argued that the funds could be taken from the government's sinking fund, the pool of money that it collected to pay off existing debt. In his time, the Treasury determined arbitrary amounts to be collected each year and set aside to be used at a later date when money the government had borrowed would come due; this money was collected through the tax system and would be saved to pay off the bonds that had been issued to borrow the money in the first place. All of the borrowing during Keynes's time, as well as the sinking fund for paying off the debt, were accounted in the ordinary budget; the Treasury had adopted a policy of counting the capital budget in the ordinary budget, so the money being collected for the eventual payment of existing government debt was already counted in the ordinary (current) budget. Keynes argued first for creating a separate capital budget in 1924. Then, in 1929, for instance, in 'Can Lloyd George do it?', he argued that if the sinking fund were suspended for two years, the funds being collected for the eventual payment of outstanding debt could be used to support the construction of new homes or new roads. Since the use of the money in the sinking fund would generate income to replace the amount borrowed, Keynes did not see why these funds could not be fruitfully employed.

Keynes was fighting a multi-faceted battle with the Treasury, however. His proposals for public works financed as capital expenditure required not only that he persuade the authorities to undertake such projects, they also required that the ordinary budget be correctly redefined as separate from the capital budget *and* that he convince them to use the sinking fund (which would be a part of the newly, correctly defined capital budget) to finance the projects. Keynes continued to write about the correct accounting for capital expenditures through the last years of his life during the Second World War, when he was working as a special consultant to the Treasury. In the course of his work on the White Paper on *Full Employment* (1944) and the *National Debt Enquiry* (1945), he insisted repeatedly that it was no part of his intention to argue for deficits in the ordinary budget. It has been taken as evidence of Keynes's limited impact on the Treasury's thinking that the White Paper on *Full Employment*, which contains a commitment to maintaining full employment after the war, and which makes this commitment in the context of demand management through the budget, nonetheless holds firm to the anachronistic accounting framework that folds the capital budget in the ordinary budget and, thus, supports the pursuit of full employment through adjustment of the size of the budget surplus, *not* through the use of budget deficits.[5]

Thus, demand management policy from Keynes's own point of view was not only something that could (and should) be used to dampen as well as stimulate the economy, it did not necessarily involve running government budget deficits. The caricature of Keynes created by Buchanan and Wagner (1977) is not a serious portrait of John Maynard Keynes.

KEYNESIAN ECONOMISTS AND KEYNES

Another irony of the image of Keynes as an advocate of constant and increasing deficits is that it helped lead to an image of him as someone uninterested in monetary policy. During the height of the anti-Keynesian counter-revolution in the 1960s and 1970s, a clear line existed in the minds of most economists and financial journalists between Keynesians, whose primary interest was fiscal policy, and monetarists, whose primary interest was monetary policy. Now, it is true that Keynes had an idea of monetary policy that has few, if any, adherents today; but he had clearly articulated ideas about what monetary policy could achieve and how it should be conducted.

In a nutshell, following the publication of the *General Theory* Keynes espoused a consistent argument that monetary policy should be kept loose, or easy. He argued in the *General Theory* that the object of monetary policy should be to set interest rates low and to keep them low; he believed that this would encourage as much private investment in new capital as possible. This argument does not imply that monetary policy is ineffective, or unimportant, but it does suggest that it not be used counter-cyclically. Keynes never seriously wavered from this position during the last ten years of his life.[6]

His position was often interpreted, however, as meaning that monetary policy was unimportant or ineffective.[7] Certainly, the young economists who formed the bulwark of the Keynesian revolution following the Second World War were overwhelmingly interested in fiscal policy; this group showed little interest or concern with monetary policy. But Keynes saw a clear role for monetary policy.

Nor did the young Keynesians' policy recommendations necessarily demonstrate complete fealty to Keynes's positions on fiscal policy. During the Second World War, Keynes had disagreements with young Keynesians on both sides of the Atlantic about how to design postwar fiscal policy.[8] The young Keynesians in America and Britain were heavily interested in adjusting taxes as a means of causing changes in household expenditure. Keynes had never shown much belief in the efficacy of adjusting consumption, and so argued instead for policies that would affect investment.

But Keynesians of all stripes made it a central claim of their writings that they were close disciples of Keynes's thought. Two of the highest-profile postwar Keynesians, Abba Lerner and Alvin Hansen, certainly staked such claims. Lerner is the author of one of the first major expositions of Keynesian economic policy, *The Economics of Control* (1944), a book that advocated a degree of fiscal fine-tuning that goes beyond anything Keynes ever argued for during his lifetime. Lerner had known Keynes in England before Lerner emigrated to the United States, and Keynes clearly admired Lerner's analytical abilities; but the question of how closely their ideas about economic policy matched is an open one at best.[9] But Lerner always claimed Keynes's imprimatur for his own work. Lerner's review of the *General Theory* in the *International Labor Review* (1936), which is more in the nature of a summary and restatement of the analytical model in Keynes's book, had been read by Keynes before it was published, and Lerner (1936: 435) said, in his prefatory comments, 'It should be added that the article has been read in manuscript by Mr. Keynes himself, who has expressed his approval of it.' Lerner often spoke in his later writings about deficit-spending (as opposed to model-building) as if all his work carried this same stamp of approval.

Another well-known example of claiming Keynes for the Keynesian economic policy came in Alvin Hansen's famous text, *A Guide to Keynes* (1953). Written as a reader's guide to the *General Theory*, Hansen's book became a staple of graduate and undergraduate education in the 1950s and 1960s. Hansen carefully mixed together his guide to Keynes with his own policy recommendations on deficit-spending and so shaped a generation's understanding of Keynes and of Keynesian economic policy. It is interesting to note, however, a caveat to Hansen's interpretation, carefully tucked away near the end of the book.

With respect to the two leading policy dogmas – the gold standard and the balanced budget – Keynes attacked the first directly but the second rather vaguely, though he staunchly supported loan expenditure as a means of raising Aggregate Demand. . . He never explored the implications of a growing public debt, the problems of debt management, or the important role of public debt as a means of providing adequate liquid assets in a growing economy.

(Hansen, 1953: 219)

Thus, Hansen admitted that Keynes had not advocated 'constant and growing deficits'. The quotation also makes it clear that he conflated Keynes's statements about 'loan-financed expenditure' with his own ideas about government budget deficits.[10]

It is not, therefore, surprising that people came to view the policy recommendations of mainline Keynesians like Lerner and Hansen as the policy recommendations of Keynes himself. They had worked hard to create that impression. The same kind of conflation was perhaps even easier in Britain, where leading Keynesian economists had studied under Keynes at Cambridge and, in some cases, had even helped him in offering comments of early drafts of the *General Theory*. James Meade, for instance, a leading British Keynesian who had a pleasant humility about his apprenticeship under Keynes, was still identified in the minds of most economists with Keynes's own ideas. Meade became one of the most articulate and effective spokesmen for Keynesianism after Keynes's death; but while he was working in the Treasury with Keynes during the Second World War, Meade had made policy suggestions with which Keynes had clearly not agreed.[11] There was certainly much in common between Keynes and the Keynesians, not least Keynes's well-articulated attacks on the efficacy of 'policy dogmas' such as the Gold Standard and the idea that the government is helpless to do anything constructive during a depression. Likewise, both Keynes and the Keynesians saw a role for government spending in smoothing the business cycle. But to the extent that Lerner and Hansen implied that Keynes had supported their ideas of burgeoning government deficits, they had no ally in John Maynard Keynes, whose ideas about financing public works projects as self-paying capital projects were a world away from the kind of deficit arguments that Hansen and Lerner made.

POLITICIANS AND DEMAND MANAGEMENT?

On the basis of the argument so far, that there is a clear distinction between what Keynes and the Keynesians might have wished for counter-cyclical economic policy, one might suppose that the next logical question would be whether the politicians who implemented demand management policies followed Keynes or the Keynesians in fashioning their policies. When Peter Hall (1933: 367) reported, 'One of the most striking findings of this study is the degree to which Keynes's ideas about demand management were resisted or ignored in many nations', was he telling us that the politicians followed the Keynesians rather than Keynes?

No, that is not Hall's point. What he is saying is that the politicians in many countries followed neither Keynes nor the Keynesians.

This might seem to indicate that demand management had not really been widely adopted in mid-century. But while it is true that some countries with highly successful economies in the three decades after the Second World War (e.g. West Germany and Japan) did not embrace demand management until near the end of that period, and even then with limited, short-lived enthusiasm, the more complex reality is that demand management was widely adopted, but was only adopted in a very few places under the guise of Keynes's influence.

The United States is an excellent example of this phenomenon. During his campaigns for the presidency in 1932 and 1936, Franklin Delano Roosevelt had run on a promise of balancing the budget and had been able in his first administration to limit his deficits to the amount that his administration spent on relief projects. Roosevelt was only swayed to deliberately run a deficit in 1938, after the economy slid into recession in 1937 immediately following his second inauguration (March 1937). However, the impetus to purposely submit a budget in 1938 that was in deficit came not from John Maynard Keynes or his followers.[12]

The recession of 1937 posed a crisis for the administration. By 1936, the economy had returned to its level of industrial output in 1929, but there was still significant unemployment; thus, when the economy began to slow down, the implications were dire. The situation posed a political crisis for the administration because they were at a total loss for how to address the economy's slide back into recession. Neither of their primary economic policies from the First New Deal had proven durable or effective: these were the National Industrial Recovery Act, an effort to establish industrial cartels to limit output and so raise prices, and a reflationary plan to buy gold in order to drive up commodity prices. The National Industrial Recovery Act had eventually been declared unconstitutional because it encouraged illegal collusion between firms, and the gold-buying scheme had been abandoned in less than a year of its adoption because it raised the price of gold but not of basic commodities. During the election campaign of 1936, Roosevelt had been careful to remind people that the country had turned back towards prosperity, but was equally careful not to claim credit that any of his own policies had been directly responsible for the upturn.

Thus, Roosevelt faced the 1937 recession as a longtime advocate of balanced budgets and with no good alternative strategy for addressing a slowdown in economic activity. The impetus to purposely run a deficit in the 1938 budget came from a small group of government economists who were commissioned through the suggestion of Harry Hopkins, a New Deal administrator who was about to be named Secretary of Commerce. Hopkins suggested to Roosevelt that he get some staff researchers to contact the heads of government departments and find out what was happening with the federal budget and with the economy. In response, Roosevelt created a small working group, including Laughlin Currie, Leon Henderson and Isador Lubin; this group discovered that there was a direct correlation between the size of government expenditure and the performance of the economy. In 1936, the last instalment of a First World War veteran's bonus had been paid; in 1937, not only had the bonus ceased, but the tax to support the new social security system had been levied for the first time. This change in fiscal position exactly mirrored the changing fortunes of the economy, and Hopkins took the results to Roosevelt to argue that this showed the necessity for a fiscal stimulus to turn the economy back out of recession.

Within a few years, young economists who were familiar with Keynes's work would enter the government and create a Keynesian beachhead within the Roosevelt administration, but the initial arguments for using fiscal policy to stimulate the economy had been without reference to, or influence from, John Maynard Keynes or the Keynesians. Herbert Stein (1969: 131), widely regarded as the leading historian of American fiscal policy, has argued that 'it is possible to describe the evolution of fiscal policy in America up to 1940 without reference to [Keynes]'. Harold James (1989) has told an analogous story for interwar Germany in his excellent essay, 'What's so Keynesian about Deficit Spending?' James points out that the country was so destabilized during the 1920s that the only way to form a democratic government was through the policies that led to deficits: business groups demanded tax cuts, while labour groups and farmers demanded spending programmes. In the face of a possible revolution, the deliberate decision to undertake deficits provided 'the only available social cement' (James 1989: 234). Keynes's writings played no part in the deliberations or decisions of this democratic calculus. Likewise, the impetus for running a fiscal deficit in interwar France was not the result of Keynes's influence. In fact, Pierre Rosanvallon (1989: 172–83) explains that the *General Theory* was not translated until 1942, and that very few in France read it in English before the end of the Second World War.

The interesting thing in each of these cases is that Keynes's name *did* eventually get attached to the counter-cyclical use of fiscal policy in these countries. Different reasons for this *ex post* labelling have been proffered, such as the rise of the collection of national economic statistics (which reflected the analytical categories in the *General Theory*), the success of Keynes's book in debunking the verities of the old economic dogmas and the rise of the welfare state. But whatever the reasons, it is clear that Keynes's role in the twentieth-century revolution in the use of demand management is more complex than the old stylized history allows. Keynes was less the cause of that revolution than he was the name around which its early successes were consolidated. The Keynesian revolution arose for a plethora of reasons which must be fleshed out in the case of each country.

Perhaps only in Britain and Canada can it be said that Keynes (or the Keynesians) was (were) directly responsible for the implementation of counter-cyclical demand management policies. In the British case, the exact nature of Keynes's influence and successes has been hotly debated, although he clearly influenced the use of fiscal policy to dampen inflation and construct the wartime budgets after 1941.[13] In Canada, the direct effect of young Keynesians and their influence in Ottawa to undertake the use of counter-cyclical fiscal policy has been well documented.[14] But beyond these two cases, demand management emerged in the interwar period through a process of discovery and democratic experimentation in several industrialized nations without any direct reference to Keynes or his writings. One could correctly paraphrase Herbert Stein in regards to these countries and say, 'it is possible to describe the evolution of fiscal policy in *most industrialized democracies* up to 1940 without reference to [Keynes]'.

PROTO-KEYNESIANISM BECOMES KEYNESIANISM

In order to deal with the awkward fact that demand management (particularly deficit-spending) arose in so many countries without reference to Keynes's writings, Peter Hall and his contributors developed the word 'proto-Keynesian' to describe the widespread phenomenon of 'non-Keynesian' or 'pre-Keynesian' arguments for deficit-spending. Thus, demand management and the use of deficits in the interwar period in Sweden, Japan, the United States, France, Italy and Germany were 'proto-Keynesian'. Such policies were, after all, widespread, and they did not rely on the authority of Keynes's name for their justification. Indeed, if 'proto-Keynesian' means arguments for deficit-spending (or public works projects) before Keynes had articulated a theoretical model in the *General Theory* that could be used to justify such action, then Keynes's own arguments for the Liberal Party in the 1920s for the use of public works projects must be labelled 'proto-Keynesian'.

The real crux of the matter, then, in trying to understand how Keynes's name became attached to counter-cyclical fiscal policy would thus seem to be Keynes's theoretical model in the *General Theory*. Widely seen at mid-century as the cutting edge of economic theory, his model of aggregate demand carried the day and served as the *ex post* imprimatur for a revolution in fiscal policy that had actually taken place without reference to him or his writings. His model served as the means for economists and economic policy-makers around the world to speak a common language and think of themselves as engaged in a common enterprise. As mentioned above, this sense of common purpose was undoubtedly made much easier by the emergence of national income accounting in the 1930s and 1940s (Patinkin 1976). It is difficult to remember that when the Great Depression hit in 1929, there were no figures for gross national product that could be used to compare output with the previous year. No one could say with authority just how much output had fallen.

The revolution in national income accounting was just beginning to take place in the 1930s, and it happened that the categories of measurement that emerged matched the categories in Keynes's *General Theory* perfectly. Since Keynes uses some preliminary figures produced by one of the pioneers of national income accounting, Simon Kuznets, in his book, it might be appropriate to say that Keynes's work was shaped by the emerging revolution in macro-economic measurement. But whichever way the influences run between the measurers and Keynes, the fact is that macroeconomic statistics were born at virtually the same time as his theoretical apparatus took centre stage. This not only made new empirical work possible, it also made it possible for researchers in different countries to see themselves as engaged in the same emerging moment in economic science and economic management. Keynes was not directly responsible for the revolution in economic statistics, but in retrospect his work seems perfectly fit for the moment when that revolution took place; it provided a common theoretical framework for people in all countries to use in analyzing their new data. The Keynesian revolutions in economic policy and economic theory, thus, benefited greatly from the revolution in national income accounting.

Likewise, it has been widely observed that the prosperity brought on in the United States by the wartime economy between 1939 and 1945 lent credence to Keynes's ideas in the eyes of many.[15] More recently, Robert Higgs (1992) has argued that the US wartime economy is not properly understood as an example of successful demand management, but rather as a successful example of a command-and-control economy; but be that as it may, in the decades following the Second World War, the rise in output and employment during the war years was widely seen as proof that government expenditure could lift an economy out of a slump. 'The elimination of unemployment during World War II was one of the greatest influences on postwar views about the role of government in attaining and maintaining high employment and production, and the possibility of avoiding serious depressions in the future.'[16]

Of equal importance with the rise of national income accounting and the wartime boom must be the rise of the welfare state after the war. The advent of the welfare state in the Western democracies was just as uneven and locally determined as the rise of demand management, but, like demand management, it grew rapidly at midcentury. This was a common transnational response to the terrible dislocations of the Great Depression; and just as the various experiments in fiscal policy were being consolidated after the war under the banner of Keynesianism, the welfare state was beginning to arise. In Britain, the early form of the welfare state was proposed in the Beveridge Report (1942), and this depended explicitly on the assumption that demand management would be used successfully in the postwar period to maintain employment at a high and steady level. A high level of employment would be needed both to help sustain tax revenues for financing the welfare state, as well as helping to minimize the number of people who would need help.

But whether this same calculus was explicit in every country, it is certainly the case that a common ideology developed across the industrialized democracies in the three decades following the war. In some form, this ideology involved the belief that the state could (and should) work to maintain full employment and to provide some level of social benefit. Taken together, demand management and the welfare state were two of the central planks of social democracy. The apparent success of the welfare state and the ability to keep most people in work between 1945 and 1975 lent tremendous cachet to Keynes's name. His ideas about economic management seemed inseparable from the postwar prosperity.

WHAT BECAME OF KEYNESIANISM?

Given the association of Keynes's name with the programme that involved the welfare state and the idea that the government had a positive role to play in the economy, it is not surprising that Keynes became the focus of much of the attack by the right against economic management in the 1970s and 1980s. The counter-revolution against the government's role in the economy entailed both a microeconomic and a macroeconomic component, but the single most common target of the right was Keynes.[17] His theoretical models, the policies associated with his name and even his character became the subject of frequent attack. Indeed, the theoretical revolution begun by Milton Friedman in the economics profession and the political revolution symbolized by the rise to power of Margaret Thatcher and Ronald Reagan were explicitly pitched against Keynes and his ideas.

At this point, we might say that a new idea of Keynesianism rose in the public arena. This Keynesianism was seen as a tired, failed set of ideas that had led to the terrible combination of high inflation and high unemployment. Since Keynesian economic policy had been understood to be able to handle either of these problems taken alone, but unable to handle them both together, and since it was argued to have led to their appearance together, its days as a positive force in economic policy circles were over in the eyes of many. With the election of Thatcher and Reagan, Milton Friedman's monetarism was widely seen to have won the battle of ideas, and Keynesianism had lost. The right wanted to reduce the government's role in the economy and very much wanted to reduce social benefit; defeating Keynes and Keynesianism was a central part of that effort.

This effort, on a fuller reading of Keynes's own work, is somewhat paradoxical. That the right would want to attack Keynesianism is altogether understandable, given its iconic status as the theory and policy behind the welfare state and the idea of demand management by the state. But Keynes himself had not argued for many of the things that the right was attacking, and so the attacks against Keynes himself were misplaced and aimed at a straw man.

Perhaps the one thing that Keynes had done that was an honest provocation to the right was his insistent rhetoric of revolution, both as regards theory and policy. As Donald Moggridge (1986: 357) has noted, 'Keynes self-consciously employed a rhetorical device' of revolution that heavily shaped subsequent interpretations and understandings of his work. In his *General Theory*, the device took the form of the juxtapositon of his own work against 'classical economics'. In his popular writings, he often made the same sort of false dichotomy between his own position and that of his opponents. In the theoretical case, the 'classical school' simply did not exist in the simple form that Keynes claimed; likewise, in the policy arena, Keynes did not face the unified opposition that he often claimed for himself.[18] Thus, in some sense, we can say that what goes around comes around: in creating false dichotomies to make his own position look more 'revolutionary', Keynes created straw men to knock down. His opponents would often treat him in the same way in the 1960s and 1970s.

But beyond this irony, there lies the more interesting fact that demand management has made a thorough comeback in the last two decades. Today one finds few arguments of the type made by Alvin Hansen or Abba Lerner, but one does find the regular use of the tools of demand management. Sometimes this use is measured and to good effect; but sometimes it is not. The discretionary use of interest rates by the Federal Reserve Bank during the last twenty years in the United States has been exceptionally successful. On the other hand, the large fiscal stimulus created by the Thatcher government's deficits in the mid-1980s led to a short-term growth spurt that caused considerable economic dislocation when the bubble burst in the early 1990s.[19] But the regular use of fiscal and monetary policy today is much more like the subtle arguments buried in Keynes's own writings than it is to either the Keynesian theories that developed after his death or the policy rules that were demanded by the right when they attacked Keynesianism at the end of the twentieth century.

Thus, if we absent the rhetoric of revolution and absent the decades of fighting between left and right, we may have settled into a world where the responsible use of demand management tools sometimes can occur, much as Keynes had hoped. There is, of course, no guarantee of their responsible use, but we have seen that demand management can be used responsibly and that it does not necessarily lead to the ruin of an economy. The world is more complex than the straw men that economists of all stripes are wont to use. Perhaps in the shadow of that knowledge, we can now turn to a fuller understanding of Keynes's actual policy arguments, as opposed to his rhetoric, and begin to use those arguments to help in the formation of policies to avoid inflation and unemployment.

NOTES

I wish to thank Roger Backhouse and Gordon Sellon for reading earlier drafts of the essay. I alone retain responsibility for any errors that remain.

1   In addition to Laidler (1999), see Laidler (1991) and O'Brien (1993).
2   See Peden (1988) for a discussion of the debates around exactly how much the Treasury may have learned from Keynes. Peden's essay in this volume offers an excellent summary of Keynes's interactions with the Treasury.
3   Keynes also came to understand and absorb his critics' argument that businessmen might not embrace government programmes and that they might, in fact, be frightened by them. See Bateman (1996).
4   See JMK VII: 128, fn 1. Peter Clarke (1997) explains the one occasion on which he can find Keynes unequivocally supporting a deficit in the ordinary budget.
5   See Peden (1988: ch. 6). As Peden notes (p. 48), the Treasury continued to argue against using a capital budget because they believed that politicians would be tempted to include in it expenditure of a 'non-self liquidating nature'.

6 Monetary economists today generally agree with Keynes that interest rates are the best instrument for conducting monetary policy. Few monetary economists today, however, believe that the central bank can hold interest rates at a low level indefinitely. The common assumption of why this cannot be done is that the loose (or easy) monetary policy will eventually lead to inflation and that inflationary expectations among bond traders will cause long-term interest rates to be bid up. One can argue in Keynes's defence that he was only thinking of the conditions at the time he was writing, when the British economy had been performing poorly for well over a decade; but he does not qualify his statements in this way. One can also view the Federal Reserve's recent spell (2001–4) of record low interest rates as an application of Keynes's argument.

7 This confusion on the part of Keynesian economists may also be attributed to a mistaken belief that an argument made by Keynes in the *General Theory* about the possibility of a liquidity trap, when central bankers are unable to drive interest rates any lower because of the public's willingness to hold infinite amounts of cash, was a general statement about monetary policy in all circumstances. Since, however, Keynes says that the liquidity trap is only a theoretical possibility, but had not happened to his knowledge, this is clearly a mistake on the part of those who used his argument to dismiss the efficacy of ever using monetary policy.

8 See Barber (1990) for the American story; see Peden (1990) for the British story.

9 David Colander (1984) carefully considers the difference between Keynes's and Lerner's policy prescriptions.

10 A central difference between Keynes and Hansen is that Hansen espoused a theory of 'secular stagnation', whereas Keynes held no such view. Hansen's theory entailed an argument that new opportunities for private capital investment had been exhausted and this would require increasing levels of government expenditure to sustain a growing population. This led Hansen to conclude that there would be a need for growing levels of government borrowing. But, again, Keynes never embraced Hansen's theory or its implicit pessimism about the prospects for private capital accumulation.

11 See Peden (1990).

12 A nice summary of this story appears in Barber (1990).

13 See Peden (1988) for an excellent survey of the extensive literature on the nature and extent of the Keynesian Revolution in Britain.

14 Granatstein (1982), Owram (1986) and Campbell (1987) have told the Canadian story from very different perspectives. In particular, Campbell

adds a somewhat different perspective from Granatstein and Owram in arguing that while Keynes's own writings influenced the early adoption of demand management, the eventual form of postwar demand management had a very limited Keynesian character.

15 See, for instance, Walter Salant (1989).

16 For a fuller discussion, see Walter Salant (1989: 45–6), from whom this quotation was taken. Notice that Salant is only making claims about views caused by the economic boom during the war, not about the causes of that boom. See also Higgs (1992).

17 Michael Bernstein (2002) has provided great detail of the attack against Keynes and macroeconomic management in the 1970s and 1980s. Bernstein seems particularly unaware, however, of how advances in microeconomics contributed to the neo-liberal counter-revolution. Backhouse (2005) provides a much more rounded picture of the microeconomic dimension of the counter-revolution as well as the right-wing funding sources that supported it.

18 Although he did face a unified and articulate opposition in the form of the 'Treasury view', a strong argument against government intervention in the economy that was developed, articulated and enforced by a group of men who had no formal training in economics.

19 One of the enduring ironies of the history of fiscal policy is that Margaret Thatcher ran more government budget deficits than any other British prime minister in the second half of the twentieth century. And as Roger Backhouse (2002) has shown, her deficits in the mid-1980s led to a bubble whose bursting caused severe economic dislocation in the early 1990s.

BIBLIOGRAPHY

Amariglio, J. 1988. The Body, Economic Discourse, and Power: An Economist's Introduction to Foucault. *History of Political Economy*
20: 583–613.

1990. Economics as Postmodern Discourse. In Warren J. Samuels ed.
Economics as Discourse. Boston: Kluwer.

and D. F. Ruccio. 1995. Keynes, Postmodernism, Uncertainty. In Sheila
Dow and John Hillard eds. *Keynes, Knowledge and Uncertainty*. Aldershot: Edward Elgar.

2003. *Postmodern Moments in Modern Economics*. Princeton, NJ: Princeton University Press.

Andrews, D. R. 2000. Continuity and Change in Keynes's Thought: The
Importance of Hume. *European Journal of the History of Economic
Thought* 7: 1–21.

Annan, N. 2002. Keynes and Bloomsbury. In Roger Louis ed. *Still More
Travels with Britannia*. London: I. B. Taurus.

Backhouse, R. E. 1985. *A History of Modern Economic Analysis*. Oxford:
Blackwell.

1997. The Rhetoric and Methodology of Modern Macroeconomics. In
B. Snowdon and H. Vane eds. *Reflections on the Development of
Modern Macroeconomics*. Cheltenham: Edward Elgar.

1998. The Transformation of U.S. Economics, 1920–1960, Viewed
through a Survey of Journal Articles. In Mary S. Morgan and Malcolm
Rutherford eds. *From Interwar Pluralism to Postwar Neoclassicism*.
Annual supplement to vol. XXX of *History of Political Economy*,
85–107.

2002. The Macroeconomics of Margaret Thatcher. *Journal of the History
of Economic Thought* 24: 3, 313–34.

2005. The Rise of Free Market Economics: Economists and the Role of the
State since 1970. In Steven Medema and Peter Boettke eds. *The Role of*

Government in the History of Political Economy. Annual supplement to vol. 37 of *History of Political Economy* (forthcoming).

and J. Biddle. 2000. The Concept of Applied Economics: A History of Ambiguity and Multiple Meanings. In Roger E. Backhouse and Jeff Biddle eds. *Toward a History of Applied Economics*. Annual supplement to vol. 32 of *History of Political Economy*, 1–26.

and D. Laidler. 2004. What was Lost with IS-LM. In M. de Vroey and K. D. Hoover (eds.) *The IS–LM Model: Its Rise, Fall and Strange Persistence*. Annual supplement to vol. 36 of *History of Political Economy*, 25–56.

Barber, W. J. 1990. Government as a Laboratory for Economic Learning in the Years of the Democratic Roosevelt. In Mary O. Furner and Barry Supple eds. *The State and Economic Knowledge*. Cambridge: Cambridge University Press.

Barkai, H. 1993. Productivity Patterns, Exchange Rates and the Gold Standard Restoration Debate of the 1920s. *History of Political Economy* 25: 1–37.

Barr, N. 2004. *The Economics of the Welfare State*. 4th edn. Oxford: Oxford University Press.

Barro, R. J. and H. I. Grossman. 1971. A General Disequilibrium Model of Income and Employment. *American Economic Review* 61: 82–93.

Bateman, B. W. 1987. Keynes's Changing Conception of Probability. *Economics and Philosophy* 3: 97–120.

1988 G. E. Moore and J. M. Keynes: A Missing Chapter in the History of the Expected Utility Model. *American Economic Review* 78(5): 1098–1106.

1990. Keynes, Induction and Econometrics. *History of Political Economy* 22(2): 359–79.

1996. *Keynes's Uncertain Revolution*. Ann Arbor: University of Michigan Press.

2005. Scholarship in Deficit: Buchanan and Wagner on John Maynard Keynes. *History of Political Economy* 37(2): 185–90.

and J. B. Davis (eds.) 1991. *Keynes and Philosophy: Essays on the Origins of Keynes's Thought*. Aldershot: Edward Elgar.

Bell, A. O. (ed.) 1980. *The Diary of Virginia Woolf, Volume III, 1925–1930*. London: Hogarth Press.

Bell, C. 1914. *Art*. London: Chatto and Windus.

1928. *Civilization*. In *Civilization and Old Friends*. Chicago: University of Chicago Press, 1973.

Bentham, J. 1962. *The Works of Jeremy Bentham* (ed. John Bowring). New York: Russell and Russell.

Bernstein, M. A. 2001. *A Perilous Progress: Economists and Public Purpose in Twentieth-Century America*. Princeton, NJ: Princeton University Press.

Besomi, D. 2000. On the Spreading of an Idea: The Strange Case of Mr Harrod and the Multiplier. *History of Political Economy* 31: 347–9.

Blaug, M. 1975. Kuhn versus Lakatos, or Paradigms versus Research Programmes in the History of Economics. *History of Political Economy* 7: 399–419.

1980. *The Methodology of Economics.* Cambridge: Cambridge University Press.

1990a. *John Maynard Keynes: Life, Ideas, Legacy.* London: Macmillan.

1990b. Second Thoughts on the Keynesian revolution. In M. Blaug ed. *Economic Theories: True or False.* Cheltenham: Edward Elgar.

1999. The Formalist Revolution or What Happened to Orthodox Economics after World War II? In R. E. Backhouse and J. Creedy eds. *From Classical Economics to the Theory of the Firm: Essays in Honour of D. P. O'Brien.* Cheltenham: Edward Elgar.

Bonadei, R. 1994. John Maynard Keynes: Contexts and Methods. In z-Alessandra Marzola and Francesco Silva eds. *John Maynard Keynes: Language and Method.* Aldershot: Edward Elgar, pp. 13–75.

Booth, Alan. 1983. The 'Keynesian Revolution' in Economic Policy-Making. *Economic History Review,* 2nd series, 36: 103–23.

Boumans, M. 2001. A Macroeconomic Approach to Complexity. In Arnold Zellner, Hugo A. Keuzenkamp and Michael McAleer eds. *Simplicity, Inference and Modelling: Keeping It Sophisticatedly Simple.* Cambridge: Cambridge University Press.

Bradford, F. A. 1935. Book review of A. Kitson, *The Banker's Conspiracy which Started the World Crisis. American Economic Review* 25: 142.

Brentano, F. 1969. *The Origin of our Knowledge of Right and Wrong.* London: Routledge. Translated by R. Chisholm.

1973. *The Foundation and Construction of Ethics.* London: Routledge. Translated by E. H. Schneewind.

Brittan, S. 1977. Can Democracy Manage an Economy? In R. Skidelsky ed. *The End of the Keynesian Era.* Reprinted in Brittan 1996.

1988. *A Restatement of Economic Liberalism.* London: Macmillan.

1996. *Capitalism with a Human Face.* London: Fontana.

Broad, C. D. 1922. A Treatise on Probability by J. M. Keynes. *Mind* n.s., 31: 72–85.

Brügger, N. 2001. What about the Postmodern? The Concept of the Postmodern in the Work of Lyotard. *Yale French Studies* 99: 77–92.

Buchanan, J. M. and R. E. Wagner. 1977. *Democracy in Deficit: The Political Legacy of Lord Keynes.* New York and London: Academic Press.

Cagan, P. 1956. The Monetary Dynamics of Hyperinflation. In Milton Friedman ed. *Studies in the Quantity Theory of Money*. Chicago: University of Chicago Press.

Cain, N. 1979. Cambridge and its Revolution: A Perspective on the Multiplier and Effective Demand. *Economic Record* 55: 108–17, June.

Cairncross, A. and N. Watts. 1989. *The Economic Section 1939–1961*. London: Routledge.

Campbell, R. M. 1987. *Grand Illusions: The Politics of the Keynesian Experience in Canada, 1945–1975*. Peterborough: Broadview Press.

Carabelli, A. 1988. *On Keynes's Method*. Basingstoke: Macmillan.

Cartwright, N. 1989. *Nature's Capacities and their Measurement*. Oxford: Clarendon Press.

Childs, P. 2000. *Modernism*. London: Routledge.

Clarke, P. F. 1988. *The Keynesian Revolution in the Making, 1924–1936*. Oxford: Clarendon Press.

　1977. Keynes, Buchanan and the Balanced Budget Doctrine. In John Maloney ed. *Debt and Deficits*. Cheltenham: Edward Elgar.

　1998. *The Keynesian Revolution and its Economic Consequences*. Cheltenham: Edward Elgar.

Clower, R. W. 1965. The Keynesian Counterrevolution: A Theoretical Appraisal. In F. H. Hahn and F. P. R. Brechling eds. *The Theory of Interest Rates*. London: Macmillan.

　1967. A Reconsideration of the Microfoundations of Monetary Theory. *Western Economic Journal* 6: 1–9. Reprinted in Donald A. Walker ed. *Money and Markets: Essays by Robert W. Clower*. Cambridge: Cambridge University Press, 1984.

　2004. Trashing J. B. Say: The Story of a Mare's Nest. In K. Vela Velupillai ed. *Macroeconomic Theory and Economic Policy: Essays in Honour of Jean-Paul Fitoussi*. London: Routledge.

　and A. Leijonhufvud. 1973. Say's Principle: What It Means and Doesn't Mean. *Intermountain Economic Review*, Fall. Reprinted in A. Leijonhufvud, *Information and Coordination: Essays in Macroeconomic Theory*. Oxford: Oxford University Press, 1981.

Coates, J. 1996. *The Claims of Common Sense: Moore, Wittgenstein, Keynes and the Social Sciences*. Cambridge: Cambridge University Press.

Coats, A. W. 1969. Is There a Structure of Scientific Revolutions in Economics? *Kyklos* 22: 289–95.

Coddington, A. 1983. *Keynesian Economics: The Search for First Principles*. London: Allen and Unwin.

Colander, D. 1984. Was Keynes a Keynesian or a Lernerian? *Journal of Economic Literature* 22: 1572–5.

2000. The Death of Neoclassical Economics. *Journal of the History of Economic Thought* 22(2): 127–43.

Collins, J. 1984. *The Omega Workshops*. Chicago: University of Chicago Press.

Craine, R. and G. Hardouvelis. 1983. Are Rational Expectations for Real? *Greek Economic Review* 5(1): 5–32.

Cristiano, C. 2004. Il giovane Keynes: politica ed economia (1903–1914). PhD thesis, Università degli Studi di Firenze.

Cullenberg, S., J. Amariglio and D. Ruccio. 2001. *Postmodernism, Economics and Knowledge*. London: Routledge.

Currie, L. 1934. *The Supply and Control of Money in the United States*. Cambridge MA: Harvard University Press.

Dasgupta, A. K. 1985. *Epochs of Economic Theory*. Oxford: Blackwell.

Davidson, P. 1972. *Money and the Real World*. London: Macmillan.

1995. Uncertainty in Economics. In Sheila Dow and John Hillard eds. *Keynes, Knowledge and Uncertainty*. Aldershot: Edward Elgar.

Davis, J. B. 1994a. *Keynes's Philosophical Development*. Cambridge: Cambridge University Press.

(ed.) 1994b. *The State of Interpretation of Keynes*. Boston and London: Kluwer.

2003. *The Theory of the Individual in Economics*. London: Routledge.

Debreu, G. 1959. *The Theory of Value*. New York: Wiley.

De Marchi, N. B. and M. Blaug (eds.) 1991. *Appraising Economic Theories: Studies in the Methodology of Research Programmes*. Aldershot: Edward Elgar.

De Vroey, M. 2004. The History of Macroeconomics Viewed against the Background of the Marshall–Walras Divide. In Michel De Vroey and Kevin D. Hoover eds. *The IS-LM Model: Its Rise, Fall, and Strange Persistence*. Annual supplement to vol. 36 of *History of Political Economy*.

Deutscher, P. 1990. *R. G. Hawtrey and the Development of Macroeconomics*. Basingstoke: Macmillan.

Dillard, D. 1948. *The Economics of JM Keynes: The Theory of Monetary Policy*. London: Crosby Lockwood.

Dimand, R. W. 1988. *The Origins of the Keynesian Revolution: The Development of Keynes's Theory of Output and Employment*. Aldershot: Edward Elgar.

Dimsdale, N. H. 1981. British Monetary Policy and the Exchange Rate, 1920–38. *Oxford Economic Papers*, n.s., 33 supplement: 306–42.

1988. Keynes on Interwar Economic Policy. In W. Eltis and P. Sinclair eds. *Keynes and Economic Policy: The Relevance of the General Theory after Fifty Years*. Basingstoke: Macmillan.

Dostaler, G. 2005. *Keynes et ses combats*. Paris: Albin Michel.

Dow, S. C. 1991. Are There any Signs of Postmodernism within Economics? *Methodus* 3(1): 81–5.

Durbin, E. 1985. *New Jerusalems: The Labour Party and the Economics of Democratic Socialism*. London: Routledge.

　1988. Keynes, The British Labour Party and the Economics of Democratic Socialism. In F. Hamouda and S. N. Smithin eds. *Keynes and Public Policy after Fifty Years*. Aldershot: Edward Elgar.

Ely, R. T. 1936. The Founding and Early History of the American Economic Association. *American Economic Review* 26: 141–50.

Esty, J. 2004. *A Shrinking Island*. Princeton, NJ: Princeton University Press.

Felix, D. 1995. *Biography of an Idea: John Maynard Keynes and the General Theory of Employment, Interest and Money*. New Brunswick, NJ: Transaction Publishers.

Fitzgibbons, A. 1988. *Keynes's Vision: A New Political Economy*. Oxford: Clarendon Press.

　2000. *The Nature of Macroeconomics: Instability and Change in the Capitalist System*. Cheltenham: Edward Elgar.

Fletcher, G. A. 2000. *Understanding Dennis Robertson*. Cheltenham: Edward Elgar.

Forster, E. M. 1905. *Where Angels Fear to Tread*. New York: Alfred A. Knopf.

　1910. *Howards End*. London: Edward Arnold.

　1927. *A Passage to India*. New York: Harcourt, Brace.

　1928. *The Collected Tales of E. M. Forster*. New York: Alfred A. Knopf, 1947.

　1951. *Two Cheers for Democracy*. London: Edward Arnold, 1972.

Friedman, M. 1942. Discussion of the Inflationary Gap. *American Economic Review*. Revised and reprinted in M. Friedman ed. *Essays in Positive Economics*. Chicago: University of Chicago Press, 1953.

　1943. Methods for Predicting the Onset of 'Inflation'. In C. Shoup, M. Friedman and R. P. Mack eds. *Taxing to Prevent Inflation: Techniques for Estimating Revenue Requirements*. New York: Columbia University Press.

　1949. The Marshallian Demand Curve. In M. Friedman ed. *Essays in Positive Economics*. Chicago: Chicago University Press.

　1955. Leon Walras and his Economic System: A Review Article. *American Economic Review* 45(5): 900–9.

　1968. The Role of Monetary Policy. *American Economic Review* 58: 1, March.

　1969. *The Optimum Quantity of Money and Other Essays*. Chicago: Aldine.

　2004. Reflections on A Monetary History. *Cato Journal*, winter.

and A. J. Schwartz. 1963a. *A Monetary History of the United States, 1867–1960*. Princeton, NJ: Princeton University Press.

1963b. Money and Business Cycles. *Review of Economics and Statistics* 45(1, part 2: supplement). Reprinted in Friedman, 1969.

Fry, R. 1909. An Essay in Aesthetics. Reprinted in Goodwin 1998.

1920a. Retrospect. Reprinted in Goodwin 1998.

1920b. *Vision and Design*. London: Chatto and Windus.

1924. *The Artist and Psycho-Analysis*. New York: Doubleday, Doran.

1926. Art and Commerce. Reprinted in Goodwin 1998.

Furner, M. O. and B. Supple (eds.) 1990. *The State and Economic Knowledge*. Cambridge: Cambridge University Press.

Gadd, D. 1975. *The Loving Friends: A Portrait of Bloomsbury*. New York: Harcourt Brace Jovanovich.

Garnett, D. 1923. *Lady into Fox*. New York: Alfred A. Knopf.

1925. *The Sailor's Return*. New York: Alfred A. Knopf.

Gernalzick, N. 2001. From Classical Dichotomy to Differential Contract: The Derridean Integration of Monetary Theory. *Wiener Slawistischer Almanach* 54 (special issue): 363–73.

Gerrard, B. 1991. Keynes's General Theory: Interpreting the Interpretations. *Economic Journal* 101: 276–87.

Gillies, D. A. 2000. *Philosophical Theories of Probability*. London and New York: Routledge.

and G. Ietto-Gillies. 1991. Intersubjective Probability and Economics. *Review of Political Economy* 3(4): 393–417.

Gluck, M. 1986. Toward a Historical Definition of Modernism: Georg Lukacs and the Avant-Garde. *Journal of Modern History* 58(4): 845–82.

Gold, J. 1981. *The Multilateral System of Payments: Keynes, Convertibility and the International Monetary Fund's Articles of Agreement*. Washington: International Monetary Fund.

Goodwin, C. D. 1998. *Art and the Market: Roger Fry on Commerce in Art*. Ann Arbor: University of Michigan Press.

2000. Economic Man in the Garden of Eden. *Journal of the History of Economic Thought* 22: 405–32.

Goux, J.-J. 1990. *Symbolic Economies*. Ithaca, NY: Cornell University Press.

Granatstein, J. L. 1982. *The Ottawa Men: The Civil Service Mandarins, 1935–1957*. Toronto: Oxford University Press.

Gray, R. T. 1999. Buying into Signs: Money and Semiosis in Eighteenth-Century German Language Theory. In Martha Woodmansee and Mark Osteen eds. *The New Economic Criticism*. London: Routledge.

Groenewegen, P. 1995. *A Soaring Eagle: Alfred Marshall, 1842–1924*. Aldershot: Edward Elgar.

Haberler, G. 1937. *Prosperity and Depression*. 2nd edn. Geneva: League of Nations.

1946. *Prosperity and Depression*. 3rd edn. New York: United Nations.

Hacking, I. 1975. *The Emergence of Probability*. Cambridge: Cambridge University Press.

1990. *The Taming of Chance*. Cambridge: Cambridge University Press.

Hall, P. (ed.) 1989. *The Political Power of Economic Ideas: Keynesianism across Nations*. Princeton, NJ: Princeton University Press.

Hammond, J. D. 1996. *Theory and Measurement: Causality Issues in Milton Friedman's Monetary Economics*. Cambridge: Cambridge University Press.

Hands, D. W. 1985. Second Thoughts on Lakatos. *History of Political Economy* 17(1): 1–16.

Hansen, A. 1953. *A Guide to Keynes*. New York: McGraw-Hill.

Harcourt, G. C. and S. Turnell. 2003. On Skidelsky's Keynes. Unpublished paper.

Harrod, R. F. 1951. *The Life of John Maynard Keynes*. London: Macmillan.

Hawtrey, R. G. 1913. *Good and Bad Trade*. London: Constable.

Hayek, F. A. 1931. *Prices and Production*. London: Routledge.

1944. *The Road to Serfdom*. London: Routledge and Kegan Paul.

1960. *The Constitution of Liberty*. London: Routledge and Kegan Paul.

Heertje, A. and P. Heemeijer. 2002. On the Origin of Samuelson's Multiplier-Accelerator Model. *History of Political Economy* 34(1): 207–18.

Henderson, H. D. 1995. *The Inter-War Years and Other Papers*. Oxford: Clarendon Press.

Hendry, D. F. and M. S. Morgan (eds.) 1995. *The Foundations of Econometric Analysis*. Cambridge: Cambridge University Press.

Hicks, J. R. 1937. Mr Keynes and the 'Classics': A Suggested Interpretation. *Econometrica* 5: 147–59.

1939. *Value and Capital: An Inquiry into Some Fundamental Principles of Economic Theory*. Oxford: Clarendon Press. 2nd edn, 1946.

1965. *Capital and Growth*. Oxford: Oxford University Press.

1983. IS-LM: An Explanation. In Jean-Paul Fitoussi ed. *Modern Macroeconomic Theory*. Oxford: Blackwell.

Higgs, R. 1992. Wartime Prosperity: A Reassessment of the U.S. Economy in the 1940s. *Journal of Economic History* 52: 1.

Holroyd, M. 1971. *Lytton Strachey: A Biography*. Harmondsworth: Penguin.

Hood, W. C. and T. C. Koopmans (eds.) 1953. *Studies in Econometric Method*. Cowles Commission Monograph 14. New York: Wiley.

Hoover, K. D. 1988. *The New Classical Macroeconomics: A Sceptical Inquiry*. Oxford: Blackwell.

2004a. Lost Causes. *Journal of the History of Economic Thought* 26 (2): 149–64.

2004b. Milton Friedman's Stance: The Methodology of Causal Realism. Unpublished typescript, University of California, Davis.

2006. The Past as the Future: The Marshallian Approach to Post-Walrasian Econometrics. In D. Colander (ed.) *Beyond the Dynamic, Stochastic General Equilibrium Model*. Cambridge: Cambridge University Press.

Howson, S. 1973. 'A Dear Money Man'? Keynes on Monetary Policy, 1920. *Economic Journal* 83: 456–64.

1975. *Domestic Monetary Management in Britain 1919–38*. Cambridge: Cambridge University Press.

1980. *Sterling's Managed Float: The Operations of the Exchange Equalisation Account, 1932–39*. Princeton, NJ: Department of Economics, Princeton University.

1988. Cheap Money and Debt Management in Britain, 1932–51. In P. L. Cottrell and D. E. Moggridge eds. *Money and Power*. Basingstoke: Macmillan.

1993. *British Monetary Policy 1945–51*. Oxford: Clarendon Press.

2001. Why Didn't Hayek Review Keynes's *General Theory*? A Partial Answer. *History of Political Economy* 33: 369–74.

and D. Moggridge (eds.) 1990. *The Wartime Diaries of Lionel Robbins and James Meade, 1943–45*. Basingstoke: Macmillan.

and D. Winch. 1977. *The Economic Advisory Council, 1930–1939: A Study of Economic Advice during Depression and Recovery*. Cambridge: Cambridge University Press.

Hutchison, T. W. 1977. *Keynes v. the Keynesians . . .?* London: Institute of Economic Affairs.

Huyssen, A. 1984. Mapping the Postmodern. *New German Critique* 33: 5–52.

Jaffé, W. 1983. *William Jaffé's Essays on Walras* (ed. D. A. Walker). Cambridge: Cambridge University Press.

James, H. 1989. What is Keynesian about Deficit Financing? The case of Interwar Germany. In Peter Hall ed. *The Political Power of Economic Ideas: Keynesianism across Nations*. Princeton: Princeton University Press.

Jameson, F. 1991. *Postmodernism; or, The Cultural Logic of Late Capitalism*. Durham, NC: Duke University Press.

Johnson, E. S. 1978. Keynes as Literary Craftsman. In Elizabeth S. Johnson and Harry G. Johnson eds. *The Shadow of Keynes*. Oxford: Blackwell.

Johnstone, J. K. 1954. *The Bloomsbury Group*. London: Secker and Warburg.

Kahn, R. F. 1931. The Relation of Home Investment to Unemployment. *Economic Journal* 41: 173–198, June.

1976. Unemployment as Seen by Keynesians. In G. D. N. Worswick ed. *The Concept and Measurement of Involuntary Unemployment*. London: Allen and Unwin.

1984. *The Making of Keynes' General Theory*. Cambridge: Cambridge University Press.

Kandinsky, W. 1911. *Über das Geistige in der Kunst*. 10th edn. Bern: Benteli.

Kates, S. 1994. The Malthusian Origins of the *General Theory*: Or, How Keynes Came to Write a Book about Say's Law and Effective Demand. *History of Economics Review* 21: 10–20, winter.

King, J. E. 2002. *A History of Post Keynesian Economics since 1936*. Cheltenham: Edward Elgar.

Klaes, M. 2001. Begriffsgeschichte: Between the Scylla of Conceptual and the Charybdis of Institutional History of Economics. *Journal of the History of Economic Thought* 23(2): 153–79.

Klamer, A. 1993. Modernism in Economics: An Interpretation beyond Physics. In Neil de Marchi ed. *Non-Natural Social Science: Reflecting on the Enterprise of More Heat than Light*. Annual supplement to vol. 25 of *History of Political Economy*, 223–48.

1995. The Conception of Modernism in Economics: Samuelson, Keynes and Harrod. In Sheila Dow and John Hillard eds. *Keynes, Knowledge and Uncertainty*. Aldershot: Edward Elgar.

2001. Late Modernism and the Loss of Character in Economics. In Cullenberg, Amariglio and Ruccio: 2001.

Klein, L. R. 1944. *The Keynesian Revolution*. London: Macmillan. 2nd edn 1968.

Knight, F. H. 1921. *Risk, Uncertainty and Profit*. Chicago: University of Chicago Press, 1971.

Knüvener, T. 2005. Landhaus Lemke. Galinski www.galinsky.com/buildings/lemke/

Koopmans, T. C. 1950. *Statistical Inference in Dynamic Economic Models*. Cowles Commission Monograph 10. New York: Wiley.

Krauss, R. E. 1981. The Originality of the Avant-Garde. In Rosalind E. Krauss ed. *The Originality of the Avant-Garde and Other Modernist Myths*. Cambridge, MA: MIT Press, 1985.

Kregel, J. A. 1973. *The Reconstruction of Political Economy: An Introduction to Post Keynesian Economics*. London: Macmillan.

Kuhn, T. S. 1962. *The Structure of Scientific Revolutions*. Chicago: University of Chicago Press. 2nd edn 1970.

Laidler, D. E. W. 1991. *The Golden Age of the Quantity Theory*. Princeton, NJ: Princeton University Press.

1999. *Fabricating the Keynesian Revolution*. Cambridge: Cambridge University Press.

Lakatos, I. 1970. Falsification and the Methodology of Scientific Research Programmes. In I. Lakatos and A. Musgrave eds. *Criticism and the Growth of Knowledge*. Cambridge: Cambridge University Press.

Latsis, S. J. 1976. *Method and Appraisal in Economics*. Cambridge: Cambridge University Press.

Lavington, F. 1921. *The English Capital Market*. London: Methuen.

1922. *The Trade Cycle*. London: P. S. King and Son.

Lawson, T. 1985. Uncertainty and Economic Analysis. *The Economic Journal* 95: 909–27.

and H. Pesaran. 1989. *Keynes' Economics: Methodological Issues*. London: Routledge.

Leijonhufvud, A. 1968. *On Keynesian Economics and the Economics of Keynes*. Oxford: Oxford University Press.

1981. The Wicksell Connection. In A. Leijonhufvud, *Information and Coordination*. Oxford: Oxford University Press.

1998. Mr Keynes and the Moderns. *European Journal of the History of Economic Thought* 1998. Also in Luigi Pasinetti and Bertram Schefold eds. *The Impact of Keynes on Economics in the 20th Century*. Cheltenham: Edward Elgar, 1999.

Lerner, A. 1936. Mr. Keynes' 'General Theory of Employment, Interest, and Money'. *International Labour Review* 435–54, October.

LeRoy, S. F. 1995. On Policy Regimes. In Kevin D. Hoover ed. *Macroeconometrics: Developments, Tensions and Prospects*. Boston: Kluwer.

Loasby, B. J. 1976. *Choice, Complexity and Ignorance*. Cambridge: Cambridge University Press.

Lorraine, D. 1988. *Classical Probability in the Enlightenment*. Princeton, NJ: Princeton University Press.

Lovejoy, A. O. 1936. *The Great Chain of Being*. New York: Harper and Row, 1960.

Lucas, R. E. Jr. 1972. Expectations and the Neutrality of Money. *Journal of Economic Theory* 4: 103–24, April.

1976. Econometric Policy Evaluation: A Critique. In K. Brunner and A. H. Meltzer eds. *The Phillips Curve and Labor Markets*. Supplement to *Journal of Monetary Economics*, January.

1981. Methods and Problems in Business Cycle Theory. Reprinted in Lucas, *Studies in Business Cycle Theory*. Oxford: Blackwell.

and T. J. Sargent. 1978. After Keynesian Macroeconomics. Reprinted in R. E. Lucas Jr. and T. J. Sargent eds. *Rational Expectations and Econometric Practice*. London: George Allen and Unwin, 1984.

Lyotard, J.-F. 1979. *La condition postmoderne*. Paris: Editions de Minuit.

1984. *The Postmodern Condition*. Manchester: Manchester University Press. Translated by Geoff Bennington and Brian Massumi.

1985. Note on the Meaning of 'Post-'. In J.-F. Lyotard ed. *The Postmodern Explained*. Minneapolis: University of Minnesota Press, 1992. Translated by Julian Pefanis and Morgan Thomas.

1987. Rewriting Modernity. In J.-F. Lyotard ed. *The Inhuman: Reflections on Time*. Cambridge: Polity. Translated by G. Bennington and R. Bowlby.

Malthus, T. R. 1820. *Principles of Political Economy*. Reprinted (with Ricardo's *Notes*) in P. Sraffa ed. 1956. *Works and Correspondence of David Ricardo* vol. II. Cambridge: Cambridge University Press for the Royal Economic Society, 1956.

Mandel, E. 1975. *Late Capitalism*. Revised edn, translated by Joris De Bres. London: Verso.

Marcuzzo, M. C. 2002. The Collaboration between J. M. Keynes and R. F. Kahn from the *Treatise* to the *General Theory*. *History of Political Economy* 34(2): 421–47.

2005. Sraffa at the University of Cambridge. *European Journal for the History of Economic Thought* 12: 425–52.

and A. Rosselli (eds.) 2005. *Economists in Cambridge: A Study through their Correspondence, 1907–1946*. London: Routledge.

Marshall, A. 1871. Money. In J. Whittaker ed. *The Early Economic Writings of Alfred Marshall*, 2 vols. London: Macmillan.

1885. The Present Position of Economics. In A. C. Pigou ed. *Memorials of Alfred Marshall*. London: Macmillan, 1925.

1920. *Principles of Economics*. 8th edn. London: Macmillan, 1972.

1923. *Industry and Trade*. London: Macmillan.

1961. *Principles of Economics* (ed. C. Guillebaud), 2 vols. London: Macmillan.

and M. P. Marshall. 1879. *Economics of Industry*. London: Macmillan.

Marx, K. 1847. *The Poverty of Philosophy*. New York: International Publishers, 1966.

Marzola, A. 1994. Rhetoric and Imagination in the Economic and Political Writings of J. M. Keynes. In Alessandra Marzola and Francesco Silva eds. *John Maynard Keynes: Language and Method*. Aldershot: Edward Elgar.

Matthews, R. C. O. 1968. Why Has Britain Had Full Employment since the War? *Economic Journal* 78: 555–69.

McCloskey, D. N. 1983. The Rhetoric of Economics. *Journal of Economic Literature* 21(2): 481–517.

1994. *Truth and Persuasion in Economics*. Cambridge: Cambridge University Press.

2001. The Genealogy of Postmodernism: An Economist's Guide. In Cullenberg, Amariglio and Ruccio, 2001.

McLuhan, M. 1964. *Understanding Media*. London: Routledge and Kegan Paul.

Meade, J. 1990. *The Cabinet Office Diary, 1944–46*. In S. Howson ed. *Collected Papers*, vol. IV. London: Unwin Hyman.

Meisel, P. and W. Kendrick. 1985. *Bloomsbury/Freud: The Letters of James and Alix Strachey 1924–1925*. New York: Basic Books.

Menger, C. (1950) *Principles of Economics* (ed. and translated by James Dingwall and Bert F. Hoselitz). Glencoe, IL: Free Press.

Middleton, R. 1982. The Treasury in the 1930s: Political and Administrative Constraints to Acceptance of the 'New' Economics. *Oxford Economic Papers*, n.s., 34: 48–77.

1985. *Towards the Managed Economy: Keynes, the Treasury and the Fiscal Policy Debate of the 1930s*. London: Methuen.

Mill, J. S. 1844. On the Influence of Consumption upon Production. In *Essays on Some Unsettled Questions in Political Economy*. 2nd edn. London: Longmans, Gree, Reader and Dyer, 1874.

1848. *The Principles of Political Economy with Some of their Applications to Social Philosophy*. 7th edn. 1871. Reprinted in 2 vols. J. M. Robson ed. Toronto: University of Toronto Press, 1965.

Mini, P. V. 1991. *Keynes, Bloomsbury and the General Theory*. New York: St. Martin's.

Mirowski, P. E. 1994. Some Suggestions for Linking Arbitrage, Symmetries, and the Social Theory of Value. In Amitava Dutt ed. *New Directions in Analytical Political Economy*. Aldershot: Edward Elgar.

2002. *Machine Dreams*. Cambridge: Cambridge University Press.

Mises, L. von. 1966. *Human Action: A Treatise on Economics*. 3rd edn. Chicago: Henry Regnery.

Modigliani, F. 1944. Liquidity Preference and the Theory of Interest and Money. *Econometrica* 12: 45–88.

Moggridge, D. E. 1972. *British Monetary Policy 1924–1931: The Norman Conquest of $4.86*. Cambridge: Cambridge University Press.

1986. Keynes and His Revolution in Historical Perspective. *Eastern Economic Journal* 12: 357–68.

1990. Keynes as Editor. In D. J. Hey and D. Winch eds. *A Century of Economics: 100 Years of the Royal Economic Society*. Oxford: Blackwell.

1992. *Maynard Keynes. An Economist's Biography*. London: Routledge.

2005. Keynes, Art and the State. *History of Political Economy*, 37: 537–57.

Moore, G. C. 2005. Evangelical Aesthete: Ruskin and the Public Provision of Art. *History of Political Economy*, 37: 483–508.

Moore, G. E. 1903. *Principia Ethica*. Cambridge: Cambridge University Press.

1922. *Philosophical Studies*. London: Kegan Paul.

1966. *Ethics*. Oxford: Oxford University Press.

1993. *Principia Ethica* (ed. T. Baldwin). Revised edn. Cambridge: Cambridge University Press.

O'Donnell, R. M. 1989. *Keynes, Philosophy and Economics: The Philosophical Foundations of Keynes's Thought and their Influence on his Economics and Politics*. Basingstoke: Macmillan.

O'Brien, D. P. 1993. *Thomas Joplin and Classical Macroeconomics*. Brookfield, VT: Edward Elgar.

Owram, D. 1986. *The Government Generation: Canadian Intellectuals and the State 1900–1945*. Toronto: University of Toronto Press.

Pasinetti, L. L. 1999. J. M. Keynes's 'Revolution' – the Major Event of Twentieth-Century Economics? In Luigi Pasinetti and Bertram Schefold eds. *The Impact of Keynes on Economics in the 20th Century*. Cheltenham: Edward Elgar.

Patinkin, D. 1948. Price Flexibility and Full Employment. *American Economic Review* 38: 543–64.

1956. *Money, Interest and Prices*. Evanston, IL: Row, Peterson.

1965. *Money, Interest and Prices*. 2nd edn. New York: Harper and Row.

1976. Keynes and Econometrics: On the interaction between the Macroeconomic Revolutions of the Interwar Period. *Econometrica* 44: 1091–1123.

1976. *Keynes's Monetary Thought: A Study of its Development*. Durham, NC: Duke University Press.

1982. *Anticipations of the General Theory*. Chicago: University of Chicago Press.

and J. C. Leith (eds.) 1977. *Keynes, Cambridge and the General Theory*. London: Macmillan.

Peacock, A. 1993. Keynes and the Role of the State. In D. Crabtree and A. P. Thirlwall eds. *Keynes and the Role of the State*. London: Macmillan.

Peden, G. C. 1980. Keynes, the Treasury and Unemployment in the Later Nineteen-Thirties. *Oxford Economic Papers* n.s., 32: 1–18.

1983. Sir Richard Hopkins and the 'Keynesian Revolution' in Employment Policy, 1929–1945. *Economic History Review* 2nd series, 36: 281–96.

1988. *Keynes, the Treasury and British Economic Policy*. Basingstoke: Macmillan.

1990. Old Dogs and New Tricks: The British Treasury and Keynesian Economics in the 1940s and 1950s. In Mary O. Furner and Barry Supple eds. *The State and Economic Knowledge*. Cambridge: Cambridge University Press.

2000. *The Treasury and British Public Policy, 1906–1959*. Oxford: Oxford University Press.

(ed.) 2004. *Keynes and his Critics: Treasury Responses to the Keynesian Revolution, 1925–1946*. Oxford: Oxford University Press.

Phelps, E. S. 1967. Phillips Curves, Expectations of Inflation and Optimal Unemployment over Time. *Economica* 34: 254–81.

1990. *Seven Schools of Macroeconomic Thought*. Oxford: Oxford University Press.

Pigou, A. C. 1912. *Wealth and Welfare*. London: Macmillan.

(ed.) 1925. *Memorials of Alfred Marshall*. London: Macmillan.

1933. *The Theory of Unemployment*. London: Macmillan.

1936. Mr J. M. Keynes' General Theory of Employment, Interest and Money. *Economica* 3: 115–32.

1943. The Classical Stationary State. *Economic Journal* 53: 343–51, June.

Plumptre, A. F. W. 1947. Keynes in Cambridge. *Canadian Journal of Economics and Political Science* 13: 366–71, August.

Popper, K. 1934. *Logik der Forschung*. Tübingen: Mohr.

1963. *Conjectures and Refutations*. London: Routledge.

Presley, J. R. 1978. *Robertsonian Economics*. Basingstoke: Macmillan.

1992. J. M. Keynes and D. H. Robertson: Three Phases of Collaboration. In J. R. Presley ed. *Essays on Robertsonian Economics*. Basingstoke: Macmillan.

Pressnell, L. S. 1987. *External Economic Policy since the War, Volume I: The Post-war Financial Settlement*. London: Her Majesty's Stationery Office.

Raffaelli, T. 2003. *Marshall's Evolutionary Economics*. London: Routledge.

Ramsey, F. P. 1922. Mr. Keynes on Probability. *The Cambridge Magazine* 11(1): 3–5.

1926. Truth and Probability. In F. P. Ramsey, *The Foundations of Mathematics and other Logical Essays*, ed. R. B. Braithwaite. London: Routledge and Kegan Paul, 1931. In Ramsey 1978.

1927. Facts and Propositions. In Ramsey 1978.

1978. *Foundations: Essays in Philosophy, Logic, Mathematics and Economics* (ed. D. H. Mellor). London: Routledge and Kegan Paul.

Redmond, J. 1984. The Sterling Overvaluation in 1925: A Multilateral Approach. *Economic History Review*, 2nd series, 37: 520–32.

Ricardo, D. 1817. *Principles of Political Economy and Taxation*. 3rd edn 1821. Reprinted in P. Sraffa ed. *The Works and Correspondence of David Ricardo, Vol. I*. Cambridge: Cambridge University Press for the Royal Economic Society, 1956.

Robbins, L. C. 1934. *The Great Depression*. London: Macmillan.

Robinson, E. A. G. 1990. Fifty Years on the Royal Economic Society Council. In D. J. Hey and D. Winch eds. *A Century of Economics: 100 Years of the Royal Economic Society*. Oxford: Blackwell.

Robinson, J. 1937. *Essays in the Theory of Employment*. Oxford: Blackwell.

1973. *Collected Economic Papers*. Vol. IV. Oxford: Blackwell.

1974. History versus Equilibrium. *Indian Economic Journal* 21(3): 202–13.

1978. *Contributions to Modern Economics*. Oxford: Blackwell.

Rosanvallon, P. 1989. The Development of Keynesianism in France. In Peter Hall ed. *The Political Power of Economic Ideas: Keynesianism across Nations*. Princeton: Princeton University Press.

Rosser, J. B. Jr. 2001. Alternative Keynesian and Post Keynesian Perspectives on Uncertainty and Expectations. *Journal of Post Keynesian Economics* 23(4): 545–66.

Ruccio, D. F. 1991. Postmodernism and Economics. *Journal of Post Keynesian Economics* 13: 495–510.

Runde, J. and S. Mizuhara (eds.) 2003. *The Philosophy of Keynes's Economics: Probability, Uncertainty and Convention*. London: Routledge.

Russell, B. 1904. Review of *Principia Ethica* by G. E. Moore. *Independent Review* 2: 328–33, March.

1914. *The Problems of Philosophy*. 2nd edn. Introduction by J. Skorupsky. Oxford: Oxford University Press, 1998.

1922. A Treatise on Probability. *The Mathematical Gazette* 119–25.

Rymes, T. K. 1989. *Keynes's Lectures, 1932–1933*. Ann Arbor: University of Michigan Press.

Salant, W. 1989. The Spread of Keynesian Doctrines and Practices in the United States. In Peter Hall ed. *The Political Power of Economic Ideas: Keynesianism across Nations*. Princeton, NJ: Princeton University Press.

Samuelson, P. A. 1939a. Interactions between the Multiplier Analysis and the Principle of Acceleration. *Review of Economics and Statistics* 21(2): 75–8.

1939b. A Synthesis of the Principle of Acceleration and the Multiplier. *Journal of Political Economy* 47(6): 786–7.

1955. *Economics*. 3rd edn. New York: McGraw-Hill.

Sanfilippo, E. 2005. Keynes's Valuable Opponent and Collaborator: The Correspondence between Keynes and Robertson. In M. C. Marcuzzo and A. Rosselli eds. *Economists in Cambridge: A Study through their Correspondence, 1907–1946*. London: Routledge.

Sargent, T. J. 1982. Beyond Demand and Supply Curves in Macroeconomics. *American Economic Review* 72: 382–89, May.

1984. Autoregresssions, Expectations, and Advice. *American Economic Review* 74(2): 408–15.

Scanlon, T. 1998. *What We Owe to Each Other*. Cambridge, MA: Harvard University Press.

Schmiechen, J. A. 1988. The Victorians, the Historians, and the Idea of Modernism. *American Historical Review* 93(2): 287–316.

Secrest, M. 1986. *Kenneth Clark: A Biography*. New York: Fromm.

Sellon, G. H. Jr. (ed.) 2002. *Rethinking Stabilization Policy*. Kansas City: Federal Reserve Bank of Kansas City.

Shackle, G. L. S. 1967. *The Years of High Theory*. Cambridge: Cambridge University Press.

1973. *Epistemics and Economics*. Cambridge: Cambridge University Press.

Shell, M. 1982. *Money, Language, and Thought*. Berkeley: University of California Press.

Shone, R. 1976. *Bloomsbury Portraits*. London: Phaidon, 1993.

Sidnell, M. 1984. *Dances of Death: The Group Theatre of London in the Thirties*. London: Faber.

Simon, H. A. 1953. Causal Ordering and Identifiability. In Herbert A. Simon. *Models of Man*. New York: Wiley, 1957.

2001. Science Seeks Parsimony, not Simplicity: Searching for Patterns in Phenomena. In Arnold Zellner, Hugo A. Keuzenkamp and Michael McAleer eds. *Simplicity, Inference and Modelling: Keeping it Sophisticatedly Simple*. Cambridge: Cambridge University Press.

Skidelsky, R. 1983. *John Maynard Keynes, Volume I: Hopes Betrayed, 1883–1920*. London: Macmillan.

1992. *John Maynard Keynes, Volume II: The Economist as Saviour, 1920–1937*. London: Macmillan.

2000. *John Maynard Keynes, Volume III: Fighting for Britain, 1937–1946*. London: Macmillan.

2003. *John Maynard Keynes, 1883–1946: Economist, Philosopher, Statesman*. London: Macmillan.

Smith, A. 1776. *An Inquiry into the Nature and Causes of the Wealth of Nations*. London.

Sokal, A. D. and J. Bricmont. 1999. *Intellectual Impostures*. 2nd edn. London: Profile.

Solow, R. M. 1997. How did Economics Get that Way, and What Way did it Get? *Daedalus* 126: 39–58.

and J. E. Stiglitz. 1968. Output, Employment and Wages in the Short Run. *Quarterly Journal of Economics* 82(4): 537–60.

Spalding, F. 1983. *Vanessa Bell*. London: Weidenfeld and Nicolson.

1997. *Duncan Grant*. London: Chatto and Windus.

Stansky, P. 1996. *On or about 1910: Early Bloomsbury and its Intimate World*. Cambridge, MA: Harvard University Press.

Stein, H. 1969. *The Fiscal Revolution in America*. Chicago: University of Chicago Press.

Stigler, G. J. 1988. *Memoirs of an Unregulated Economist*. New York: Basic Books.

Strachey, L. 1918. *Eminent Victorians*. London: Collins.

Suppe, F. 1977. *The Structure of Scientific Theories*. Urbana: University of Illinois Press.

Taylor, M. P. 1992. The Dollar-Sterling Exchange Rate in the 1920s: Purchasing Power Parity and the Norman Conquest of $4.86. *Applied Economics* 24: 803–11.

Thirlwall, A. P. (ed.) 1976. *Keynes and International Monetary Relations*. London: Macmillan.

Thomas, M. 1983. Rearmament and Economic Recovery in the Late 1930s. *Economic History Review*, 2nd series, 36: 552–79.

Tinbergen, J. 1939. *Statistical Testing of Business-Cycle Theories, vol. II: Business Cycles in the United States of America, 1919–1932*. Geneva: League of Nations.

   1940. On a Method of Statistical Business-Cycle Research: A Reply. *Economic Journal* 50: 141–54.

Townshend, H. 1937. Liquidity-Premium and the Theory Of Value. *Economic Journal* 47: 157–69.

Upchurch, A. 2004. John Maynard Keynes, the Bloomsbury Group and the Origins of the Arts Council Movement. *International Journal of Cultural Policy* 10(2): 203–17.

Veblen, T. 1899. *The Theory of the Leisure Class*. New York: Macmillan.

   1900. The Preconceptions of Economic Science. *Quarterly Journal of Economics* 14(2): 240–69.

Verdon, M. 1996. *Keynes and the 'Classics': A Study in the Language, Epistemology and Mistaken Identities*. London: Routledge.

Wagner R. E. and J. Burton. 1978. *The Economic Consequences of Mr Keynes*. London: Institute of Economic Affairs.

Warming, J. 1932. International Difficulties Arising out of the Financing of Public Works during a Depression. *Economic Journal* 42: 211–24, June.

Weatherson, B. 2002. Keynes, Uncertainty, and Interest Rates. *Cambridge Journal of Economics* 26(1): 47–62.

Weinberg, J. R. 1936. *An Examination of Logical Positivism*. London: Routledge, 2000.

Weston, R. 1996. *Modernism*. New York: Phaidon.

Whitworth, M. 2000. Virginia Woolf and Modernism. In Sue Roe and Susan Sellers eds. *The Cambridge Companion to Virginia Woolf.* Cambridge: Cambridge University Press.

Wicke, J. 1996. Coterie Consumption: Bloomsbury, Keynes, and Modernism as Marketing. In Kevin J. H. Dettmar and Stephen Watt eds. *Marketing Modernisms.* Ann Arbor: University of Michigan Press.

Wicksell, K. 1898. *Interest and Prices.* Translated by R. F. Kahn 1936. London: Macmillan for the Royal Economic Society.

Williams, R. 1980. The Significance of 'Bloomsbury' as a Social and Cultural Group. In Derek Crabtree and A. P. Thirlwall eds. *Keynes and the Bloomsbury Group.* London: Macmillan.

Williamson, J. 1983. Keynes and the International Economic Order. In D. Worswick and J. Trevithick eds. *Keynes and the Modern World.* Cambridge: Cambridge University Press.

Wilson, T. 1982. Policy in War and Peace: The Recommendations of J. M. Keynes. In A. P. Thirlwall ed. *Keynes as a Policy Adviser.* Basingstoke: Macmillan.

Wittgenstein, L. 1922. *Tractatus Logico-Philosophicus.* German text and translation by D. F. Pears and B. F. McGuinness, introduction by B. Russell. London: Routledge and Kegan Paul, 1961.

  1974. *Letters to Russell, Keynes and Moore* (ed. G. H. von Wright). Oxford: Blackwell.

Wolcott, S. 1993. Keynes versus Churchill: Revaluation and British Unemployment in the 1920s. *Journal of Economic History* 53: 601–22.

Woodford, M. 2003. *Interest and Prices: Foundations of a Theory of Monetary Policy.* Princeton, NJ: Princeton University Press.

Woolf, L. 1925. *Fear and Politics.* London: Hogarth Press.

  1931. *After the Deluge.* New York: Harcourt, Brace.

  1935. *Quack, Quack!* New York: Harcourt, Brace.

  1953. *Principia Politica.* London: Hogarth Press.

  1913. *The Village in the Jungle.* Oxford: Oxford University Press, 1981.

Woolf, V. 1915. *The Voyage Out.* London: Hogarth Press, 1975.

  1924. *Mr. Bennett and Mrs. Brown.* London: Hogarth Press.

  1925. Modern Fiction. In Virginia Woolf ed. *The Common Reader.* Vol. I. London: Vintage, 2003.

  1927. *To the Lighthouse.* New York: Harcourt, Brace.

  1925. *Mrs. Dalloway.* New York: Modern Library, 1928.

  1931. *The Waves.* Oxford: Blackwell, 1993.

  1941. *Between the Acts.* London: Penguin, 1992.

  1977. *A Change of Perspective: The Letters of Virginia Woolf 1923–1928* (eds. N. Nicolson and J. Trautmann). London: Hogarth Press.

1983. *The Flight of the Mind: The Letters of Virginia Woolf 1888–1912* (eds. N. Nicolson and J. Trautmann). London: Hogarth Press.

1986. *The Essays of Virginia Woolf* (ed. Andrew W. McNeillie). Vol. I. New York: Harcourt, Brace.

Wright, G. H. von (ed.) 1974. *Ludwig Wittgenstein: Letters to Russell, Keynes and Moore*. Oxford: Blackwell.

Young, W. 1987. *Interpreting Mr Keynes: The IS-LM Enigma*. Boulder, CO: Westview Press.

INDEX